FACES
IN THE
CROWD

FENG JICAI

Translated by
Olivia Milburn

SINOIST

Published by Sinoist Books (an imprint of ACA Publishing Ltd)
London - Beijing

info@alaincharlesasia.com ☎ +44 20 3289 3885
www.sinoistbooks.com

Published by Sinoist Books (an imprint of ACA Publishing Ltd) in arrangement with People's Literature Publishing House

Author: Feng Jicai **Translator:** Olivia Milburn **Editor:** Matthew Keeler

Original Chinese Text © 俗世奇人全本 *(su shi qi ren quan ben)* 2020, People's Literature Publishing House, Beijing, China

ALL RIGHTS RESERVED. NO PART OF THIS PUBLICATION MAY BE REPRODUCED IN MATERIAL FORM, BY ANY MEANS, WHETHER GRAPHIC, ELECTRONIC, MECHANICAL OR OTHER, INCLUDING PHOTOCOPYING OR INFORMATION STORAGE, IN WHOLE OR IN PART, AND MAY NOT BE USED TO PREPARE OTHER PUBLICATIONS WITHOUT WRITTEN PERMISSION FROM THE PUBLISHER.

English Translation text © 2023 ACA Publishing Ltd, London, UK. A catalogue record for *Faces in the Crowd (The Complete Collection): 54 Extraordinary Tales of Tianjin* is available from the National Bibliographic Service of the British Library.

This novel is entirely a work of fiction. The names, characters and incidents portrayed in it are the work of the author's imagination. Any resemblance to actual persons, living or dead, events or localities is entirely coincidental.

Paperback ISBN: 978-1-83890-601-6
eBook ISBN: 978-1-83890-602-3

Sinoist Books is honoured to be supported using public funding by Arts Council England.

FOREWORD
BY JULIA LOVELL

Since the beginning of the post-Mao era (1976 onwards), Feng Jicai has established himself as a cultural figure of exceptional range. He threw himself into successive phases of the 1970s and 1980s literary thaw: Scar Literature (which openly confronted the traumas of the Cultural Revolution), modernism, magical realism and debates about Chinese culture and tradition. As the compiler and editor of collections of oral histories, he has been preoccupied with remembrance of the Cultural Revolution, an issue which remains highly sensitive and controversial in China today. His writing covers a bewildering breadth of styles and subject matter, including the historical novel, futuristic, environmental fiction and documentary literature, and he has argued for freedom of artistic criticism in China.

And Feng is far more than a writer. He trained as a painter (which gives his writing an imagistic quality), he is a connoisseur and collector of antiquities, and he has worked with local communities in his native Tianjin to preserve China's cultural heritage against a backdrop of the crash modernisation that has been state policy since the 1990s.

The stories that make up *Faces in the Crowd* – beautifully translated by Olivia Milburn – encapsulate the diverse concerns of Feng Jicai's career. A series of vignettes drawn from Tianjin life in the late 19th and early 20th centuries, the book takes in physicians, comics, actors, wrestlers, paint slingers, antique dealers, gangsters, generals, restaurateurs, embarrassingly honest mynah birds, fishermen, famous farts, and a drunkard who sweats alcohol out of his feet. Each literary sketch is prefaced by a deft visual likeness, testament to Feng's cultural ambidexterity. The local specialities of Tianjin – the city's cheap but potent liquor, sesame paste noodles, exceptionally delicious steamed buns, revolutionary hairstyles – have their own personalities and agency, and periodically intervene in local and national affairs. *Faces in the Crowd* is an extraordinary literary memorial to a city that the destruction and dislocations of the 20th century transformed beyond recognition.

Professor Julia Lovell is an author, academic and literary translator. Her works include *The Opium War*, which won the 2012 Jan Michalski Prize for Literature, and the widely acclaimed translation of Lu Xun's *The Real Story of Ah-Q*. She teaches modern Chinese history and literature at Birkbeck College, University of London.

FACES IN THE CROWD
The Complete Collection

54 EXTRAORDINARY TALES OF TIANJIN

FENG JICAI

Translated by
OLIVIA MILBURN

Sinoist Books

AMAZING PEOPLE APPEAR IN EVERY GENERATION: A SHORT PREFACE TO THE EXPANDED EDITION OF FACES IN THE CROWD

BY FENG JICAI

I've already written two collections of *Faces in the Crowd* so why do I continue to write more? It is because these two books have become a platform on which the amazing people of my hometown can appear. Besides which, remarkable men and women keep on cropping up, one after the other, and they all hope that their best tales will find a place here. They've all done extraordinary things, and they're very insistent—it's hard to say no. So each time one of them comes to my attention I've written another story, until in the end I had eighteen new pieces, and that's how this book came into being: *Faces in the Crowd: The Complete Stories*.

Tianjin is a city with its own unique features. Ordinary people like to have a good chin-wag after dinner and they often come back to the ever-popular subject of the amazing people that have now and again made a home here. There's no admiration here for the upper classes: they like to talk about the extraordinary ordinary people living around them. These characters also throw an interesting light on the likes and dislikes of local people, and a regional identity is deeply ingrained in them. Regional identity lies at the very heart of any local culture and this is a topic that I love exploring and presenting to the rest of the world. This is another reason why I continued writing the stories that make up this book.

I'm sure someone's going to ask me if I plan to continue writing? Writers are all emotional creatures so their plans are never to be relied on. The best situation for any writer is to be like a horse on a loose rein. A horse has its own personality and should be left free to respond to events as they occur; but the reins are my pen.

November 2019

INTRODUCTION

Tianjin is a port city, and its residents have come from all over the place; naturally, their characters are very different. In ancient times, this was the border between the kingdoms of Zhao and Yan, whose inhabitants were extremely tough; the water here is salt, and the soil is alkaline, giving a harsh and fierce character to its people. In the last century or so, in every disaster and catastrophe that has confronted China, these were the first people to feel its effects, and because of this all kinds of remarkable individuals have been produced here, some of whom went on to play a role in the destiny of nations, but even more found only a local fame. I have heard many stories about them, and remembered them for a long time; occasionally I have been able to use them in novels such as *The Magic Braid* and *Three-Inch Golden Lotus*; however, they were just appendages to the main story and not fully integrated characters. These people had amazing skills and experienced remarkable things, quite unbelievable, and wouldn't it be a shame if we forgot all about them? Recently I suddenly had the idea that I should write all this down and allow people in later generations to enjoy these tales so that everyone can know what happened here. That is how I came to start writing this collection. Everyone gets their own chapter, and each is entirely independent. However, I have brought them together under one title: *Faces in the Crowd: 54 Extraordinary Tales of Tianjin*.

First one book and then another,
One crowd of folks followed by t'other;
Amazing people on all sides,
More than my pen can cover!

On the surface they're ordinary guys:
But each one can give you a surprise.
Open your eyes and keep careful watch,
And then you'll see them in a whole new guise.

I
SEVEN DOLLARS SU

DOCTOR SU'S full name was Su Jinsan, and in the early years of the Republic, he opened a clinic in the Foreign Concession. He was very highly skilled indeed – supposedly the best in all of Tianjin – and it even happened that when a racehorse belonging to a foreigner strained a shoulder or broke a leg, it was taken to him for treatment.

He was a tall man in a long robe, with bony but strong hands, and although he was now over fifty, he still had red lips and beautiful white teeth. His eyes were as bright as lamps, and he wore a goatee beard which he oiled until it shone a glossy black. When he spoke, the sound seemed to come rumbling out of his belly, loud and resonant; if he'd thought to go into the theatre, he could have been a real rival to the great Peking Opera star Jin Shaoshan. When the doctor was working, his movements were clean and quick. When someone was brought to him with a strained tendon or a broken bone, what would he do? He would gently touch the wound with his fingers, probing it, and then he would immediately understand what was going on underneath. Suddenly, as fast as homing pigeons, like a flash of lightning, his hands would fall, and then you would hear a "crick-crack"... Before the patient even had time to feel any pain, the broken bone had been set. He would then apply an ointment and put on splints, after which his patient would be sent home to rest and recuperate. If his patient ever came back, it was to bow deeply and thank the doctor for his help or to hand over a congratulatory inscription as a formal expression of esteem.

People who possess an unusual skill also develop strange habits. Doctor Su had an odd rule: if you came to him for treatment, it didn't matter whether you were rich or poor, his greatest friend or a complete stranger, you had to put seven silver dollars down on the table before he was prepared to even look at you... if you didn't do that, he would just ignore your presence. What kind of rule is that? But that was the rule he set! People cursed him and said that all he cared about was the money, but to him, his professional skill was worth seven silver dollars, and so his inflated nickname was coined: Seven Dollars Su. People called him Doctor Su to his face, but behind his back, they called him Seven Dollars Su – nobody remembered that his real name was actually Su Jinsan.

Doctor Su liked playing cards, and one day, having some free time on his hands and two card-playing friends visiting, they were still lacking one player, so he thought to invite Doctor Hua (the dentist who had his office a little further down the street) to join them so they would have a proper table. Just when the game was at its height, all of a sudden Zhang Si the rickshaw puller burst in on them and stood leaning against the door frame. He was supporting his left elbow with his right hand, and his face was covered with sweat; the little rag hung around his neck was sopping wet. He'd obviously broken his arm, and it was murderously painful. But rickshaw pullers live from hand to mouth; how could he possibly pay seven silver dollars? He said he'd have to owe Doctor Su and pay him back a bit at a time, and as he said this, he was huffing and puffing with the pain. But Doctor Su didn't pay the slightest attention: he was too busy looking at his cards and calculating his next move, playing away just the same as before. He might have been happy, or sad, or shocked, or pretending not to be shocked – who could tell? He was concentrating on the game. One of his card-playing friends couldn't stand it anymore and jerked his finger towards the door. Doctor Su's eyes never left his cards. The nickname of Seven Dollars Su was now pretty much set in stone.

Doctor Hua the dentist, who was known far and wide as a kind and good man, excused himself on the grounds he was going for a pee. Having got up from the table, he went out into the rear courtyard, snuck out through the back gate, and made his way round to the front road. From a distance, he called over Zhang Si – who was still leaning against the door – and fished out seven silver dollars for him. He didn't wait for Zhang Si to thank him; he turned straight round and went back the way he had come. He returned to sit down at his place by the table and carried on playing cards as if nothing had happened.

A little bit later, Zhang Si hobbled back into the room and slapped down the seven silver dollars on the table with a sharp ring. Faster than if a button had been pushed, Doctor Su materialised in front of Zhang Si. Rolling up his sleeves, he put Zhang Si's arm down on the table and started feeling the bone, moving his hands up and down, pulling and pressing here and there. Zhang Si hunched his shoulders, pulled in his head, shut his eyes, and gritted his teeth, preparing to be overwhelmed by agony, but all Doctor Su said was: "It's been set." All that remained for him to do was to smear some ointment on and get the arm splinted, and he also gave Zhang Si a couple of sachets of powdered medicine to take by mouth; that would clear his blood and help with the pain. Zhang Si pointed out that he didn't have the money to pay for medicine, but Doctor Su just said: "It's a present from me." Then he went back to the card table.

In today's game, first someone won, and then he lost, and so they kept playing right through until it got dark, by which time their stomachs were rumbling with hunger, and everyone decided it was time to go home. As they were leaving, Doctor Su stuck out his bony hand and held Doctor Hua back: he wanted to talk to him. When his two card-playing friends had gone, he picked seven dollars out of the pile of silver coins left on the table in front of where he'd been sitting and put them in the palm of Doctor Hua's hand. When Doctor Hua exclaimed in amazement, Doctor Su said: "I should explain... You mustn't think that I'm completely heartless, but I cannot change the rules that I have set for myself!"

Doctor Hua took what he had said away with him and thought about it for three days and three nights, but in the end he decided that he had no idea what on earth Doctor Su was talking about. However, he always had a great deal of respect for Doctor Su, and how he had behaved on this occasion, and the strong principles he believed in.

2
MASTER LI, THE PAINT SLINGER

IN ANY PORT, the people are as tough as can be. Those with a skill in hand use their dexterity to make a living, and every single one of them has some trick up the sleeve. Thanks to their skills, they get to eat well, they have confidence in themselves, and they can walk down the middle of the road. The unskilled survive on scraps, they slump in misery, and they creep along the edge of the pavement. This isn't a rule that anyone has set, but it is how life in a port city is lived. If all the world's a stage, then anyone with ambitions wanted to succeed in the Tianjin theatre. People in Tianjin loved the theatre and understood its rules, they had sharp eyes and ears, and they knew exactly who was on the way up and who was down and out. If you performed well, the audience would be there to shout its praise as loudly as if the emperor were there in their midst – and there were plenty of famous players who got their start in Tianjin and went on to fame and fortune. But if it turned out there was nothing much to you, if you didn't rise to the challenge, if your performance

fell flat, then the audience would start catcalling. If you were really unlucky, the next stage was them smashing their teacups down, so you found yourself with clumps of tea leaves and splashes of tea ruining your costume and make-up. Theatres are to be found everywhere, but no other audience could be as tough as the one in Tianjin. There is no point in complaining about it, either, because the conditions there resulted in some really amazing people honing their skills. They came from every walk of life, in all shapes and sizes, people of unbelievable ability – Liu the stonemason; Zhang the figure maker; Wei the kite maker; Wang the machine maker; Li the paint slinger, and so on and so forth. The people of Tianjin put these men's surnames together with their business and used that as their nickname. After a while, everyone forgot what they were really called. Their nicknames though were something to conjure with in this port city.

Master Li the paint slinger worked for a builders out on Hebei Avenue. His job was working with whitewash, and that was all he did. If he was painting a room for you, you didn't need to swathe the place in sheets – just leave everything sitting there, and it would all be beautiful. The really amazing thing was that he always wore black when he was slinging his paint, but when he finished, there wasn't so much as a speck on him. You'd better believe this was true! He'd made a rule about this: he wouldn't charge for whitewashing if he got any paint on himself. If he couldn't keep the paint off his clothes, he'd have starved to death long ago, wouldn't he?

That was the story at any rate. Not everyone believed it. People who didn't know anything about the business and who'd never seen the man in action didn't believe it; other painters angrily insisted that it couldn't possibly be true.

One day, Master Li the paint slinger took on an apprentice called Cao Xiaosan. As an apprentice, his job was to make the tea, light cigarettes, and follow along behind carrying any equipment that might be needed. Cao Xiaosan had heard all about his master's amazing skill, and he wasn't quite sure he believed it – this time he was going to see for himself.

That day, which was his first out working with the master, they were going to be painting a western-style house on Zhennan Road in the English Concession, which had just been built by Li Shanren. When they arrived, Master Li went and chatted to the site manager: you could see the master got a lot of respect from those in the know. He would only paint one room per day. This house had nine rooms, so he'd be working there for nine days. Before starting work, he opened up the square case he was carrying: sure enough, he was going to be wearing a black jacket and black trousers, and even a pair of black cloth shoes. When he was dressed in his black work-clothes, he was ready to deal with the bucket of whitewash at his feet.

In a room, you have a ceiling and four walls, and you paint the ceiling first and then the walls. Ceilings are very difficult to paint – when a brush thick with whitewash is being lifted up, how can anyone avoid drips? And when it drips, the drops land on the paint slinger. But when Master Li was on the other end of the brush, the paint stayed put. The brush touched the ceiling, and immediately it turned white, smooth and even, snowy and pure. Some people said it was all in the handling of the brush; others that he mixed his paint to a secret recipe. Cao Xiaosan had no idea how to explain it. He saw the master's arm moving slowly back and forth, as regular as a metronome, as calmly as if he were moving to music. Every time he raised the brush, the paint-covered bristles were slapped against the wall with a satisfying "pok" sound. "Pok... pok... " one stroke after another, covering the surface evenly and without gaps, until the walls were as white as snow. However, Cao Xiaosan was more interested in whether or not there was any paint on Master Li.

When Master Li was working, he had a particular custom: every time he finished a wall, he would sit down for a bit on a stool, smoking a pack of cigarettes and drinking a cup of tea, and only afterwards would he tackle the next wall. Then Cao Xiaosan took advantage of the fact that he had to pour the tea and light the cigarettes to get a really good look at Master Li's clothes. Every time he finished a wall he would inspect him, but from start to finish he couldn't find so much as a speck of paint on him. In all of those black clothes, he found the master a deeply awe-inspiring sight.

But when Master Li finished painting the last wall and sat back down, and Cao Xiaosan came and lit his cigarette, he saw a spot of white on his trousers, about the size of a pea. White on black is so much more eye-catching than black on white. Damn! All of these stories weren't holding up to scrutiny, there was nothing special about him at all, and the towering image built up in the tales told of him was crumbling. However, he was worried about making his master look bad, so he didn't dare to say anything – he didn't even dare look at him. But he couldn't stop himself from glancing at the spot.

Just at that moment, Master Li suddenly spoke: "Xiaosan, you've noticed the spot of white on my trousers, haven't you?

You think I didn't earn my reputation, that it's all a trick, don't you? Silly boy! Come and have a good look…"

As he spoke, Master Li pinched the fabric of his trousers in his fingers and lifted it slightly, and the white spot immediately disappeared. When he let go again, the white spot was back. How odd! He looked again, and this time he realised the white spot was a hole in the fabric! He must've just carelessly burned a small hole with cigarette ash. His white underpants were showing through the hole, and it looked just like a spot of whitewash had landed on him!

Master Li looked at Cao Xiaosan standing there dumbfounded. He laughed and said: "Do you think I got my reputation for nothing? Don't fool yourself. You have a hell of a lot to learn!"

On his first day as an apprentice, Cao Xiaosan saw things and learned things that other people would take a lifetime to understand!

3
BOOZING GRANNY

BARS COME in all shapes and sizes, but the little tavern on Shoushan Street was one of the very lowest kind. There was no sign hung up on the street (in fact, it didn't even seem to have a name), there weren't any seats inside, and no snacks were sold at the bar – all they had there was one jar of wine. The people who went there to drink were all at the bottom of the ladder: day-labourers, rickshaw pullers, and coolies. Some of them might have a lump of savoury sausage clutched in one hand, or they might have a few five-spice peanuts in a pocket... coming through the door they would order up an ounce or two of alcohol, which they would drink all by themselves propped up against the corner of the wall, or leaning against the windowsill. If it happened that a bunch of people turned up at the same time, they would take their bowls of wine outside and stand leaning against a tree. They would sip their wine and savour each drop – that was just fine!

This particular bar only sold one kind of wine, made from sweet potatoes, cheap and strong. The cats people kept as pets up and down Shoushan Road never got lost, because if they happened to run away, they could always find their way back by following the smell of alcohol. This wine wasn't prized for its flavour, but for its kick – sipping it was like sipping acid. You had to swallow it down quick before it ruined your tongue and your lips, or wrecked your teeth and your throat, or even got at your eyes. But once you'd got it down, it would leap into action, going straight to your head, making you woozy and confused: it really did have a kick like a mule! It was just like one of the firecrackers people set off on New Year's Eve: it exploded as soon as you set light to it, filling the sky with flashes of red. That is why this kind of wine was called Firecracker. Now good wine ought to be rich and warming, something to be savoured slowly; it certainly shouldn't go straight to your head. But the poor are struggling to survive from one day to the next. When they are bone-tired, or depressed, why shouldn't they relax and cheer themselves up with a bit of cheap booze with some go to it that would make them feel all light-headed and silly?

One of the people who'd really let themselves go like this was Boozing Granny. Every afternoon, this one old woman would turn up at the tavern, as regular as clockwork, her clothes in rags like a beggar, her hair a complete bird's nest, and her face as black as soot. There was nobody who knew what she really looked like and nobody who knew what she was called: they just knew that she was always to be found drinking in this one bar, and so she was given the nickname Boozing Granny. When she came through the door, she would always start by pulling out a small square bundle wrapped in a cotton handkerchief; when she opened that, there was a parcel wrapped in newspaper inside, and sometimes the newspaper was brand new, while other times it was old; then when she opened the paper parcel, there was yet another parcel inside, this time done up in nice wrapping paper, as if there were a piece of jade jewellery inside or something; and then when she opened the parcel done up in wrapping paper, there were a couple of coppers inside! She would plonk the money down on the bar, and the barkeeper would pour her the usual three-quarters of a bowl of Firecracker. She would then grab the bowl and, craning her neck, raise it to her lips, tipping the contents down her throat with a single flip, just like any other alcoholic. But once Granny got her two feet out of the door, she seemed to be trying to move them in every direction at once.

She would wobble off down the road weaving from side to side, and then when she'd gone about one hundred steps, she'd hit a crossroads where there was traffic pounding back and forth, a place where accidents often happened. However, you wouldn't need to worry about Granny – she might seem to be completely sodden with drink, but every time she got to that crossroads she'd suddenly come to her senses with a start! Then she seemed just like everybody else – you wouldn't have guessed she'd had a drop to drink, and she'd cross the road safe and sound. This happened day after day, and nothing ever went wrong. The people up and down Shoushan Road loved to watch Boozing Granny's wandering steps as she moved about in an alcoholic stupor – wobbling and wavering, first twirling this way and then twisting that, like a lotus leaf tossed in the wind... And then when it was raining and she was soaked through, she looked like an umbrella slowly swirling down the road... But how could it be that Boozing Granny always sobered up the moment she got to the crossroads? Was it that Firecracker had only a very limited effect, or did Boozing Granny have some superhuman ability to come round from it in a trice?

The secret to any good wine is in its keeping. The barkeeper was a right bastard, and he watered his wine. Alcoholics might see the rest of the world through a glass, darkly, but when it comes to what they are tipping down their throats, they know exactly what end is up – but in this case, nobody wanted to complain openly: he let them drink there, and that was good enough. If the barkeeper was an arsehole, he would have to pay for it in other ways; here he was at nearly sixty without chick or child, so the chances were that he'd be the last of his family. But then one day the barkeeper's wife started having strange cravings for hot and sour foods, and it turned out that she was pregnant! When the barkeeper went to offer prayers of thanks to Buddha, he found himself making all kinds of resolutions, swearing that from now on he was going to turn over a new leaf, that he'd sell wine just as it was ordered, and that he'd never water it or swap for ersatz again.

And it was on this very day that Boozing Granny went to her regular watering hole and went through the usual rigmarole of fishing out her bundle and opening the parcel one layer at a time, then buying her wine, craning her neck as she raised the bowl to her lips... but this time she was tipping real Firecracker down her throat instead of the usual rubbish, and the real thing had plenty of quality to it. On this occasion, Boozing Granny was reeling before she even got out of the bar. Today, she gave a very fine show of wobbling and weaving as she walked down the road: her arms would be heading off to the left while her legs were going right, and the more she whirled about, the faster she went. To begin with, she was moving like a bird caught in an updraft, but by the end she was wheeling about like a black whirlwind! The people on Shoushan Road were watching in alarm and puzzlement, but they didn't have much time to think about it – Boozing Granny was already at the crossroads, and she hadn't sobered up at all: she just went charging out into the traffic on the highway without a second thought, and you can imagine what happened next...

After that, Boozing Granny was never seen on this street again. However, it would happen that from time to time the other regulars in the little bar would mention her. They agreed that she was a real drinker. She would just swallow her wine without a thought about snacks, and she would knock it back in a single gulp. She couldn't care less about anything else – she just wanted to feel the fire of the alcohol. She also wasn't interested in interfering with other people in the tavern, and she never gossiped; she would pay her money and drink her wine, and having drunk it she would leave. She never, ever ran a tab. A real drinker enjoys the drinking and doesn't disturb anyone else in the process.

When the barkeeper heard that, he suddenly remembered that the day Boozing Granny had her accident was the day that he didn't cut the wine in her bowl. It was all his own fault! It was very confusing for him: sometimes it is not at all clear what the right thing to do is. Was he wrong to have cheated his customers, or was he wrong to have started giving them the real thing? How could it be that for decades he'd been selling cheap and nasty ersatz wines without any problems and everyone had been drinking it up perfectly happily, but the moment he gave them the proper stuff, they got themselves into such terrible trouble?

4
DEAD BIRD

THE PEOPLE of Tianjin like a good joke, and that's why lots of people there have nicknames. Some people have nicknames that you can use to their faces, while others have nicknames you can only call them behind their backs… it all depends on how they got it in the first place. To have a nickname, something funny must have happened to you, but every story is different; some of these stories make a good laugh for everyone, but others you have to be careful how you tell them. He Taotai's nickname was one of those – Dead Bird.

He Taotai wasn't much to look at; in fact, he looked like a pig. However, we must not go by appearances, and you can't judge a book by its cover. He had two remarkable talents – one was licking the boots of his superiors, and the other was keeping birds.

There is a real art to keeping your superiors happy. The whole day you are wandering around in their wake, but it is not

enough to keep close behind them or make sure you stay out of their way. If you lag too far behind then you aren't right on the spot when they need you, in which case your superiors are going to get cross; if you are too close, you'll be tripping over them the whole time, in which case they are going to get annoyed. And you also can't be trotting along like a little dog at their heels. You need to develop a real feel for what it is that they want, and you need to understand what kind of people you are dealing with so that when you put in a word, you do so at the right time, and you don't end up saying the wrong thing. You whisper in their ears just when they need your help. When they shout at you, you say that you deserved it. When your superiors are shouting at you, it doesn't mean that you have done anything wrong – sometimes they need to take their anger out on someone and they'll feel better afterwards. If you can't control yourself, if you furrow your brow or purse your lips, if you show even the slightest signs of irritation yourself, your superiors will remember it and hold it against you. After that, as time goes on, promotion will slip from your grasp, and you'll find yourself in a worse and worse position. Anyway, it's an impossible task but He Taotai was good at it – he made it look natural. People said that He Taotai was just a natural born bootlicker. Letting his superiors use him as a punching bag came easy to him because he simply didn't have the feathers to ruffle, and you could kick him until he was down and out without getting so much as a squeak out of him – so he was a natural, right?

Having explained how good he was at licking the boots of his superiors, it's time to talk about keeping birds.

Keeping birds is a very different kind of ability. You can put a bird in a cage, you can give it some grain and a few worms to eat, and fresh water, but that isn't necessarily going to keep it chipper. Birds have their different needs: if you don't give them what they want, they'll close their eyes and ruffle their feathers, pulling in their wings. Birds have their own personality: if you don't make them happy, they won't sing, they won't even move – they'll just sit there looking stuffed. People said that He Taotai must have been a bird himself in a past life. He understood birds – it didn't matter what kind. In passing through his fat little hands, their feathers would become sleeker, they would be hopping about happily, and they'd be singing away as loudly as the opera stars in the Heavenly Blessings teahouse when they got to the grand finale.

The second year, the day after the official start of summer, a Mr Lin who worked in the Customs and Excise Office came back after a holiday to his old hometown of Changzhou in Jiangsu Province, and he brought with him a mynah bird. This mynah bird had a big fat stomach, thick legs and strong claws, with glossy black feathers all over and a bright golden-yellow beak; when it got going, you could hear it quite clearly out on the main road. He Taotai was thrilled: "Even a cock in full crow doesn't make as much noise as that."

Mr Lin smiled and said: "It can't really speak though. It's been very slow to learn. Whatever I try, it won't learn, but if I say something without thinking, it'll remember that. However, with your training, I'm sure it will turn out to be a very fine bird."

He Taotai smiled too. "In three months, I'll have made it a master storyteller," he said.

As it turned out, the mynah bird was like a high-spirited

thoroughbred colt – it was not going to be so easy to train it. He Taotai tried everything; it just would not learn. He Taotai cursed it: "Stupid bird!" The next day it bellowed "Stupid bird" from dawn to dusk. You could try telling it to shut its beak, but it wouldn't listen. Everyone in front and back could hear it clear as a bell, and it was impossible for anyone to have their regular midday nap that day. He Taotai had to cover up the cage for most of the day, and then it finally came to a rest. When it got late, Madame He was worried that the poor bird would be suffocating under there, so she got the maid to take the cover off its cage. The moment the bird was revealed, it asked Madame He: "Are you suffering from a heat rash, dear?" That gave her a real turn. But when she thought about it, she remembered that her husband had asked her that very question a couple of days earlier; they hadn't thought anything of it at the time, but the bird was paying attention. This made Madame He giggle for hours. When He Taotai got home, she told him all about it. Before she had the opportunity to call on the mynah bird to go through its paces, it spoke up of its own accord: "Are you suffering from a heat rash, dear?"

He Taotai was so amused that he burst out laughing. "That bird!" he said. "It can even imitate the tone of my voice."

"I had no idea the tiresome thing was so clever," Madame He said.

After that, He Taotai trained the bird even more carefully. As time went on, he managed to get it to learn a few phrases like "Welcome to my humble home" and "Please take the seat of honour" and "Wonderful to see you, sir!", but it wouldn't say them nicely. But it picked up quick enough on a few everyday conversations between He Taotai and his wife, like the heat rash thing, and that amused their guests so much they would start laughing, and pretty soon the whole house was rocking with mirth.

The prefect said: "Really, Mr He, that bird is a testament to how clever you are."

He Taotai was pleased with his bird and pleased with himself. However, we don't need to go into that.

On the ninth day of the ninth month, a festival was held at the Yuhuang Pavilion outside the city walls to the east – the people of Tianjin would head out there to enjoy the view: as the saying goes, on the ninth of the ninth you climb up high. That day, the weather was lovely, and the view from the top of the pavilion was particularly fine. Everyone was in an excellent mood, and there wasn't a cloud in the sky. On this occasion, the Manchu viceroy of Zhili Province, Hitara-Hala Yulu, also joined the company heading to the Yuhuang Pavilion, and he was in a very cheerful frame of mind; he even climbed up the rickety-rackety ladder that went through to the second storey of the Qingxu Pavilion. The civil and military officials in his entourage were all kept busy running back and forth, trying to make him happy. He Taotai was naturally one of their number. He pointed out the sails of boats going in and out of the mouth of the Sancha Estuary and said a few flattering words, which pleased Yulu very much. As they descended, He Taotai happened to mention that his home was not very far away and he would be honoured if the viceroy would come and visit him. Under normal circumstances, the viceroy would never demean himself by visiting the home of a subordinate. However, he was in an unusually good mood that day, and so he agreed. He Taotai's palanquin led the way, and the other officials followed in a magnificent procession.

He Taotai had his mynah bird in a cage hung up in the main reception room. The moment Viceroy Yulu came in through the door, the mynah piped up: "Welcome to my humble home!" It spoke unusually clearly, and Yulu heard it perfectly well.

The viceroy was obviously delighted and said: "That bird is really quick off the mark."

He Taotai then put in his own word: "It's because you've come, sir. Normally it won't speak so nicely, no matter what."

When tea was served, the mynah bird suddenly spoke again: "This tea is made with first flush leaves."

Yulu was startled and then turned his head to speak to the mynah in its cage: "No, that can't be right. Think of the time of year – this cannot possibly be first flush, now can it?"

Everyone was now enjoying this, and the sound of laughter filled the room. Everyone was making fun of the silly mynah bird.

"You are absolutely right, sir," He Taotai said. "I never taught it to say that, but every so often that bird will just come out with something, and I have no idea where it got it from."

The prefect laughed and said: "You don't always pay attention to idle remarks, but the bird is listening. I daresay that you were drinking a nice cup of tea one time and it has remembered what you called it!"

Now Yulu laughed and said: "If you've got some good tea to hand, you should let me try it. I am the viceroy after all!"

Everyone laughed at that. However, the mynah bird had caught the title of "viceroy", and now it suddenly flapped its wings, fluffing up the black feathers all over its body. Then it spoke in a loud and crystal-clear, furious voice: "The viceroy is an absolute bastard!"

Everyone in the room froze. The entire company had heard what it said, but while they were sitting there stunned, the mynah bird repeated its comment: "The viceroy is an absolute bastard!" It spoke as clearly and as frankly as ever. Yulu slapped his hand down on the table with a thud, and the tea-things were swept onto the floor. In thunderous tones, he roared: "How dare you!"

He Taotai fell to his knees. In a voice so faint it could hardly be heard, he said: "I never taught the mynah…" But as he spoke these words, they stuck in his throat. He realised that the mynah bird was just repeating what he said every time he came home after Yulu had been kicking him around. Why was that the only thing it had remembered? Was it trying to get him killed? He could feel cold sweat trickling down his body.

When he came to his senses, Yulu and the other officials had gone; he was left kneeling all on his own in the middle of the reception room. He suddenly jumped to his feet and made a dash at the mynah, screaming: "You've ruined me! I'm going to rip you wing from wing! You're a dead bird!"

He grabbed hold of the cage with both hands, but he put too much force into it – the cage broke, and the bird flew off. Even though he made a swipe for it, he didn't catch it. The mynah flew out of the window and came to a stop in a tree outside. Clearly, it had been studying what He Taotai had just said because it now called to him: "Dead bird!"

He Taotai called for his servants to bring sticks to beat it out of the tree. Some of them threw bricks at it, and others tried to climb the tree to get it. The mynah just hopped backward and forward at the very top of the tree. The whole time it was screaming: "Dead bird! Dead bird! Dead bird!" In the end, it took to its wings and flew away, and soon disappeared completely from view.

After that, He Taotai was known to one and all by the nickname Dead Bird. And when his nickname was explained, this is the story they told.

5
STRONGMAN ZHANG

STRONGMAN ZHANG'S real name was Zhang Jinbi, and he was noted in Tianjin for his physical prowess. He wasn't just huge; he was also enormously strong. That is why he was called Strongman.

The people of Tianjin – old and young – liked and respected him, and they praised him highly. However, Tianjin folks have their own way of praising people. There was an incident involving Strongman Zhang that illustrates this perfectly; at the time nobody really knew much about it, and it has now been completely forgotten, so let me set it down here.

There was a business selling stone and timber at Houjiahou, called the Unity-is-Strength yard. Right by the front entrance of the yard, there was a huge and heavy granite boulder in the shape of a padlock, with the shackle being stone too. A line of Chinese characters had been carved into it:

Anyone who can lift this stone lock will be rewarded with one hundred silver dollars.

The people at Unity-is-Strength had set up this padlock to prove the quality of their stonework.

Once they had put their stone in position, nobody ever lifted it – in fact, nobody ever managed to move it even fractionally, so just think how heavy it must have been! It seemed embedded in the earth, as if you were going to have to lift that too if you wanted to raise it!

One day, Strongman Zhang happened past Houjiahou and saw the stone lock. He read the characters inscribed on it. He bent down and got his hands on it, moving it gently. It began to swing back and forwards as if he were shaking a bamboo winnowing basket. That brought a lot of people out to watch. Then they saw his hand grasp the shackle, and as he straightened up, the huge stone boulder was lifted into the air as easy as could be. His arm was straight as an arrow, and he had a smile on his face, for all the world as if he were lifting nothing more than a bunch of flowers!

The crowd was bellowing its acclamations as Strongman Zhang lifted the stone. He didn't put it down right away, either, since he waited until the workmen at Unity-is-Strength went and got their boss to come out to see for himself. After that, he put the stone back where he found it. The boss came forward smiling: "Oh, Mr Zhang is here. Do come this way and have a cup of tea!"

When Strongman Zhang heard that, he put it to him straight: "Now, boss, there's no need for all of this fuss. You say right there on that stone lock that anyone who lifts it will be rewarded with one hundred silver dollars. Go and get me the money, since I don't have all day!"

Nobody would have imagined that the boss of the Unity-is-Strength yard would pay not the slightest attention to what Strongman Zhang had said. He waited until Strongman Zhang had finished speaking, and then he said evenly: "Mr Zhang, you've clearly read what it said on the top of the stone, but have you read what it says underneath?"

Strongman Zhang started. Just now he'd been feeling pleased with himself; he simply hadn't seen that it said anything on the bottom of the stone. And it wasn't just him; nobody had noticed. Strongman Zhang thought this one over and decided the boss was trying to weasel out of it – he didn't want to give him the money – and so he thought that having lifted the thing once, he wouldn't have the strength to lift it a second time. Anyway, he hefted the stone up over his head all over again, and when he raised his eyes, he saw there really was another line of writing carved on the base:

But if it is Strongman Zhang, that doesn't count.

When you put that together with what it said on the top, it read:

Anyone who can lift this stone lock will be rewarded with one hundred silver dollars, but if it is Strongman Zhang, that doesn't count.

When everyone saw that, they fell about laughing. These people knew right from the start that Strongman Zhang was the only person who could possibly lift this bloody thing. And the second line showed their respect for him, their admiration – Strongman Zhang understood that very well.

He put down the stone lock and threw his head back with a bellow of laughter, before walking off in triumph.

6
FIFTH MASTER FENG

FIFTH MASTER FENG originally came from Ningbo in Zhejiang. The Feng family produced only two kinds of children: businessmen and scholars. The Feng family also ran to brains; their noggins were like the nested ivory puzzle balls carved by Weng Wuzhang of Guangdong – one layer after another, and each one different. So when the Feng family went into business they made themselves super-rich; and when they became scholars, they passed the civil service examinations with flying colours and went on to dazzling official careers. In Fifth Master Feng's generation, there were five boys and two girls, and he was the youngest of the family, so his older brothers were off in Shanghai or Tianjin opening factories and establishing their business empires when he was growing up, and they were very successful. Only Fifth Master Feng was left at home, working his way through his books. He was as thin as a rake, and bony with it, but with soft, white skin like the belly of a fish. He didn't look like a thrusting businessman – this was a scholar pure and

simple. But he was no ordinary bookworm because if you read a sentence from any classic text, he could recite the next line from memory, and Wang Anshi, who had been prime minister of China during the Song dynasty, was supposedly the only person who had ever been able to perform a feat like that. Everyone was deeply impressed by his erudition, and he wrote a truly beautiful hand. Everyone agreed that in this generation of the Feng family, it was the Fifth Master who was by far the cleverest.

When Fifth Master Feng was twenty-five, his parents having passed away, he sold the house and land and moved with the rest of the family up to Tianjin, where he was going to throw in his lot with his older brothers and see if he could make something of his life.

He was an ambitious man, but Tianjin was a city of merchants – they used their pens to write out their accounts, and that was all. Since nobody there had the slightest interest in reading books, it was natural that they despised scholars. To put it another way, if there is a book lying on the ground, and a gold bar lying next to it, which one are you going to pick up? Seeing that other people were getting rich all around him, Fifth Master Feng was struck green with envy, and he made up his mind that he was going to go into business too. But having made this decision, he had no idea how to go about it.

When Chinese people start on a get-rich-quick scheme, the first thing they think of is opening a restaurant. Food is the most important consideration for people, so they will spend money on food; you need three meals a day or you just don't have the strength to work, and in this way, every penny you earn ends up in the hands of restaurant owners. In Tianjin, businessmen have all the money, and more than half their deals are made over the dinner table. Besides which, Tianjin is a centre for salt production, and they lay it on their food with a heavy hand; Ningbo is just the same, and so the flavour should go down well. So Fifth Master Feng made up his mind: he would open a restaurant specialising in Ningbonese food.

He found a suitable location, off the bustling market at Majiakou, and put up a building, which he was going to call Optimus restaurant. He picked an auspicious day, hung up his shingle and cut the ribbon, all to the deafening sound of firecrackers going off, and then he was open for business. Fifth Master Feng was wearing a long robe in indigo figured silk, with a gold watch-chain glittering across his chest in a refined blend of east and west, and his hair had been slicked back with pomade so he looked like the epitome of a successful businessman as he stood in the main room greeting his guests, welcoming all who came. As an educated gentleman, he was very polite, and he spoke well which gave everyone a good impression. Besides which, the Optimus was the only Ningbonese speciality restaurant in the whole of Tianjin, and both river fish and shrimp were Tianjin favourites anyway – when they'd been through the hands of the cook hired in from Ningbo, they were as delicious as they could be.

So after its grand opening, the restaurant was packed to the rafters day after day, and in the evening they had such a turnover that they had to reset each table twice. In the blink of an eye, a river of gold and silver poured into the cashbox, so Fifth Master Feng was much relieved. But as time went on, profits dwindled. This puzzled Fifth Master Feng: they were making money hand over fist, so the cash was definitely coming in, but where was it going after that? Then he cast up his accounts again... and he was actually in the red!

One day, one of the kitchen apprentices, who'd been hired in from Ningbo, plucked up the courage to tell him that very few of the chickens, ducks, fish and pork that were being bought for the kitchens actually made it as far as the customers – the majority were being handed over to the staff to be thrown over the back wall, and there was someone on the other side to collect. How much of the profits of the Optimus were being thrown over the wall every day?

After Fifth Master Feng had calmed down a bit, he reminded himself with pride of how he had learned each and every one of the *Twenty-Four Histories* off by heart: was he going to let them get away with ripping him off like this? It was time to teach them a lesson they wouldn't forget in a hurry. With the sole exception of the fat cook, who he'd brought with him from his old home, all of the rest of the staff were fired. After this root and branch extermination, he brought in a whole new team, and he installed an electric fence by the back wall. He thought that this was going to be enough, but his accounts stayed obstinately in the red. What on earth was going on?

Then a granny who lived next door to the Optimus whispered to him that every evening when the rubbish truck came past, ringing its little bell, they were hauling about eight bin-loads out of the restaurant, but only the top layer was rubbish; underneath there were steel drums stuffed with salt fish, wine, and other foodstuffs. Clearly, his staff were still in league with people on the outside to steal from him, and they were using this method to smuggle the stuff out. Why not go right ahead and just fill the bins every day with his money? Fifth Master Feng was on the spot the next evening when the rubbish truck came past and made sure that the allegation was investigated – sure enough, it was quite true. In a rage, he fired his staff a second time. He might have a whole new workforce, but the deficits in his account books seemed impossible to shift.

Fifth Master Feng had every confidence in his own abilities, and he was right there in the restaurant day after day with his eyes and ears open, patrolling the place and keeping an eye on everything, and he could not find anything wrong. Scholars spend their day in thought, so when they find themselves caught up in the kaleidoscope of real life, they prove the truth of the saying: "Those who think themselves clever are the real idiots." The Optimus restaurant was like an old football, leaking air at every seam as it deflated in front of your very eyes. A successful business can be compared to the human body: as long as it keeps on breathing, it will survive, but once it stops there is nothing that you can do. The few customers they had never bothered to come back; the place was dying on its feet, and the staff all found better things to do. Sometimes they were only switching on the lights in half the restaurant.

Fifth Master Feng was getting very worried now.

One day, his own little servant boy told him that he'd heard gossip to say that the real thief at the Optimus was none other than the cook, who'd come with him from his home in Ningbo. Apparently, he was next door to a kleptomaniac: he stole all day every day, and there was nothing that he wouldn't try and make off with. He wouldn't go home in the evening until he had something to take with him, and he was very good at lifting things right out from under your eyes so that you wouldn't notice a thing. Fifth Master Feng refused to believe it: the fat cook had cooked for his own father way back when, and the fat cook's father had cooked for his grandfather – the family had worked for the Fengs for generations. If even someone like that was a thief, was there anyone you could trust?

However, by this time, Fifth Master Feng had been in business for two years, and during that period he'd seen a lot of sycophantic grins and heard an awful lot of lies – he wasn't completely wet behind the ears any more. That evening, just when the Optimus was closing its doors and putting out the lights, Fifth Master Feng went and sat in the entrance with his servant. He pulled out a wicker chair and positioned it in a place where he could catch any breeze, and lay there staring at the ceiling. He said he was relaxing in the cool of the evening, but he was there to catch a thief.

He did not have long to wait before the fat cook raked out the embers in his stove and came out of the kitchen, heading for home. He was naked from the waist up, wearing just a huge pair of white trousers and with his feet rammed into an old pair of cloth shoes. He had a sweat-rag slung around his neck, and he carried a paper lantern. He glanced at his boss but seemed in no hurry to go home – he was happy to take a moment to stand there and gossip. His whole attitude seemed to be: Take a good look, why don't you?

As Fifth Master Feng chatted with him about this and that, he was bringing a pair of very sharp scholarly eyes to bear and measuring him up very carefully – there was nowhere to hide anything on his bare head or body, and he could hardly have stuffed something in his armpit, now could he? That beaten-up pair of shoes couldn't hold as much as a packet of cigarettes! His trousers were enormous, but with the breeze blowing back and forth through the dining area, every bulge of his legs and buttocks was clearly revealed, so he couldn't possibly be concealing anything there. Could he maybe have hidden something in the rag worn over his shoulders? Just as this thought crossed his mind and before he could say anything on the subject, the fat cook unwound the towel from around his neck and threw it carelessly at the little servant boy, saying: "It's nice and cool out here so I won't be needing this. Do you mind hanging it up on the line out in the back courtyard?" After that, he said goodbye to Fifth Master Feng, picked up his lantern, and stomped off into the night.

Fifth Master Feng told his servant boy to spread the towel out, but there was nothing there at all. He'd been suspecting an innocent man.

The very next day, the servant found out that on that evening the fat cook had been concealing his ill-gotten gains in the lantern. The base of his lantern, which had the wax candle fixed in it, wasn't made of wood but from a lump of frozen meat. He'd managed to steal nearly twenty pounds of meat that way! Right under Fifth Master Feng's nose, he'd lit the lantern and walked away. That was really smart!

Fifth Master Feng heard him out. For the next three days, he didn't say a word, and then on the fourth day, he closed the Optimus. People encouraged him to resume his education, to go back to his ivory tower, but he just shook his head and sighed. If you are going to study, you have to believe that you can learn things from books. If an educated man can't even deal with a pig-ignorant illiterate, how can he justify his studies?

7
BLUE EYES

IN THE ART and antiques trade, there are two sides pitted against each other: those who make fake works of art, and the experts who track them down. The forgers rack their brains and use every trick of their trade in the hope of evading the sharp and critical eyes of the experts; the experts rely on their keen eyesight to see what is really going on, to evade the traps set for them, and to put their finger on the mistake that shows the fake for what it really is, pulling that one wrong out of a mountain of rights, until it stands revealed in the bright light of day.

There was one particular expert whose name was Blue Eyes. He worked at Riches Antiques on Guodian Street, and his expertise was in painting. Blue Eyes was actually called Jiang Zaitang, but everyone called him Blue Eyes. People in Tianjin like to give people nicknames like this; they are fun and easy to remember. Blue Eyes got his name from the spectacles he wore for his short sight, with lenses as thick as the bottom of a glass bottle that had a blueish shine to them that really did make him

look like he had blue eyes. But the whole point of Blue Eyes was his eyes: people said he could look at a painting in the pitch dark and he'd still be able to tell if it was real or not. This may sound like some kind of wizardry, but there was nothing wrong with his abilities. Blue Eyes was amazing to watch in action – if he was looking at a fake, his eyes would dull over, but when he was looking at the real thing, there would be a sudden flash of blue light.

On the day in question, a young man dressed like a student came to the shop, carrying a scroll painting in one hand. The label stuck on it read "*Lake Vista in Springtime* by the monk Dadizi". Blue Eyes barely glanced at it; he knew that whatever it said on the label, it wouldn't mean a damn thing – if you want to know if a painting is genuine, you have to look at it. He unrolled it, and quick as a flash, half a foot of the painting was revealed. That was Blue Eyes' way; it didn't matter how big or small the whole painting was, he would only ever look at half a foot. As to whether the artwork was real or fake, his verdict would depend on what that half a foot told him, but he wouldn't look at even an inch more. Blue Eyes was face-to-face with this half a foot, and his spectacles flashed with a blue light. He raised his head and asked his visitor: "How much are you planning to sell this for?"

The man was in no hurry to open negotiations on the price. Instead, he said: "I've heard that Third Master Huang from over on the west side has made a copy of this painting."

Third Master Huang was the best forger in Tianjin. Everyone in the art world was afraid of him. But Blue Eyes carried on regardless. He said: "I don't care about any Third Master Huang. You just tell me how much you want for this painting."

"Two," the visitor said. That meant that he wanted twenty bars of gold.

It wasn't a pittance, but it wasn't unreasonable either, so after a bit of bargaining, the price was agreed at eighteen bars.

From that day onwards, the art world in Tianjin was buzzing with the news that Riches Antiques over on Guodian Street had bought a landscape painting by the famous artist and monk Dadizi, also known as Shitao. The ink lines representing the water of the lake were particularly well done – you could really see the shallows, it was amazingly fluid – and then up above was a long inscription. What a treasure! Some people said it had originally come from a princely mansion in Beijing. The man who sold it clearly had no idea what he had; Blue Eyes had pulled a fast one! It had cost him a lot of money, but nothing like what the thing was worth. A painting by Dadizi of this quality hadn't been seen on the art market in Tianjin in a decade or more. In those days, there weren't any newspapers, so everything relied on word of mouth. The more people spoke about it, the better they made it out to be, and soon news had spread far and wide. People came in droves to look at that painting, and Riches Antiques was packed to the rafters from morning until night.

Well, once everyone had made enough fuss, some ugly rumours started to be heard. About three months after the sale, people started to say that the Dadizi painting at Riches Antiques wasn't all it was cracked up to be. It was very impressive when you saw it for the first time, but once you'd looked at it on several occasions, it came to seem lifeless and thin. The difference between a real work of art and a fake is that the real thing can stand up to being looked at, and the fake can't. Once rumours to this effect had started to circulate, another bit of news was added to the mix – some people said that it was a copy made by Third Master Huang over on the west side of the city! Saying that made Blue Eyes look completely incompetent, didn't it?

Blue Eyes knew what he was about and didn't pay any attention. But the more he tried to ignore what people were saying, the more the rumours grew. In the end, there was a lot of corroborative detail. There was the story about how someone had seen the real painting in a house over by Zhenshi Street. Now people turned up in droves yet again, coming to Riches Antiques to look at the painting, but this time it was to admire the techniques that Third Master Huang had used to put one over on Blue Eyes. This kind of battle of wits was great fun!

By this time, Mr Tong, the boss of Riches Antiques, was starting to get worried, and he said to Blue Eyes: "I have faith in you, but the gossip is killing us. The store is in chaos day after day. How about we find someone to tell us where this other painting is? If there really is an identical painting, we need to be able to put it on show, make everyone see which one is real and which is the fake, and that will prove we were in the right all along."

Blue Eyes could hear that the boss wasn't sure, but there was nothing he could do to put a stop to all the rumours other than go along with what he said – they had to be able to put the two paintings on show together. If someone was out to cause trouble for them, they had to win fair and square by making the whole thing public.

Mr Tong went and found You Xiaowu. You Xiaowu was what they called a "sewer rat" in Tianjin in those days: he went absolutely everywhere and heard everything that was going on. They sent You Xiaowu off to find out what this was all about, and the next day he had news for them. There really was another painting by Dadizi, also called *Lake Vista in Springtime*, and it belonged to a family called Cui who lived over on Zhenshi Street! Neither Mr Tong nor Blue Eyes had ever even heard of these Cui people. Mr Tong got You Xiaowu to take Blue Eyes over there to have a look at it. Blue Eyes had to go, and when he arrived at their house, his spectacles flashed blue light all over again. He was stunned!

This was the real thing. The painting back at the shop was a fake! The size, the colours, the painting, they were identical – even the seals had been copied exactly. But somehow the spirit of the thing was different – you see, this painting really had life to it!

He had no idea how he could have made such a mistake. Standing face-to-face with this painting, he wished he could disappear through a crack in the floor. In the last twenty years, he hadn't been wrong about one single work of art. Blue Eyes was a legend in the art world. If he said it was real, it was real; if he said it was a fake, it was a fake; nobody ever questioned his attributions. But this time he'd got it wrong, and when people found out, his reputation would be ruined. When it comes to authenticity of art, you have to be right every time. If you make a mistake just once, you're done for.

He didn't say a word. When he got back to the shop, he told the boss the truth. Riches Antiques depended on Blue Eyes; if he went down, then the business was ruined. Mr Tong thought about it overnight and decided that they had to buy the Cui family's Dadizi painting, no matter what it cost. Once they had both paintings in hand, the real one and the copy would be whichever they said it was. But they couldn't appear in this themselves, so they'd have to spend money to hire someone to appear as the purchaser, who would then go to the Cui house with You Xiaowu to buy the painting. They were not expecting that the Cui family would ask the earth for their picture. They announced that if they didn't get the price they wanted, they weren't going to sell. In this kind of situation, you have the worst of all possible worlds: one side that has to buy whatever the cost, and the other that refuses to sell. The man acting as the buyer knew exactly what he had to do, though, because right before he set off, Mr Tong told him: "Even if it costs me everything I own, you have to get that painting for me." So, in the end, he gave way, and it cost him seventy bars of gold to buy the painting – in other words, more than three times as much as the first one.

When the scroll arrived at Riches Antiques, Mr Tong breathed a sigh of relief. Even though having to spend all that money was a terrible wrench, he'd saved the company name. He told the shop boys to hang both paintings up on the wall so that he could have a good look at them. When the paintings were up, Blue Eyes came to have a look, and his spectacles flashed blue all over again. He stood there as if he'd been poleaxed. It couldn't possibly be true, and yet it was – the first painting was genuine, and the one they'd just bought was the fake!

If the two hadn't been put right next to each other, it would have been impossible to tell which one was the original and which was the copy – that was how good the man was, and he was the very best!

What on earth was Blue Eyes doing? Where had his eyes been lately?

Blue Eyes practically had a heart attack on the spot. It took him three days to work the whole thing out from start to finish, and then he realised it had all been a trap cunningly laid for him by Third Master Huang, and he'd walked right into it. He'd bought the real painting at a good price, but he'd paid a fortune for the fake. He suddenly remembered that right at the beginning, the young man dressed as a student had said to him: "Third Master Huang has copied this painting." Right? He'd told him straight out that there were two versions of the same painting, one real and one copy. If he made a mistake, whose fault was that? Clearly, this wasn't about the money for Third Master Huang, this was personal. He wanted to show that even when you own the real thing, you would still go out and buy his copy. That's a nasty trick to play on anyone! When he understood that, when he realised exactly what had happened, he had to accept that he was done for. Blue Eyes packed up his stuff and left Riches Antiques. After this, not only did he never reappear in the Tianjin art world, nobody ever saw hide nor hair of him again. Someone said that he got terribly sick, took to his bed, and died. He never recovered from the blow!

Thinking about it, there is another dreadful thing – Third Master Huang got him, but he only ever saw his brushstrokes. The man himself never appeared, and he didn't even get to see his face.

The only good thing about any of this is that in the end, he worked out that Third Master Huang had been behind it all. He knew exactly who was responsible for his death.

8
YANG BA AND HIS MOUTH

TIANJIN IS a wonderful place that has produced all kinds of amazing people, including two real masters who sold *chatang* – they got famous selling this perfectly ordinary and traditional snack food. One of them was dark-skinned, fat, and straightforward – his name was Yang Qi, or Yang the Seventh. The other was pale-skinned, thin, and quick-witted, and people called him Yang Ba – the Eighth. The names suggested that they were brothers, but in fact, they weren't related at all: they just happened to both have fathers with the surname Yang. Yang Ba's original name was Ba meaning "hopeful" but it is pronounced just the same as Ba meaning "eighth", and Yang Ba was obviously younger than Yang Qi, so people made the mistake of thinking they were the seventh and eighth sons of the family. However, when it came right down to it, the two of them were very close, better than the best of friends: there are plenty of real brothers that couldn't match up to them. Yang Qi was the one who could cook, so he dealt with making the stuff; Yang Ba

had the mouth, so he was out there chatting to the customers. Even though there were just the two of them in the business, and they were more staff than bosses, they did much better for themselves than many a larger enterprise.

Yang Qi had two particular tricks up his sleeve in the cooking.

When most people make *chatang*, once they've cooked up their glutinous rice noodles, they top them with some sesame paste – but that means the good bit comes first, and as you eat, the flavour gets more and more boring. Yang Qi improved on this. He'd put half the glutinous rice noodles in the bowl and then put in a layer of sesame paste, then add the rest of the noodles, and then top with more sesame. That way there'd be flavouring the whole way through to the bottom of the bowl.

His other trick was that instead of using whole sesame seeds, he'd roast them a bit in an iron wok first, and then use the end of a rolling pin to mash them. Mashed to a paste, the delicious scent would come out. The sesame seeds had to be toasted a lovely golden brown but not burned – if they weren't golden they wouldn't have the flavour, but if overdone they'd go bitter. Crushing the seeds was also an art – too coarse, and the texture would be gritty; too smooth, and there'd be nothing to get your teeth into. This is something that everybody knows, but most people won't take trouble over. Good cooks need to hone their skills – no different from painters or calligraphy masters.

It doesn't matter how good you are, how high quality your food is – if you want it to sell well, you need people to promote it. The product is three-tenths of your success, while marketing is seven-tenths: if enough people say so then the dead can come back to life, and some bit of rubbish can become a must-have item. Marketing is all in how you tell it. When the time came and it was necessary for someone to appear and jolly everyone along, saying just the right thing, trimming his sails to the wind, and making friends with one and all – then it was all down to Yang Ba and his mouth.

One day, the great statesman Li Hongzhang came to Tianjin, and the local officials and taotais were all racking their brains: what could they give His Excellency to eat? What would please him? He was a huge figure in the capital – he'd have eaten his fill of rare delicacies years ago, so if they wanted to surprise him, it would have to be with some local speciality. But Tianjin's local specialities were really too coarse and vulgar: their fish stew ran to lots of little bones which might so easily get stuck in the great man's throat, while their fried *mahua* dough twists were so hard he might break a tooth. After three days of thinking about it, they still hadn't reached any kind of decision. Fortunately, the prefect was the sort of person who likes to walk his patch, visiting every lane and alley, and he'd eaten everything they had for sale there, so he could recommend "Yang Family *chatang*" – besides which *chatang* is soft and sweet, good to eat and posing not the slightest risk to His Excellency. The other officials all thought this was a great idea. This was how Yang Ba got catapulted into fame and fortune.

That afternoon, His Excellency Li Hongzhang had listened to a performance of the local opera *The Lotus Blossoms are Falling*, and he'd been enjoying himself, for it was all great fun. Afterwards, he went for a relaxing pee, and then feeling a little bit peckish, he decided he'd like a snack. The prefect quickly called on "Yang Qi and Yang Ba" to serve their *chatang*. Today, the two young men were dressed up for their high-society debut in new clothes from top to toe: blue trousers and jackets, white handkerchiefs and socks, and they'd scrubbed their hands so hard with soap that they nearly took the top layer of skin off – that's how clean they were! The two of them came in together to place the bowl of *chatang* on the table in front of Li Hongzhang, and afterwards, they took five paces back and stood with their arms by their sides. They said they were waiting for further orders, but in fact, they were hoping for a reward.

His Excellency Li Hongzhang was just about to taste this famous Tianjin speciality, his fingertips were touching the edge of the bowl... and then his eyes looked at the contents, his brows suddenly wrinkled in a frown, his face became thunderous, and with a violent swipe from his arm, the bowl of *chatang* fell to the floor with a thud. The porcelain bowl was smashed to smithereens, and the steaming *chatang* spread across the floor. The officials present were shocked into silence, and Yang Qi and Yang Ba instantly fell to their knees. But nobody knew why His Excellency was so angry.

The officials present were all flummoxed, but Yang Ba realised pretty much straight away what must have happened. In the blink of an eye, he'd worked out that His Excellency had never had *chatang* before, and he didn't know what the paste on top might be. He was thinking they must be the sort of filthy street-traders who dropped mud in the food, and that was why he was so angry. If that was correct, they now had a serious problem.

If he said it was sesame paste and not some bit of muck that had fallen in by mistake, then it would make His Excellency look ignorant and foolish – how could he not realise it was sesame? If he didn't explain, then he was effectively admitting that he'd given a bowl of filth to His Excellency. Either way, he was looking at a beating now and bankruptcy for his business later. But right now it was crucial to stop His Excellency opening his mouth and complaining that he'd been given something disgusting and dirty to eat. Once he said that, it would be impossible to get him to change his mind. So he had to come up with an excuse that would allow him to get in ahead.

Quick as a flash, an idea sprang into Yang Ba's mind: that was it! His head hit the floor with a resounding thud, and he kowtowed with all his might as he said: "Your Excellency! I had no idea that you don't like sesame paste – I'm so sorry! Please forgive me! I won't make the same mistake again!" When he had finished, he kowtowed again.

Li Hongzhang now realised that the brown stuff he'd noticed in the *chatang* wasn't unmentionable filth but merely sesame paste. Having grasped that point, he thought to himself that Tianjin was the watershed for nine rivers, and the people living there had to be quick on the uptake – it's a centre for commercial activity too, and that makes sure people stay on the ball. This young man selling *chatang* was clearly pretty bright; not only had he realised immediately that he'd made the mistake of thinking the sesame paste was some bit of filth, but he'd managed to clear the whole thing up in a way that gave him face. The magistrates and taotais standing about the room weren't a patch on this young man. Impressed and pleased with Yang Ba's quick thinking, he said: "It's not your fault that you didn't know! Now although it is true I am not fond of sesame paste (and here he was making sure that he got out of an awkward situation gracefully), your *chatang* is justly famous throughout Tianjin, and you deserve a reward! Let me present you with one hundred taels of silver!"

Those present were amazed and baffled. If he didn't like the *chatang*, why was he giving them such an enormous reward? Was he completely stupid? Meanwhile, Yang Ba was down on his knees kowtowing and thanking him for his kindness. He knew exactly what he meant.

After that, Yang Ba was famous the length and breadth of Tianjin. "Yang Family *chatang*" was now known to one and all as "Yang Ba's *chatang*". Yang Qi gradually faded from the scene, and nobody even noticed. Yang Ba wasn't ashamed of having taken over like that, because it was his own mouth that had made him famous – after all, the great Li Hongzhang never even tasted the *chatang*!

9
YOUNG MASTER CAI

Young Master Cai had a very special talent – selling the family silver.

How much family silver did the Cai family have? Nobody was quite sure of the answer to that question. But it was known that they were one of the richest families in Tianjin, they'd made their money in the salt monopoly, and that once they got rich, they went into government, and also over the generations they produced numerous collectors of art and antiques. Back at the time of the Boxer Rebellion in 1900, the Old Master and Madame had fled the fighting and ended up dying far away from home. Their oldest son was already living in Shanghai by then, where he was in business; he had his own family there and owned a successful company. So the stuff left back at home was all the property of the Young Master now. He didn't know how to do anything other than sell things and live off the proceeds. All these years, from the time he was a youth to the beginnings of old age, he had eaten the bread of idleness. But people said that it would take three generations to pick the Cai family clean of everything.

When Mr Huang, the owner of the Respecting Antiquity Studio, heard people say things like that, he laughed to himself. He'd spent years dealing exclusively in the stuff coming out of the Cai family mansion. It is easy to sell things that come with a famous name attached. And Mr Huang had a good eye, so he could see at a glance that the senior generations in the Cai family had been well up to snuff when it came to buying art and antiques. Not only was there not a single fake in the place, but they'd bought the very best of the best – if you could lay your hands on it, you'd be guaranteed to be able to sell it again. More than half of what the Cai family had sold had passed through his hands, so he knew exactly what end was up in the mansion. Fifteen years ago, it had been jewellery and carved jade stones, calligraphy, paintings, and antiques coming out of the Cai house; ten years ago, it was ceramics and stone artworks, and the hardwood furniture; and five years ago, it was bag after bag of old clothes. It was all top quality, make no mistake about that, but there was a strong feeling that the river was now gradually starting to run dry. Mr Huang had also gradually changed the way he behaved towards Young Master Cai. Fifteen years ago, when he bought things from the Young Master, he'd always gone in person to the Cai mansion; ten years ago, when the Young Master had something to sell, he'd send a man to call him round, and he'd go rushing off; but for the last five years or so, it was the Young Master's turn to come to the Respecting Antiquity Studio himself, clutching his bag of old clothes under his arm.

Then Mr Huang would look down and say: "Second Master, do you mind opening your bag?" None of the apprentices even tried to help. Mr Huang would take up a ruler, and pick through the clothes in the bag one at a time, tossing them aside afterwards, while calling out the price, just like one of the dealers in old clothes that operated on Yigu Street. When it came to paying, that was left entirely to the apprentices – Mr Huang had already gone off to drink his tea or have a smoke out the back. Mr Huang thought that he knew everything there was to know about the state of the Cai family, but in the last two years, some strange things had been happening.

All of a sudden, Young Master Cai wasn't selling old clothes any more – in recent times, every few days he was sending someone to call him to come over to the Cai mansion. Then after an eternity of roundabout discussions of this and that, he would turn around and take something off the shelves behind him, and it was always an absolutely marvellous piece. First it was a large *famille vert* ceramic dish, dating to the reign of the Kangxi Emperor, and next it was a fan, painted by the great Ming dynasty artist, Shen Zhou. From the Young Master's expression and manner when he plonked the thing down on the table, they were back where they had been more than a decade earlier. Mr Huang said: "Rich families are amazing, and that's a fact! It seems like you've got a bottomless chest here, Young Master. You've been selling stuff off for nearly twenty years, and you can still find beautiful pieces like these!" Young Master Cai smiled and said lightly: "I couldn't simply sell off everything that I had inherited from my ancestors, now could I, because wouldn't I then be squandering the family fortune?" But the trouble really started when it came to discussing the price; he always wanted so much more than Mr Huang was willing to pay. This is what is called a "noose price" in the trade. If you pay it, you will never make a profit on the deal, so you might as well go ahead and kill yourself right now.

There are only two ways to buy things from people like the Cais: either you buy when they are desperate, or you buy when they are flush. Buying when they are desperate means that they have some urgent need for the money so they have to sell something – you are very lucky if you catch them in such a crisis. Buying when they are flush means that they don't need the money, and in any case, they will only sell if you offer them absolutely top dollar. In that kind of situation, it is going to be hard going. Young Master Cai had always been selling because he was desperate; what on earth could have happened that he was now flush?

One day, Mr Mao, the boss of the Pavilion of Refinement at Liulichang in Beijing came to the Respecting Antiquity Studio. There had always been a lot of dealings between their two businesses, between Beijing and Tianjin, and they frequently sent items back and forth for sale, as well as finding buyers for each other's pieces, so they were very well-acquainted.

Mr Mao spotted an item he recognised on a shelf in the shop the moment he came through the door, and went over to have a look at it – sitting on a magnificent rosewood stand there was a copy of the *Diamond Sutra* carved on eight plaques of mutton-fat jade, written in small but highly elegant clerical script calligraphy, and carved by a master hand. Each individual character was inlaid with pure gold. He turned his head to look at Mr Huang and said: "Where did you get this?" He looked confused.

"It came in about two weeks ago," Mr Huang replied. "Why?"

Mr Mao responded with a question of his own: "Who sold it to you?"

Mr Huang rolled his eyes. These people in Beijing ought to know the rules by now! In the world of art and antiques, you never ask straight out who's selling a thing, or who's bought it. He smiled and refused to say more.

Mr Mao realised that his question had been inappropriate. He now rephrased his question: "Did you get this from Young Master Cai in Tianjin? He bought it from me."

Mr Huang was amazed and couldn't help himself: "He's been selling to me for years! How could he be buying from you?"

Mr Mao picked up on this immediately: "He's always been a good customer to me, so why would he need to sell things? That's why I asked you about it just now."

The two men looked at each other, baffled.

Suddenly Mr Mao pointed at a blue-and-white Ming dynasty vase, dating to the reign of Chenghua, which was standing on another shelf, and said: "I sold that vase to him too! How much did you give him for it? He paid me a pittance… I practically gave it away."

Mr Mao still seemed to have no idea what had happened, but Mr Huang could see exactly how the scam was worked. However, he had no intention of explaining it all to Mr Mao. He waited until the man left and then immediately gave orders to all the apprentices: "Remember, from here on in we are not having any more dealings with Young Master Cai. That bastard is already far too good at this little trick!"

10
CROP-HAIRED YANG

AFTER THE EVENTS of Gengzi year (1900) in the reign of the Guangxu Emperor, social reform was in the air, and revolutionaries were popping up like mushrooms. All kinds of odd people and odd ideas came to the fore, and the Dazhigu district produced a particularly fine specimen: Crop-haired Yang. At that time, men could still get into trouble with the authorities for cutting off their queues, besides which their parents wouldn't like it, so they mostly weren't prepared to have too much off. But then, once they'd had their hair cut, there wasn't a new style to adopt yet, so they ended up with a pile of loose hair hanging down from their heads looking not unlike a haystack – this was commonly called a "horse's mane", but if you were being polite, you said they were "crop-haired". At that time, having a cropped head was very fashionable for modern and forward-thinking men.

So if this is true, what was so special about this person called

Yang going around with cropped hair? Good question. Let me explain – this one was a woman.

There was an important family in Dazhigu with the surname Yang, and they had two unmarried daughters. The oldest daughter was very quiet and refined, and she stayed at home; the second Miss Yang was lively and fun-loving, and she was out all day, dressing up and carrying on just as if she'd been a boy. She was also always following the very latest trends: whenever some new fashion got going, she was there making sure she was right on the front line. The very first time she heard the word "revolution", she went straight out and cut her hair so that she had a cropped head just like the modern young men. That was big news at the time. But she didn't care how much her family created, nor what other people said about her: she did just what she felt like, and she was having fun. But in less than a week, she started having real problems.

On the evening of the day in question, Crop-haired Yang was on her way home after listening to a lecture at the Academy of Western Studies over at Laolongtou. She was absolutely desperate for a pee. She was making for home as quickly as she could, but the faster she went, the more she felt she was about to burst. It was like floodwaters beating against a dam, trying to force a breach. She spotted a public lavatory by the side of the road and plunged straight in.

All public lavatories work on the same principle – men on one side and women on the other, with a wall between them, and it is always gents to the left and ladies to the right. Just as she was undoing the belt to her trousers, she heard one of the women squatting down start to scream in a high-pitched voice: "Hooligan! Bastard!" Then another person started screaming, and she was even louder. She was confused by all the racket and had no idea where this hooligan could be, so she hoisted up her trousers and came running out. She was surprised to find that the other women came running out too, shouting and throwing punches at her; it turned out they'd decided that she was some sex pest who'd gone to the women's lavatory to make a nuisance of himself by eying them up. Some passers-by joined in and grabbed hold of her, and now they all attacked, kicking and thumping her. Crop-haired Yang screamed: "Stop! Don't hit me! I'm a woman!" That just earned her an even worse beating: "We're hitting you for pretending to be a woman, get it!" This went on until a policeman came by on patrol, recognised that this was the second Miss Yang, and rescued her and took her home. Crop-haired Yang was bruised all over, and her face was covered with blood. When she saw her parents, she cried and had hysterics, and this carried on for a good few days, but there is no need to say more about it.

Having been beaten so badly, Crop-haired Yang didn't dare go near a public lavatory again. Even if she was so desperate that she ended up peeing in her pants, she wouldn't go in. Obviously, she couldn't use the men's, but trying to use the women's side would be even worse. For a time she didn't know anymore what she was.

She wasn't looking for trouble, but trouble came to find her.

She heard that there had been incidents in women's lavatories all over Dazhigu. The story was that a man with short hair would burst in, and then shout: "I'm Crop-haired Yang!" He'd scare the women witless, he'd get to see them in various degrees of undress, and then he'd turn round and run off. It wasn't serious, but it was annoying, and people were upset about it. And then in some places, there were horrible teenagers who thought they'd take advantage of the situation to have some fun, so from time to time they'd take up position outside the women's lavatories and then bellow: "Crop-haired Yang is coming!" It got so that the women's lavatories in that part of town were treated like haunted houses and nobody dared set foot inside one.

Crop-haired Yang simply couldn't understand it; how could being modern have got her into so much trouble? All she'd done was cut her hair, and it ended up that she couldn't use a lavatory. She had no idea whether she'd caused this situation, or whether the situation existed anyway and she had somehow or other become caught up in it. In her rage, she spent the next two months shut up in her room. Gradually, her hair grew out, and she looked like a woman again – now she could go into the women's public lavatory whenever she liked, and the place was completely peaceful, as if none of those awful things had ever happened.

11
I KNOW HIS TEETH

DOCTOR HUA WAS a dentist and very good at his job. All you had to do was open your mouth: you didn't have to tell him which tooth hurt, which tooth was giving you gyp, or which tooth was wobbly – he could tell it all at a glance. He could make your real teeth look as pretty as a set of false ones, and he could make false teeth that worked as well as your real ones. As to trying to understand how he'd come by his skill... that kept people guessing!

Doctor Hua was a lovely man, very kind and honest, and utterly law-abiding, but he had one odd failing, and that was his terrible memory. He couldn't remember people's faces; he'd see them and forget them straight away. Supposing that it was only yesterday that you went to see him about a rotten tooth, and today you bumped into him on the street and said hello, and he obviously didn't know you from Adam – wouldn't you find it insulting? You might try and excuse it on the grounds of bad eyesight, but he never wore glasses. How could it be that he had

such a terrible memory? That was another thing people speculated about.

Later on, something happened to Doctor Hua that answered all these questions in one fell swoop.

One afternoon, two plainclothes detectives arrived from the local police station. The moment they came in the door, they started questioning him: "Did a dark-skinned man come to your clinic this morning? He had a beard, puffy eyes, and a large black mole by the right corner of his mouth."

Doctor Hua shook his head and said: "I don't remember."

"How many patients did you see this morning?" the detective asked.

"This morning I only had six patients," Doctor Hua replied.

"That's odd!" the detective said. "You only saw six patients this morning so how come you can't remember? Besides which, with this man's striking appearance, even if you only caught a glimpse of him walking down the road, I reckon you'd still remember him a year later. Let me tell you, our man carried out an armed robbery at a jewellers shop over on Guyi Street last month – he's a wanted criminal. If you refuse to tell us what we want to know, does that not make you an accessory?"

Normally, Doctor Hua never got angry, but when he heard that he was furious. Bang! He thumped the table so hard that his pliers for pulling teeth leapt in the air. "We Huas have been dentists for three generations, helping people in pain, and none of us has ever been involved in any kind of illegal activity. If I say I can't remember, it's because I can't remember! I can also tell you for free that if I were to discover the location of a violent criminal, you wouldn't need to come and find me, because I'd go to you!"

The two detectives could see that the dentist was really angry: he was gritting his teeth so hard they could see his gums – he didn't seem to be putting it on. They hesitated for a moment, and then turned and went away.

One icy day, Doctor Hua really did come running into the police station. He had run so hard that he'd torn his coat. He said that the man who'd robbed the jewellers was over at the restaurant on Kaifeng Road called A Jug of Wine, drinking right at that very moment! When the police heard the news, they set off immediately, and they were able to make an arrest, bringing a serious criminal to justice.

"How did you recognise him, Doctor Hua?" the detective asked.

"Well, I was having my dinner at A Jug of Wine, and I spotted the man drinking with some others. I saw that he had a black mole by his mouth, but that was something that you had told me about – I couldn't be sure it was him. There is more than one person on this earth with moles by their mouths, and it would be dreadful to make such a serious accusation by mistake! But when he opened his mouth to laugh, I could see that incisor of his. That tooth was what he came to consult me about; I remember that perfectly – there could be no mistake! So I came rushing here to tell you!"

"I simply can't understand it," the detective said. "How did you recognise him by his teeth?"

Doctor Hua burst out laughing and said: "I am a dentist. I never notice what anyone looks like, but I know his teeth!"

The detective listened to his explanation with baffled amazement.

When this story got out, everyone's speculations were answered. He couldn't remember people, but this shouldn't be accounted a failing, because he didn't notice faces, he noticed teeth. As a dentist, all of his attention went to teeth, so no wonder he was so good!

12

THE MASTER OF CLOUD BELVEDERE

The Master of Cloud Belvedere was the name given to an educated gent living over by the Hai River. Why do I call him an educated gent? Well, he was the kind of person who would never, ever get a nickname, but when you mention him, pretty much everyone would know who he is.

This educated gent had a narrow face and thin body, his skin was yellow and dry, and his arms and legs were spindly and long – he looked like nothing so much as a rag draped over a bamboo pole to dry. However, you can't judge by appearances. He was a competent painter and calligrapher, in addition to which he could carve a beautiful seal, and he was also perfectly capable of mounting a scroll, but the professionals all said he... well, somehow or other his work was just too heavy-handed. It was for this reason that you couldn't find a single business in the whole of Tianjin that he'd written the signboard for, nor was there a restaurant or medicine shop that had one of his paintings on the wall. When it came to calligraphy and painting, he was a professional, but he was treated like an amateur. When an educated gentleman finds himself in this position, he may well feel that he has no outlet for his talents; whether he is bitter or sour about this, or bitter *and* sour, only he can tell.

The name of his studio, the Cloud Belvedere, was his own invention. He called himself the Master of Cloud Belvedere, and wrote a pair of calligraphic couplets which he hung on the wall facing the entrance: "Even though I am imprisoned among green hills," said one; "My mind wanders among the white clouds," proclaimed the other. He often recited these lines to himself. Every time he intoned them, he would close his eyes and give a little shake of the shoulders, as if he really were some kind of hermit. But in point of fact, Tianjin was a playground for all kinds of people, and the Cloud Belvedere was located right by the eastern entrance to the city's main shopping drag, so there were always hordes of shoppers stampeding past. Besides which, he had the Four Seasons restaurant right next door, and so all day every day he had the most entrancing cooking-smells, one after the other, coming in through the window – first fish, then meat, then garlic, then soy sauce… And if he shut the window? It didn't make the blindest bit of difference! The glass might keep out the smell of frying fish and broiling meat, but it didn't keep out the sights and sounds of the endless partying. One of the neighbours pointed out to him: "You might as well open the Cloud Belvedere as a restaurant too. It would make a lovely name for a restaurant – the Cloud Belvedere – it sounds very good!"

He nearly had a heart attack right then and there.

But as time passes, it may happen that your luck changes. There was an interfering type called Chen Ba who came to visit him one day with an American in tow. This man was about fifty, bald, and with prominent eyes and a huge walrus moustache, which meant that you couldn't see his mouth. Chen Ba said that this American was interested in Chinese art and antiques, particularly calligraphy and painting. This was the first time that the Master of Cloud Belvedere had ever found himself face to face with a westerner, and he was quite overcome, to the point where he didn't know what to do with his hands and feet – when he got up on a stool to hang up his paintings, he nearly went arse over tit. The American didn't even notice: he was too busy staring at the paintings on the wall. Each time he came to a new picture, he would be going wow, wow at the top of his voice, as if he'd just sprayed some delicate part of his anatomy in boiling water. Afterwards, he would work his chops a bit and splutter a few words of praise. When he was working his chops, you could see something cherry-like, red and shining, pop out from underneath that huge moustache. The Master of Cloud Belvedere stared at it: it was the old American guy's lips. In the end, he spoke to the Master of Cloud Belvedere in Chinese, spitting out one word at a time: "I... am... so... happy... Thank... you... I... am... so... happy... Thank... you..." These were probably the only words that he knew how to say, so he kept repeating them right up to the time that they said goodbye and left.

The Master of Cloud Belvedere was so delighted he almost went off his head. In his entire life, he'd never had anyone express such appreciation of his work before. Two months later, he got a letter in English. He took it to Mr Zhu, who worked at the *Ta Kung Pao* newspaper and could understand foreign languages. Mr Zhu smiled when he read this missive, and said: "I don't know what you've done to this American, but he seems to have gone insane! He says that since getting back home he hasn't been able to forget your wonderful calligraphy – he thinks about it all the time and even dreams about it at night. He says he has now come to understand that artists in China are all geniuses!"

The Master of Cloud Belvedere felt as if he were walking on air. His body felt as light as a feather. He didn't sleep a wink that night, and as soon as it got light, inspiration came to him. He wrote the words "In the Pursuit of Tranquillity You Achieve Greatness" and mounted it as a scroll with his own hands, after which he headed to the post office. When he posted it off, he included a note to say that he wanted him to hang it up on the wall; come what may, he should have a photograph taken of himself standing in front of the inscription, and send him a copy. His idea was that he wanted everyone to see it. His friends and family should see it; his neighbours should see it; the people who'd always shown their contempt for him should see it; the bosses of big companies should see it; the editors of newspapers should see it; hell, he might even take out an ad in the papers and let everyone see it! Open your eyes people! You don't like what I do, but this American guy does!

He waited at the Cloud Belvedere for three months, by which time he was feeling unhappy and discouraged about the whole thing. Finally, a letter arrived with foreign writing on the outside. He quickly ripped it open and took out the letter: it was all in foreign language, and he didn't understand a word. There wasn't a photograph. He took up the envelope again – the photograph was inside. He picked up the photograph and looked at it, feeling awkward, as if there was something not quite right. When he looked carefully, he was stunned. The American guy was standing in front of his calligraphy, but it was the wrong way up. He'd hung it upside down!

❧ 13 ☙
YANG YUELOU AND HIS FRIEND, LI JIN'AO

IN THE TWENTY-EIGHTH year of the Republic (in other words, in 1939), there was a terrible flood in the city of Tianjin, and buildings big and small found themselves standing in water. Three-storey buildings had their feet in the water; two-storey buildings were up to their waists; and little houses were covered right up to the roof. There were boats sailing up and down the roads, people used the windows to get in and out of their houses, business had stopped, wheeled traffic was impossible, and Yang Yuelou found himself trapped, along with the other members of his troupe and their horses, at the Qingyun Theatre near the Southern Market. With everything underwater, who had time and energy enough to go to the theatre? The twenty members of the troupe found themselves sleeping on the stage.

After a couple of months, the floodwaters in Tianjin started to go down, and by this time the members of the troupe, with their horses, had not only eaten through all their savings, they'd had to hock a dozen or so trunks of costumes and props at the

Prosperity pawnshop on Hebei Avenue. They waited until the waters receded, they waited until the trains were running again, and by that time Yang Yuelou was desperate to get back to Shanghai, but when it came to finding the money for the tickets, he just didn't have it. He was in such a fret that he ground his teeth until they hurt and his cheeks swelled. One of the more helpful young members of the troupe suggested a way out to him: "You'd better go and ask Li Jin'ao for help. He likes to do good deeds. If someone famous like you begged for assistance, I am sure he'd do his best."

Li Jin'ao was a big man in Tianjin in those days, a gangster boss. When it came to any kind of dangerous situation, right up to killing people, he didn't hold back: he would jump in with both feet. But even though he was a career criminal, he had some standards, and he did care about his reputation, and there were plenty of occasions when he'd helped out the little guy, robbing the rich to give to the poor. Yang Yuelou had never had anything to do with him before. But the situation was impossible – he had to go and see the man no matter how much he disliked the idea. He went with the young man to the west side of the city, up various roads and down the alleys, until he raised his eyes and stopped in amazement. A rickety fence, a gate cobbled together from a few planks of wood, and a tumbledown building; how could the famous Li Jin'ao possibly live in a hovel like this? However, the young man from his troupe stopped outside the door and called: "Second Master Li!"

At the sound of this cry, a hunched figure shuffled out of the building. Once this person got outside, he straightened up, which gave Yang Yuelou a right shock – the man was over six feet tall and had shoulders so broad he'd struggle to get through the average doorway. His face had crimsoned with age, and his stubble went unshaved. He was wearing a robe made of grey cotton which was big enough to be used as a bedsheet for any ordinary person, but it had stains all down the front. Yang Yuelou decided they must have come to the wrong place, but then the man opened a mouth the size of a bucket and said: "You were looking for me?" His voice was harsh and his expression aggressive. There could be no doubt: this was Li Jin'ao!

When they went in, the place was a wreck. The floor was filthy, and the furniture was filthy too, and it was all so beaten up over the years that nothing was in one piece. Right opposite them there was an octagonal table, but one of the legs was missing, so it was propped up on a pile of bricks. There was a teapot on the table, but it was missing its handle and lid, its spout was broken, and its bottom was cracked. Yang Yuelou started to wonder whether Li Jin'ao was genuinely poor or just pretending to be so. If he was actually as poverty-stricken as he seemed, how could he possibly help him? He was not holding out much hope for this encounter.

Li Jin'ao had been measuring up his visitor – jacket and trousers in a light pongee silk, with white silk socks, black formal shoes, and a finely woven Panama straw-hat on his head. He was holding a painted folding fan with a calligraphic inscription, mounted on fan sticks of speckled bamboo. He looked at Yang Yuelou through narrowed eyes and said: "Have we met?" His expression was aggressive; he seemed to be treating him as an enemy, and not as a guest.

The young man from the troupe made the necessary introductions and explained why they'd come. Li Jin'ao immediately got to his feet and put his hands together in a gesture of respect: "I must apologise for my manners, please don't mind me, Mr Yang. We're very lucky to have such a great star coming here to Tianjin to perform! We can't possibly let you get into difficulties! How about you go back to the Prosperity pawnshop tomorrow afternoon to collect your stuff!" He spoke so easily, you might think that nothing happened in Tianjin without his say-so. The whole thing made Yang Yuelou very nervous and suspicious – he even wondered if the whole thing might not be some kind of elaborate hoax.

The following day, in the morning, Li Jin'ao came stomping into the Prosperity pawnshop on Hebei Avenue. As he came through the door, he went straight to the high counter, raised his head, and said: "Go and tell your boss that Li Jin'ao is here to see him!" That didn't just frighten the apprentice behind the counter into galloping off at the double; all the other customers were scared witless and decided to remove themselves just as quickly as they could. The boss came hurrying forward and invited Li Jin'ao to come upstairs for a cup of tea. Li Jin'ao ignored him. He just said: "My friend, Mr Yang, has pawned several trunks of costumes and props with you, and he doesn't have the money to get them back. You tell him that he can take them away, and he can pay you back at some later date." Having said that he turned around and walked off.

Now in the afternoon of the same day, Yang Yuelou went along to the Prosperity pawnshop with a few other people to try his luck, and the moment he got in through the door he saw more than a dozen trunks lined up by the desk – his main costume trunk, the second costume trunk, the third costume trunk, the trunk of helmets, the trunk of banners and weapons, and so on and so forth. Yang Yuelou was so happy and surprised at this sight, he exclaimed in delight. Having retrieved his property in this way, he went back to Shanghai, as pleased as punch.

After Yang Yuelou had gone, Li Jin'ao's lads back in Tianjin got to hear all about it, and they were so impressed by their boss that they went in droves to the Prosperity pawnshop, wanting to pay back the money that Yang Yuelou still owed. The boss of the pawnshop wouldn't take it, but the lads just threw the money over the counter and went away. They didn't care about counting the cash, and so they ended up paying off the debt many times over. News of this reached Li Jin'ao's ears. He then reserved a couple of tables at the Heavenly Blessings restaurant in the Beidaguan shopping district and invited the lads to dinner on his own account.

Now about three months after Yang Yuelou got back to Shanghai, he sent some banknotes to the Prosperity pawnshop in Tianjin to pay his debts there. Having already taken money from the lads, the Prosperity didn't dare to get the same bill paid twice, so the boss took the money round in person to Li Jin'ao. Now what kind of person was Li Jin'ao? Not only did he refuse to take a penny, he wouldn't even look at the money – he told someone to take it and divide it up among the lads who'd originally paid what was owing. The money was now paid off, and nobody owed anything to anyone else. That ought to have been the end of it. But there was still a debt of gratitude. How was that going to be paid?

That winter, it was unusually cold in Shanghai, and the Huangpu River froze three feet thick, and the Yellow River iced over too. This didn't just mean that ocean-going boats couldn't sail upriver; any boat that was on the river that was late getting away now found itself caught in pack ice, stuck as fast as if it had been nailed in place. This meant that the coolies working on the wharfs were no longer being paid, and that was hitting men who'd come from Tianjin to find work particularly badly. They were finding it harder every day to fill their stomachs, and many were pretty much at the end of their tether. Now it so happened that Li Jin'ao was in Shanghai on business, and he saw what was going on. Just as he was worrying himself sick about the situation, he looked up and saw a poster advertising the fact that Yang Yuelou would shortly be starring in *My Beloved Wife, Yunniang*, and so he picked up his feet and went to find him.

When he arrived at the theatre, Yang Yuelou was in the middle of getting changed after the end of the performance. When he heard that a Mr Li Jin'ao from Tianjin was waiting for him outside the main entrance, he came running out with all his greasepaint still on his face. The only thing he had eyes for was the tall man standing out in the snow at the foot of the stairs. He yelled: "Second Master Li, my friend!" and came running down the steps two at a time. He slipped on an icy patch and ended up on his bottom, but when he looked up at Li Jin'ao, he was still smiling.

Yang Yuelou treated his benefactor, a man that he admired almost more than he could say, to a banquet at the Jinjiang restaurant. Li Jin'ao said: "You can feed me until my eyes bubble, Mr Yang, but you can't feed my lads who work on the wharfs along the Huangpu River – there's more than a thousand of them. Right now, the Yellow River's frozen solid, and the lads are starving, so if somebody doesn't do something soon, they're going to die."

"I'll see what I can do!" Yang Yuelou said awkwardly.

"No need," said Li Jin'ao. "All I want from you is that you

get the most famous actors in Shanghai together in one place and put on three days of performances! You give me the tickets, and I'll tell the lads to go and sell them. That won't put you to too much trouble, will it?"

"You really are amazing," Yang Yuelou said. "First you say you want me to help, and then you tell me I don't actually need to do anything. What you are asking for is as easy as pie."

The very next day, he called together all the most famous actors in Shanghai – people like Zhao Junyu, Zhou Xinfang, Huang Yulin, Liu Xiaoheng, Wang Yunfang, Liu Binkun, Gao Baisui and so on – and they agreed to put on a benefit performance at the Golden Theatre. The tickets were sold to the bosses that the lads from Tianjin normally worked for. These rich people bought a few tickets because they would get to see a performance, and they'd be helping out – going to see a benefit was their good deed for the day, so why not? There were going to be all kinds of famous actors performing together on the same stage, and they were going to be putting on romantic plays that everyone loves like *Dragon and Phoenix Happy at Last* and *The Red-Haired Steed*. What more could anyone ask for? The actors did three days of performances and saved the lives of more than one thousand frozen and starving men.

Having concluded his business, Li Jin'ao wanted to head back to Tianjin, but before he left, Yang Yuelou arranged another banquet for him. When they had eaten and drunk their fill, Yang Yuelou called for someone to bring a big bag of silver, with a red envelope stuffed full of cash, to give to Li Jin'ao. This was to pay for the expenses of his journey and also to say thank you for his kindness the year before. When Li Jin'ao saw the money, his face immediately hardened. Lowering his voice, he spoke in impressive tones: "I like to help out my friends, Mr Yang – money doesn't come into it. Just think about it, in all our dealings together, when did money ever change hands between us? Has money ever even been an issue? I put my back into helping you, and you did the same for me, but wasn't that all because it was the right thing to do? Sooner or later money runs out, but I hope our friendship will never be at an end!" Then he stood up and said goodbye.

When Yang Yuelou heard Li Jin'ao say this in such heartfelt tones, he was deeply impressed. The next day, he was due to perform in *Hua Mulan*, and he did so with unusual brio, his voice clear and vibrant, until the whole theatre was swept along in a gust of emotion.

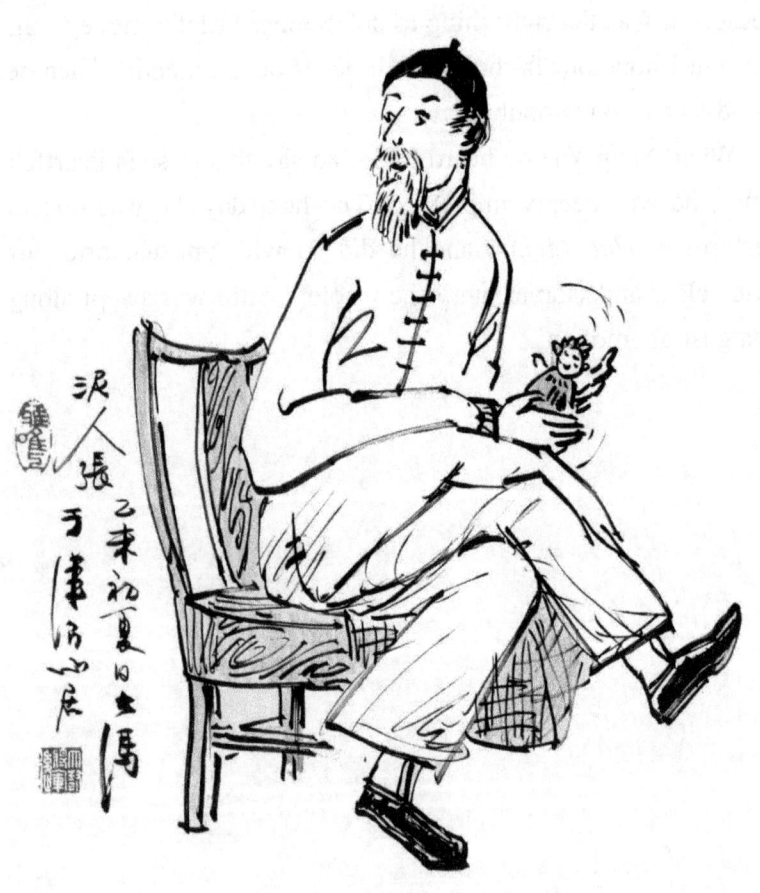

14
MASTER ZHANG, THE FIGURE MAKER

OUT OF ALL THE street artists in Tianjin, Master Zhang the figure maker, who modelled in clay, was by far the best. In fact, there wasn't anyone else who even came close.

Master Zhang's full name was Zhang Mingshan. At the time when the Xianfeng Emperor sat on the throne, back in the 1850s, he had a beat running between two spots: the Grandview Theatre in the northeast corner of the city, and the Heavenly Blessings restaurant in the Beidaguan shopping district. Sitting there, he could watch all kinds of people coming and going, and make his little portrait figures of them. There were all sorts of characters who went to the Grandview Theatre to watch the actors perform, and there were also all sorts of characters who went to the Heavenly Blessings to watch the world go by. However, there were always more of the second kind than the first.

One day, it was raining, and he was sitting inside the Heavenly Blessings restaurant having a nip of something while at the same time keeping an eye on the other diners. Just at that moment, three people came stomping in from outside. The one in the middle was very expensively got up: a man of middling height with a head like a pumpkin, and a jutting-out stomach. He clearly thought the world of himself as he came barrelling in. The maître d', who was standing by the desk at the entrance to greet new arrivals, immediately came forward burbling: "It is indeed an honour to have you here, Fifth Master Zhang... A table for three – please come this way!"

When they heard this, the other diners fell silent; some of them even put down their chopsticks to stare at the famous Fifth Master Zhang. At that time, Zhang Jinwen was famous far and wide for the enormous wealth he had accumulated in the Salt Gabelle. As a much younger man, he'd been involved in various unsavoury activities at the orders of General Hai Ren, which had ended up with the general recognising him as his fifth adopted son. This got him his nickname Two-faced Bastard. People called him Fifth Master Zhang to his face, but behind his back they called him Two-faced Bastard. Tianjin was a commercial centre – anyone with money was welcome there – and even officials walked small around such a wealthy man. But artists are something else. Artists have their own pride and don't see why they should truckle to anyone. It was for this very reason that Master Zhang sipped his wine and ate his food, looking left and right, clearly not giving a toss that he was in the presence of the great Fifth Master Zhang.

However, not long after they sat down, Two-faced Bastard's party started talking about him. There was a reedy voice that remarked: "He'll be there watching the action on the stage but all the while he'll be pinching and pulling at a ball of clay in his sleeve. When he's finished, he'll pull it out and have a look, and he'll have reproduced exactly what was there up on stage…"

Then Two-faced Bastard chimed in with his loud, coarse voice: "So where exactly is he pulling? At his sleeve? Or at the contents of his trousers?" He laughed heartily at this, for he was enjoying making fun of Master Zhang.

Everyone in the Heavenly Blessings restaurant heard what he said. Everyone was waiting to see how Master Zhang – who was not merely a fine artist but also a very brave man – got back at this Two-faced Bastard. Would he lob a lump of clay at him or what?

It seemed as though Master Zhang hadn't heard a word of this exchange; with his left hand, he reached under the table and scraped a lump of mud off his boots. His right hand was still clasping his cup of wine, and his eyes were still fixed on the food on the table – it was just his left hand that was at work shaping this lump of mud. His fingers were flying as he pinched and prodded, even faster than Baldy Liu, the juggler. At the one table, that Two-faced Bastard carried on cracking jokes about him, but everything he said was being worked into the mud by Master Zhang at the other table. Then his hand stopped, and with a "plap" sound, he slapped the lump of mud down on the tabletop and got up to go and pay his bill at the desk.

The other diners craned their necks to see: really he was a wonderful sculptor! He couldn't have got a better likeness if he'd cut that Two-faced Bastard's head off and plonked it down on the table. The pumpkin-shaped head, the protruding eyes, that expression of arrogance and entitlement… It looked more like the Two-faced Bastard than the Two-faced Bastard did – but it was just the size of a peach.

Two-faced Bastard was right there, and from just a few feet away, he could see perfectly well that the clay figure was of him. He shouted at Master Zhang's retreating back as he headed out of the door: "How do you think you are ever going to earn a penny with that rubbish – even sold off cheap, nobody would want it!"

Master Zhang, the figure maker, didn't even turn his head; he opened his umbrella and walked off. But the matter was far from over.

The very next day, the stalls up and down Guyi Street outside the North Gate of the city had row after row of little clay figures of that Two-faced Bastard on display – now there was a body attached, and it looked twice as lifelike. He was turning them out of a mould, one after another, until he had hundreds. The stalls all had a sign up in front, which said in black and white:

Sold Off Cheap: A Two-faced Bastard

The people wandering up and down Guyi Street thought this was hilarious. When they'd enjoyed the sight themselves, they went off to find a friend who'd also appreciate the joke, and then they could laugh at it together.

Three days later, that Two-faced Bastard sent someone to pay big money to buy up every single one of the figures; supposedly he even bought the mould. The figures are gone, but the story of *Sold Off Cheap: A Two-faced Bastard* has been handed down for over a hundred years, right down to the present day.

15
A BRILLIANT ROBBERY

THE AREA between the old city and the Foreign Concession was the most dangerous in Tianjin – the population was extremely mixed, and some of them made a living in really nasty ways. In the 1920s, a young couple, newlyweds, rented a little house there overlooking the street. They had a whole load of brand new furniture moved in, all shiny and bright. They pasted up red Double Happiness papercuts on the wall on either side of the front door. The morning after the wedding, the two of them went back to work. The neighbours didn't even know what they were called or anything about them.

On the third day, not long after they'd left the house and gone to work, a flat-bottomed three-wheeled cart suddenly came flying up the road. An old man was driving the cart, all skin and bone, with sunburned face and yellowed teeth, but hard as nails with it – at one glance you could tell he'd been driving this cart for years. There were two young men squatting on top, both about seventeen or eighteen, holding sticks, axes, and rope.

The three of them were grim-faced, as if they had come to deal with an enemy.

The old man stopped by the entrance to the newlywed couple's house, pulling up abruptly. The two teenagers jumped out and rushed to the door to have a look. They turned round and said to the old man: "Dad, they're not here, the door's locked!" There was indeed a large western-style padlock on it.

The old man now looked even more furious. His eyes were glaring so that you could see the whites clear round, and the veins in his face and neck were standing proud. He leapt down from the cart and started cursing: "That animal! What a right little bastard! He couldn't care less about his parents – here he is enjoying himself in the fucking lap of luxury! Boys! Get that door open for me!"

Immediately, the two teenagers got to work with their axes and broke the padlock on the door open. When the door was thrown wide, the new furniture that filled the room was there gleaming in front of them. The old man was even more annoyed at this sight, and pointing at the room, he jumped up and down screaming in a shockingly loud voice: "Will you look at that? Ungrateful little bastard! We brought you up so carefully, and now look at you! Your mother is so sick, and we don't have the money to get a doctor or buy her medicine, and you won't give us a penny – you want to spend it all on that little whore you've picked up. You're off enjoying yourself while your mother is dying! I'll show you! Boys! What are you doing just standing there? Get all of this stuff loaded up – we're taking it home! And if you dare say a word for your brother, I'll break your legs for you!"

The two young men got busy with all the boxes and suitcases

in the room, packing up all the clothes and bedding and piling it in the cart.

The neighbours all came running to watch. Hearing the old man cursing them, they learned all about what this newly married couple had been up to. Nobody could care less what happened to the possessions of the kind of bastard who would abandon his mother as she lay dying. Besides which the old man was hopping mad with rage – he looked just like one of those firecrackers that gets set off at New Year's, which explodes at the first touch. If anybody had got in his way, he'd have killed them!

When pretty much everything had been packed up, the two lads said: "Dad, we can't lift the big furniture. What do we do?"

The old man shouted in a voice like thunder: "Smash it!"

They threw themselves into the work, and then when the final last glass cup had been thrown into the room and smashed, it was all over. The old man seemed as angry as ever, as he bellowed: "We'll see what you have to say for yourself tomorrow!" Then they all took themselves off.

Nobody even bothered to close the door, and it hung open all day. The neighbours were all standing off in the distance… none of them came forward, but none of them went away either. They were waiting to see the fun when the newlyweds came home.

That afternoon, the young couple came home together, chatting and laughing. When they got to their front door, they were struck dumb. They went over to ask the neighbours what had happened, but they just drifted away. One old man came forward to speak – clearly he was horrified by the appalling way the young man had treated his parents. He said to the bridegroom: "Your father and your two brothers came by this morning – they did this. You'd better go and talk to your parents!"

When the young man heard this, he was even more dumbfounded. Unable to control himself a moment longer, he shouted: "What father? Dad died when I was three, and Mum passed away the year before last. My only family is my older sister who's married and living in Manchuria. Who are these people you are talking about?"

"What?" The old man was shocked. However, the scene had been set so well that morning that he couldn't wrap his head around it straight away. All he could say was: "But it was your dad!"

The newlyweds rushed to the police station to make a report. The case was kept open for a decade, but "Dad" was never found.

There were all kinds of weird and wonderful robberies in Tianjin in those days, but this was a real classic. The thieves arrived and made sure that everyone thought they were family, so quite apart from losing all your stuff, you also had everyone thinking it was your own fault – and there was nothing you could do about it. If you couldn't stand it anymore and told someone about it, they wouldn't even be sympathetic. They'd just laugh at you, which made it all worse. It was a nasty trick, a dirty trick... and also absolutely brilliant!

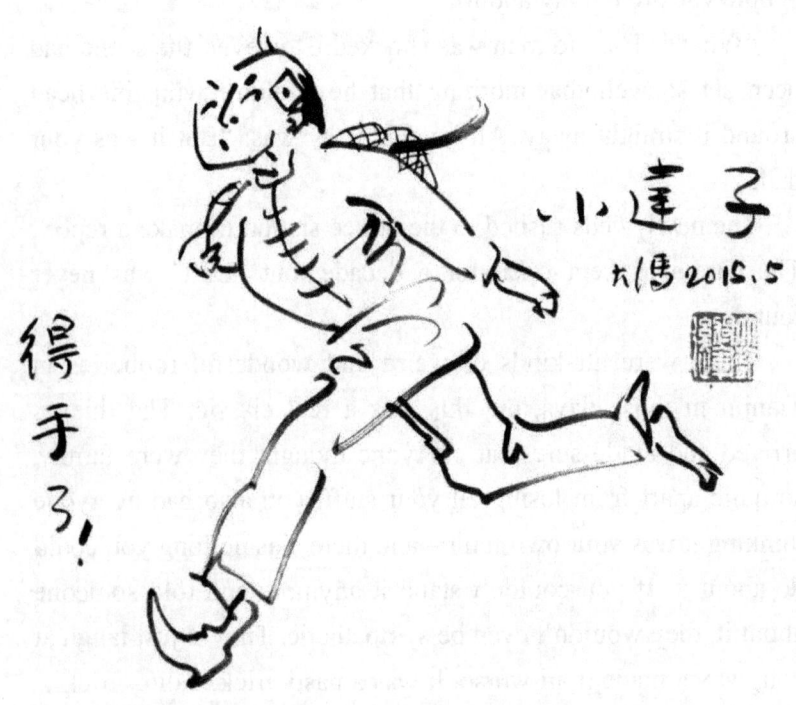

16
TARTAR

TARTAR DIDN'T LOOK like much – a short neck and short little legs, grey eyes and dusty-looking skin, which seemed as flabby and soft as a roasted sweet potato. When he stood there, he attracted no more attention than a shadow, and he could move like a puff of smoke. People said that he was a natural-born thief, and they were not wrong! Supposing that you stuck your folding money so that it was right there touching the skin on your stomach: in the blink of an eye, he'd have it in his hand and you wouldn't have felt a thing – hell, you'd still be able to feel the bills right there against your body. But to really see him at his best, you needed to see him working the trams. If you happened to be on the same tram as him, you'd better not get anywhere near him or you'd lose whatever you happened to have with you.

To give you an example, here's a young man in a suit – if he gets on the tram he's not going to get away scot-free! This is a fashionable young man, so his wallet has been parked in the back pocket of his trousers, right on the arse. The pocket isn't buttoned, and the wallet is peeping out at the top. But don't be dumb enough to think that all you have to do is stretch out your hand and yank the wallet out! The pocket is small, and the wallet is thick, so it's wedged in pretty tight, besides which the nerves in your arse are right there on the case the same as the nerves in your face – the moment someone touches that wallet, the guy's going to notice. Tartar had worked out his own way to deal with this. In this kind of situation, he'd be leaning against the pole right by the door to the tram, waiting for it to come to a halt, and as the young man got off, quick as a flash he'd have the nails of his index and middle fingers gripping the top of the wallet like pincers. When getting off the tram, people are concentrating on making their way down safely, besides which the wallet isn't grabbed out of the guy's back pocket, it's more like it is left behind unnoticed as he leaves. But having said that, you mustn't imagine that Tartar had the trams all to himself.

One day, Tartar was on the tram, and a middle-aged man got on at the Baimao Yamen stop. He had a pure-gold pocket watch hanging there glittering away on the jacket of his black suit – so vulgar! Tartar stood there not moving a muscle, waiting until the tram had almost got to Lizhan, and then he got close. The tracks there took an S-bend. As the tram moved along, it would swing back and forth, and he took advantage of this to get right in there. The watch was in his hand, and then in his pocket, faster than the eye could see. When the tram stopped at Lizhan, there were loads of people getting off, so he got lost in the crowd, removing himself from the scene as quickly as he could.

As he walked, he turned over today's haul in his mind. Suddenly, he realised that walking along up ahead was a man who looked just like the middle-aged guy on the tram. Just as this thought crossed his mind, the man turned round, and it *was* him; but the strange thing was that shining on his chest was that self-same vulgar and flashy watch! Could it be possible that he owned two? Tartar couldn't stop himself from feeling in his own pocket, and immediately he jumped – it was empty. He'd spent half his life stealing off other people, but this was the first time he'd ever experienced what it was like to be stolen from. Even more devastating, he simply could not for the life of him understand how the other man had managed to take the watch back. The man saw him standing there looking stupid and smiled brightly. That smile clearly showed contempt for his adversary, as if he were saying: "How could a dumb cluck like you with fumbling mitts and two left feet possibly hope to succeed in this line of work?" Then he stopped smiling, turned round, and walked away.

After that, Tartar never worked the trams again.

17
BIG HUI

BIG HUI WAS INDEED SURNAMED Hui, and he was huge – he had big hands and big feet, a big mouth and big ears, and so people called him Big Hui. Once they got used to calling him Big Hui, it got so nobody could remember his real name.

Big Hui was a competent guy, a good fisherman. If you put a bamboo pole in his hands, it would turn into a fishing rod; if you gave him a bent pin, that became a fish hook; hand him a fine bit of waxed thread of the kind used to sew together the soles of boots and he'd make it his line; and with a tuft of pigeon feathers tied to the line, he had a lure. With just this basic equipment, such as what you might find anywhere, he could sit by the side of a pond for seven days and pull several thousand fish out – even the fry couldn't escape.

It didn't matter what kinds of fish were there in the waters below – he would get whichever ones it was he had in mind; he could catch only males or only females, or if he wanted to, he could catch them in pairs. He pulled fish out that were heavier than he was, as well as some that were smaller than his hook.

People like to say that fishing is all about luck, but for him, it was all about patience.

The bloodworms used to catch crucian carp are tiny little things, about as thick as the fishing line itself, and they just consist of a thin layer of skin – what's inside is just red liquid. If you want to put it on a fish hook, that's not easy; if you aren't very deft, the hook goes in at an angle, and the red liquid just pours out, leaving you with just the skin. The best way is to hold the hook in your fingers and impale the worm when it opens its mouth, because then you can keep the bloodworm dangling nicely off the end… but who can do something like that?

He had all kinds of tricks up his sleeve when fishing for different species – just look at how he dealt with terrapins!

If you hook a terrapin when you are fishing, you're going to find the pole bent and the line unmoving, so you might easily imagine that you'd got the hook stuck in rocks underwater. If you then get anxious and move incautiously, the line will break. Big Hui never got nervous; he would hold still and leave the line taut. After a while, seeing the line twitch, he could be sure that the terrapin was on the move, and then he was in even less of a hurry to jerk the pole. Particularly if you've caught a big terrapin, once the fish hook is well embedded, it will use its front feet to grab a tight hold of some waterweed. Supposing that you then try and raise your catch – the line will break, and you may even snap the pole. Well, every time this happened, Big Hui would reach for one of the bronze rings he kept on his belt and thread it over the end of the pole – the bronze ring would then go hurtling down the fishing line. The terrapin down under the water would be holding on with all its might and then suddenly catch sight of a bright object speeding towards its head. It wouldn't have a clue what this might be and would raise its front feet, letting go of the waterweed. Ha! And that's the moment Big Hui would lift it out of the water with no problem.

Who had ever seen anything like it?

It is customary every New Year's that the people of Tianjin earn a bit of good karma by releasing creatures back into the wild. In particular, they release carp back into the rivers. They hope to gain merit thereby and get a bit of luck. When they release the fish, they tie a red thread onto the dorsal fin, as a sign. If the fish is caught the next year, then it gets another red thread. The year after that, it gets a third thread. The saying goes that if you catch a carp with three red threads and then release it back into the river again, that means it'll leap through the Dragon's Gate. Everything that you could wish for in the way of luck, promotion, long-life, and wealth will be yours.

You can find carp everywhere, but carp with red threads are impossible to catch. Once a fish has been hooked once, it wises up and becomes really smart. You may occasionally see a carp for sale with one red thread, but you will not see carp with two. As for those with three – well even the guys who go out with nets never catch them. If you say you'll pay good money for one, he'll tell you with a smile: "If you take all the water out of the river first, I'll catch it for you."

So what do you do? You go and find Big Hui. Once it got to the end of the year, the eight main families in Tianjin would all put in an order with Big Hui for a three-thread carp.

Big Hui would stand by the riverbank, watching the routes used by the fish. A route is a path commonly taken by fish as they move through the water. Big Hui had keen eyesight, and at a glance he could see exactly what was going on down there. Having seen exactly where the carp would congregate, he would throw some chunks of bread there. These chunks would each be bigger than a chestnut, so the smaller fish couldn't get them in their faces, but the bigger fish would gobble them up in a single bite. There wouldn't be hooks hidden in these chunks – he was just feeding the fish, pure and simple, and every day he would throw them bread just once. To begin with, the wily big fish would maybe take the risk of nibbling a bit, and once they did that they realised it was safe. The second day, they'd get another piece, and they'd start getting bolder, and then in the end they'd be gulping down the chunk of bread the moment it hit the water. By the time it got to the last few days of the month, Big Hui was ready to call it a day – he'd bait his hooks with bread and toss them in. He never failed: each time a big fat carp with a red thread hanging off it was lifted out on the end of his line.

This method will only work for catching two-thread carp. Three-thread carp will never ever take the bait. A three-thread carp has already been caught three times, and it would rather eat shit than eat bread for a second time. So what do you do? He used kid's poop as bait! Big Hui really did know absolutely everything there was to know about fish!

He knew exactly what ponds there were outside the South Gate, which ponds had which fish in them, how big those fish were, and which ponds had more fish and which had less. He could have taken every fish out of those ponds, but that was something he would never do. If he fished them dry, what would he do for an encore? Therefore, he refused to catch little fish; he'd wait until they got bigger. He also refused to catch female fish, at least until after they had spawned. The other fisherman, near and far, called him Terminator. This was not meant as an insult – they were trying to praise him.

However, this was not a good nickname to have.

It was the third year of the Republican era, one day after the summer solstice. Big Hui had been out fishing all day, and he was tired. If you have spent most of your life standing all day every day on the edge of a pond somewhere, getting burned to a crisp by the sun or blasted by howling gales, you will find it a wearing experience. He'd been at the Happy Gatherings restaurant north of the Drum Tower, eating and drinking his fill, and then he set off home with a basket of fish weaving from side to side – when he couldn't make it any further, he leaned against a wall and went to sleep. His home was off in the north part of the city, in Beichenggen, and that was a pretty good step; he walked a bit and then rested a bit, and soon it was past midnight. All confused, he stumbled out onto the main avenue. Just at that moment, a truck was passing by, and the driver was asleep. Actually, even if he'd been wide awake, he wouldn't necessarily have spotted him – it so happened that a few of the streetlights along that section of road had been knocked out by the wind. As the saying goes: when your time is up, you die! When the truck rolled over him, the old buffer driving it was so fast asleep that he didn't notice a thing. When it got light, passers-by discovered that Big Hui had been flattened by the truck and was now smeared across the surface of the road like a piece of paper. The really weird thing was that he got squashed, but the basket of fish didn't – in fact the fish were still alive in there. When the police arrived, they noticed another strange thing: the truck that ran him over was hauling fish! That gave everyone who heard about it a turn – they could feel a cold draught prickling the backs of their necks at the mere thought.

Some people said that it was all because of that dreadful nickname – they called him Terminator, so he was bound to come to a sticky end. Some people said it was a debt of karma; he'd caught so many fish that in the end the Dragon King demanded his own life in exchange. But when the story reached Pei Wenjin – Fifth Master Pei – over on the east side of the city, he gave an educated person's perspective on the matter. He said: "Each man is killed by the thing he loves."

18

LIU DAOYUAN GOES INTO HIS COFFIN ALIVE

IN TIANJIN, businessmen are as thick on the ground as hairs on a dog. But the moment your businessmen get into some kind of conflict, you'll find another kind of person popping up immediately, picking quarrels and trying to get the two parties to sue, making mountains out of molehills, putting together the evidence for a court case here and getting in good with government officials there, rushing hither and yon, and taking every opportunity to grab a bit of cash for themselves. This kind of person is an educated gangster.

Gangsters were an endless source of trouble in Tianjin. Historically they have been divided into two kinds: educated and uneducated. Your uneducated gangster goes and beats people up, causing trouble in this way or that – the moment they get to work, you have broken arms and heads split open, and there's blood all over the place. Your educated gangster, on the other hand, only needs a writing brush in his hand, and he makes his money by encouraging litigation among businessmen. You might

imagine that a writing brush is entirely innocuous, but a brush in the hands of an educated gangster always conceals a knife – black letters on white paper can kill you very dead. And when it came to educated gangsters, Liu Daoyuan was right at the top of the profession.

Whenever businessmen went to law, whoever had Liu Daoyuan on his side was guaranteed to win – the man was a master. People said that he might as well write the verdict himself while he was about it; in fact, they might as well let him judge the case, since it was up to him to determine who lived and who died. He didn't take cases about small family-owned stores or corner shops; he was only interested in big business. Big business means big bucks, and he could charge the most astronomical fees. If he'd ever found himself short of cash, there would be no need to go and borrow it; all he had to do was to go and stand by the door of one of the big companies, and the boss would come out running immediately with a sack of money, handing it over with an ingratiating grin. Now when an uneducated gangster turns up to get his protection money, they stand by the doorway looking pretty damn grim: they make it clear that not giving them the cash will have consequences. They show their teeth, and any failure to pay is paid for in blood – it is very frightening. But an educated gangster like Liu Daoyuan doesn't work that way at all. When he leans on the door, you might imagine that he was there enjoying the sunshine without a care in the world. Once you hand over the money, he turns round and walks off – there's never the slightest trouble. That's the "educated" bit in an educated gangster.

Liu Daoyuan was a rich man, but he didn't buy houses or land, he didn't gamble, and he never went to brothels – in fact, he didn't even have servants. He was a bachelor, and he lived in a house outside the West Gate, north of the Paupers' Cemetery, with his two disciples – Jin San and Ma Si – to look after him. The money that he earned went in part on his daily expenses, and whatever was left over was given away to people in need. He would be walking down the road, and he'd hear the sound of crying coming from one of the houses – it might be someone suffering terribly from poverty, or quarrelling because they didn't have the money to pay the bills – and then he'd go to the window and toss in some coins. There were plenty of people living round the Paupers' Cemetery who had been helped out by him. But nobody dared to say thank you to his face: if you tried to thank him, he'd get furious and scream abuse at you.

That is what a gangster is like: it doesn't matter whether he's educated or not. When it comes right down to it, he's a gangster through and through.

One day, he suddenly called in his two disciples, Jin San and Ma Si, and said to them: "I'm fifty-six years old now, and I have seen all there is to see in this world, but I know nothing about the next. Recently, I have been wondering – what happens to us when we die? I have an idea. I am going to pretend to be dead, and you are going to hold a funeral for me. I'll be right there in the coffin, and there'll be plenty for me to enjoy. However, while I am in my coffin, the two of you are going to have to deal with things for me. Listen up! You pair of bastards had better not get any cute ideas about nailing me into the coffin while I am still alive!"

Jin San was a quick and clever guy, while Ma Si was slow and stupid. Jin San said: "We wouldn't do a thing like that! If anything happened to you, we wouldn't know what to do with ourselves! But boss! Even though it's a great idea, when someone dies you have day after day of funeral rites – at least seven days. How are you going to spend all that time in a coffin? It's going to be pitch black in there, and there isn't much room, and it'll get stuffy... how can you cope? Besides which, what happens when you need to eat, or want a pee? I have a better idea – we'll leave the coffin empty in the main room, and you can hide in the storeroom out the back. Nobody's going to go in there. You can eat and drink to your heart's content, and the two of us can make sure you are comfortable the whole time. When the coffin leaves the house, then you can take your place inside. The lid can't possibly be nailed down, right... there has to be a crack so you can see what is going on outside!"

Liu Daoyuan laughed and said: "You are a clever little bastard. That's what we'll do!"

Pretty soon, everyone in Tianjin knew that Liu Daoyuan, their most famous educated gangster, had died. Supposedly, he'd been taken sick suddenly in the middle of the night. There was a notice of his demise put up outside the door of the Liu house, and inside they set up a mourning hall with a coffin in the middle, and his famous brush was placed on the altar in front. They also brought in some Buddhist monks to perform the seven days of ceremonies. There were plenty of people who wanted to pay their final respects too; there was a huge queue out in front of the door – it looked just like the Bian family's soup kitchen on New Year's Eve.

Liu Daoyuan was hidden in the little room off the back courtyard. He had food and drink, and a pot that he could pee in, so he was pretty comfortable. Jin San was out in front dealing with the people paying their respects, and Ma Si was running back and forth from time to time to keep the boss up to date with what was going on. To begin with, Liu Daoyuan was very pleased. People had showed him a lot of respect when he was alive, but it seemed that he got even more plaudits now he was dead. But after a couple of days, he started to feel that something was wrong. There were so many big companies he'd won court cases for – where were the bosses? There was an absolute crowd of people nobody had ever heard of in his house – were they just there to enjoy the fuss? Normally people like that wouldn't dare even turn their heads or raise their eyes when they walked past his house, but now they could come right in and have a good look around to see how an educated gangster lived. Ma Si said that Mr He, the owner of the Fushuncheng Foreign Goods Store, which he'd pretty much ruined in a court case the previous year, had come. He came marching in to stand in front of the coffin, but he didn't bow or anything like that. Instead, he spat a huge wad of phlegm onto the floor. After that, all kinds of strange things started to happen...

On the fourth day of the funeral, a huge man burst in through the door and marched towards the coffin, dragging an Alsatian dog after him. The moment he came into the room, he started cursing: "Bloody Liu Daoyuan! You're dead, but you still owe me ten bars of gold – who's going to pay me back now! I am not leaving until I have my money back!" He sat down plumb in front of the coffin and refused to move. With him there, it was impossible for anyone else to come and pay their respects. Jin San and Ma Si had never seen the man before, and they knew perfectly well he was just trying to extort money from them. First, they tried to persuade him to go away, and when that didn't work, they tried to drag him off, but the man was unexpectedly tough, and with a punch or two, both Jin San and Ma Si were on the floor with their heads spinning. Jin San and Ma Si were both educated gangsters; when it came to pen and ink they knew exactly what to do, but they weren't violent men. Since they couldn't get rid of him any other way, they decided to wait it out. When it got late and the man saw that he'd got nothing out of making all this commotion, he got up and left. Before heading out of the door, he said that he'd be back in ten days' time and he would take the house to cover the debt. The huge Alsatian he had with him jumped up and grabbed a big steamed bun off the altar, one of the offerings for hungry ghosts, and went off with it clamped in its jaws.

Ma Si was a simple soul and reported exactly what had happened to his boss. When Liu Daoyuan heard this, he was furious. "How dare that bastard come and extort money from me!" he screamed. "Since when have I ever borrowed money from anybody? I'm not dead yet! I don't know who that slob thinks he is!" He was just about to march outside and deal with the man himself.

Ma Si couldn't cope with the situation and called in Jin San. "If you go out," Jin San said, "how are you going to carry on pretending to be dead? We won't be able to keep it up. Keep your hair on, boss, and deal with him after the coffin has left the house. Won't it be fun to see everyone splutter?"

That last sentence of Jin San's was a stroke of genius. You could see Liu Daoyuan calming down right there and then. But after this, Ma Si didn't like to tell the boss what was going on out front. When Liu Daoyuan got desperate, he started to ask about the people that he knew. Had this person come? Was this person staying away? Ma Si knew perfectly well that the boss was really only interested in one of the other educated gangsters, the man known as Bouquet of Flowers. He was usually round there all the time, and he always talked about Liu Daoyuan as if he were his brother – it sometimes seemed that the two of them only wore one pair of trousers. The moment Liu Daoyuan "died", he was nowhere to be seen; he never showed his face even once. How could Ma Si tell the boss that? The less Ma Si wanted to say what had happened, the more he came to understand; his face got longer and longer, as if someone had attached a weight to the bottom of his chin. In the end, he just shut his eyes, he didn't want to know any more, and he didn't ask any further questions. He looked as though he might actually be dead.

That morning, there was a noise outside, and it didn't sound like Jin San or Ma Si. Bending his ear, he realised it was his neighbour, Qiao Erlong, the water carrier, and his son, Gouzi. They'd come over the wall and were now in the back yard. Through the wall, he could hear Gouzi say: "Dad, if Jin San and Ma Si come back, we won't have time to make it back over the wall."

"Scared, are you?" Qiao Erlong said. "Bloody useless brat! Jin San and Ma Si wouldn't hurt a fly, but you're still scared of them. Old Liu didn't leave a son and heir, did he? This stuff doesn't belong to anyone now, does it? If we don't take it, someone else will! Now come with me..."

Liu Daoyuan was so furious he felt that the top of his head might come off. When I was alive, you had plenty of money off me, he thought to himself, and you couldn't have been more polite. Now I'm dead, you're here to steal everything that isn't nailed down! Anything else I can do for you, perchance? Maybe you'd like to have my skin for a drum?"

He would have liked to kick the door down and burst out on them, but he couldn't – he wasn't going to ruin his grand scheme for a pair of cheap swindlers. The whole thing made him angry, and suddenly an idea came into his mind. In a high-pitched, feminine tone of voice, he started to yell: "Help! Thieves!" That gave Qiao and his son a right shock! They stood there gaping like a pair of idiots and then jumped and sprang, so with a crash and a bang they were back on the other side of the wall. Luckily, the monks reading sutras out front were banging their drums right at that moment, so nobody heard the racket at the back. But when Ma Si came back again, he saw that he hadn't eaten a thing: all the food had been thrown down on the floor.

The first seven days passed and nothing had gone too badly wrong – in fact, everything was fine. Jin San now put the writing brush that had been on the altar all this time into the coffin. He told people that it had to be buried with the boss, and he also said that this brush was the real thing: even Hua Shikui, the famous calligrapher, had used common-or-garden brushes – only the boss ever wrote with a proper writing-brush. Afterwards, he sneaked out to collect his boss, and when nobody was paying attention, they managed to get him into the coffin and prepared to send it out of the house. Liu Daoyuan cursed: "I don't know any more if I've had enough of bloody living, or enough of being bloody dead." However, he lay down inside the coffin.

Jin San had prepared the coffin very nicely for him. The lid was loose so he could open it whenever he liked; it was stocked with food and drink, and the pillow was just right if he felt like a nap. However, he wasn't going to have time to sleep: having "died" like this, he wanted to see exactly what everyone would do.

When the coffin was lifted up and placed on the back of the hearse, he could hear both Jin San and Ma Si start to cry. Jin San was a bright guy, and he could cry properly – he managed to get a really heart-wrenching note into his wailing. Jin San is good at this, Liu Daoyuan thought to himself, and that fool Ma Si can't even work out how to cry. However, Jin San couldn't keep it up for any length of time, and after making a lot of noise, he found himself out of voice. On his side, though, Ma Si was still going. Ma Si was slow to warm up, and he wasn't loud, but he was sincere – he wept and wailed the whole way along as if he were crying over his own father. This endless weeping was now getting on Liu Daoyuan's nerves – it was too depressing for words. He couldn't make up his mind whether the fake or real emotion was better.

They went on and on, and then Liu Daoyuan suddenly heard a racket going on outside. It was very loud, so something must clearly have happened. The hearse was now forced to a halt. He was sufficiently curious that he raised the lid of the coffin with his two hands so that a crack appeared. Looking out, he could see paper figures of servants and horses, a paper car and a paper palanquin, the ox-headed and horse-headed gods of the Underworld, silver streamers and snow-white banners, and a sea of white flowers. Both sides of the street were packed with people watching the funeral procession. What on earth could be going on that even a hearse had to stop for it? Looking past the fluttering banners, he saw a bunch of men standing up ahead with clenched fists – it was an old professional acquaintance, Teng Heizi, and his thugs who worked transportation scams. Now he suddenly caught sight of his old pal, Bouquet of Flowers, standing with them. He heard Bouquet of Flowers shouting: "That writing brush ought to be mine – who the hell does he think he is! How dare he take that brush with him to the grave? He's not getting away with this! If you don't hand it over, you aren't going anywhere!"

Liu Daoyuan could feel his head spinning, but this time he wasn't angry, he had finally come to his senses. "That's what being dead is all about," he said to himself. "I understand!" He lifted the coffin lid with a jerk of his wrists, and it fell with a crash. Then he stood up.

That not only scared the funeral procession and the onlookers into fits of screaming; even the thugs blocking the road ran away.

Liu Daoyuan stood up on the back of the hearse, and he laughed and laughed.

19
BLACKFACE

BLACKFACE COULD REFER to a type of opera make-up, but in this case, it is the name of a dog. This was, however, no ordinary dog.

Blackface was a good dog – but not the kind of loyal hound that dies trying to save its owner in a morality tale. This was a totally unique dog.

When it first appeared in the pack of stray dogs living out in the streets by Beidaguan, it was just a little puppy, and it was absolutely hideous! Probably someone had a bitch that had produced a litter of puppies, and the owner decided this one was so ugly they weren't going to keep it, so they dumped it by the side of the road. If you dump a dog, you do so at some distance from home. Dogs know where they live, and if you abandon them too close to home, they will just come running straight back.

Blackface was a pepper-and-salt mongrel – but really it was a remarkably unattractive looking animal! It was white with black spots, but the spots weren't pretty; it looked randomly splotched with ink, one patch here and one patch there. The whole of its head was black, and so black that you couldn't see its eyes, just its white teeth and a little red tongue lolling in the middle. It wasn't just people that thought it hideous – even the other strays didn't seem to like it. Beidaguan is right by the Southern Canal, so the whole area is packed with wharfs, with people coming and going, and with all kinds of businesses and food stalls, so there were lots of bins with food in them. Even if they just had the contents of a bin, the stray dogs weren't going to go hungry. But these strays were tough dogs, and they would guard their food; Blackface couldn't even get close. As a result, even after a year, it hadn't grown any bigger. It had matchstick-thin legs and a shrivelled abdomen, and its little black face was no bigger than a fist.

The biggest business out at Beidaguan was the Prosperity Seafood Company: they specialised in retailing saltwater shrimp, and freshwater langoustine, fish, and terrapins – they were famous for this far and wide. Mr Shang, one of their most senior staff members, was a very honest and upright man, who'd worked at Prosperity Seafood since he joined as a trainee when he was a young man. He'd spent his entire life working at this one company, and now at over sixty years of age, he was the most senior person in the place – he knew more about what went on in the seafood industry than he did about what was happening in his own home. Anything that happened in Beidaguan, he had his eye on. He saw that Blackface was nothing but a bag of bones and felt sorry for the poor animal, so from time to time he would tell one of the younger men to give it a bit of fish to eat. Dogs eat meat and not fish, and they really don't like raw fish because of the smell, but this puppy appreciated Mr Shang's kindness and would take a few mouthfuls even if it didn't eat the whole thing. Afterwards, it would give a couple of woofs at Mr Shang and then go off wagging its tail. Mr Shang became very fond of the beast. As time went on, a friendly feeling grew up, and it didn't seem to matter that the dog was so ugly.

One day, Mr Shang finished work and set off for home, and the puppy went along with him. Old Mr Shang's house was over at Houjiahou, so not far away, and Blackface followed him all the way, keeping a certain distance and not making a sound until it arrived at the door to his home.

Mr Shang's home was an L-shaped brick house with a courtyard attached. As he went in through the door, he looked back, and Blackface was squatting under a scholar tree beside the entrance, watching him without moving. Old Mr Shang ignored the dog and shut the door. The following day he didn't see it at all. That evening when he got off work and went home, Blackface just materialised and walked along behind him, escorting him all the way back to his house without making a sound. On the third day, old Mr Shang understood what the puppy wanted, and when he got home he held the door open and said: "Come on in. You're my dog from now on." That was how Blackface became part of the Shang family.

The neighbours were a bit puzzled by this. If old Mr Shang decided he wanted a dog, why not get a nice one? If you decided to take in a stray, why not at least choose one that looked pretty? Why bring this hideous object into the house? It would be right there with you day after day, so how could you stand it?

Old Mr Shang was a generous man, and he pretty quickly had Blackface properly fed, so it started to grow. After one year it was a grown dog, and after two years it was huge: its head was now the size of that of a small child, and it had enormous fangs and a long red tongue. It very rarely barked, but Mr Shang understood perfectly well that dogs that bite don't bark. He didn't take it out much because he was worried it would bite people, or that its size would scare them.

Actually, Blackface was a very intelligent dog; it seemed to know that it was frightening, so it wouldn't go out of the main door, and it also didn't go into the house – it spent the whole day on guard in the courtyard. If guests came to the house, it would lie down with its front paws over its head. It didn't want to draw attention by barking, and it was worried that if it did bark, the visitors would be scared off, so it just sat there with pricked ears and watchful round eyes. It was not at all like a regular guard dog, which will bark for hours at the sight of a stranger. However, one night in the early hours, a thief came over the wall into the courtyard, and the dog went bounding straight over to bring him under control. It didn't bark, but between pain and fright the thief was screaming his head off. That told old Mr Shang that the dog was worth its salt: he didn't have to worry about a thing with Blackface on guard.

Mr Shang liked to say that Blackface was a grateful dog as well as being intelligent, and it "knew its business". Old Mr Shang had spent his life working in the retail trade, and he knew all about face and company rules and how the customer is king – this dog appealed to that side of his character, and so he liked it. If anyone said something nice about Blackface, old Mr Shang would beam, as if someone had praised one of his children.

However, on one occasion Blackface got into serious trouble.

Over the course of several days, the rooms on the west of Mr

Shang's courtyard house were dismantled and repaired, and so a whole load of builders and carpenters were hard at work, toting bricks and moving cement in and out. Normally, there weren't many visitors to the house, and anyone who did come was likely to be a regular visitor, so most of the time, the main entrance was shut. The dog wasn't used to having it open to the four winds with a horde of complete strangers rushing about. Blackface was still a very young dog after all, and it was feeling threatened, so all the hairs on its body bristled. However, it knew that it wasn't supposed to scare people, so it spent all day every day squatting in front of the eastern building, not daring even to sleep. After seven or eight days of this, the old building had been dismantled, and the foundations had been dug, so they started laying the bricks for the walls, and very soon the basic framework for a house had appeared. On the day that the main roofbeam was hoisted into place, old Mr Shang invited someone to come and put a lucky talisman on it, all done up with a red silk bow. Then everyone put their backs into it, and with a cacophony of shouts, they got the main beam put into place, after which a string of firecrackers was set off. That immediately brought a host of small children into the courtyard to join in the fun, yelling at the tops of their voices.

Blackface thought that something dreadful must have happened, so it suddenly leapt to its feet and came rushing over. The children took one look at Blackface with his ugly spots, his sharp teeth and huge claws – it really was a nightmarish vision – and ran for their lives. Those on the outside pushed in, those on the inside wriggled their way out: there was a struggling chaotic mass. All you could hear was screaming and crying.

Old Mr Shang came running out to see what on earth could

be the matter just as the son of one of his neighbours fell to the ground. His head hit the stone lintel, and the skin broke, showing blood. When the neighbours arrived and saw this scene, they were very unhappy about it all and started laying into Mr Shang: "Did you set your dog on our child? Who the hell do you think you are?"

Old Mr Shang was a man who cared about his face and his public reputation; he was at a disadvantage here, and so whatever these people said, he had to put up with it. He told his family to go with the child to the doctor's while he himself went to calm down the frightened builders.

It was just at this moment that catching sight of Blackface out of the corner of one eye, he was absolutely furious. Snatching up a bamboo pole and taking two steps forward, he gave the dog a single heavy thump, cursing it all the while: "What can you do with an animal? I've done my best to keep the peace all my life, and now you've embarrassed me like this in front of everyone!"

Blackface had been badly beaten and jumped to its feet, howling and showing its teeth – it looked very dangerous. Old Mr Shang was still furious and wasn't scared in the slightest. He shouted angrily: "What do you think you're doing? Don't you dare try to bite me!"

Blackface stood there motionless, watching Mr Shang. Then suddenly it turned around and ran out of the door – vanishing like a puff of smoke. Old Mr Shang tossed the bamboo pole aside and said: "Piss off and never come back! After all, you started out as a stray, didn't you?"

Blackface never came back. Night followed day and three days passed one after the other, and they did not see hide nor hair of the beast. Old Mr Shang started to miss his dog, but he didn't say so. However, he couldn't stop himself from going out to the door to have a good look around. Was the animal really never going to come back?

Two days after that, the rafters on the roof of the building on the western side of the courtyard were up, and they started plastering and laying tiles. The door to the courtyard was open, and Blackface suddenly came back. At that time of day, old Mr Shang was at work at Prosperity Seafood, and the builders were busy at the various tasks they had in hand, so nobody paid any attention to it.

Blackface gazed around the courtyard and spotted a pool of wet freshly-mixed cement in the middle of the courtyard. Suddenly, with all the force at its command, the dog bounded at that pool of cement and landed in it with a plop, and it had thrown itself in with such force that only its hind legs and its tail remained outside. Nobody saw any of this.

That evening, when Mr Shang came home, the workmen were packing up, and someone realised that the hairy thing in the pool of cement was a dog. Pulling it out, they were very shocked: it was Blackface! It had been dead for a while and was starting to go stiff. How could it have died here? When did it die? Did the neighbours kill it and then put it here?

Everyone speculated for ages, but nobody had a clue. Old Mr Shang had been silent all this time, but in the end he provided an answer that satisfied everyone: "I know that dog. It cared about face even more than I did, and so it killed itself." Then he said with a sigh: "Since it had to die, it wanted to die in its own home."

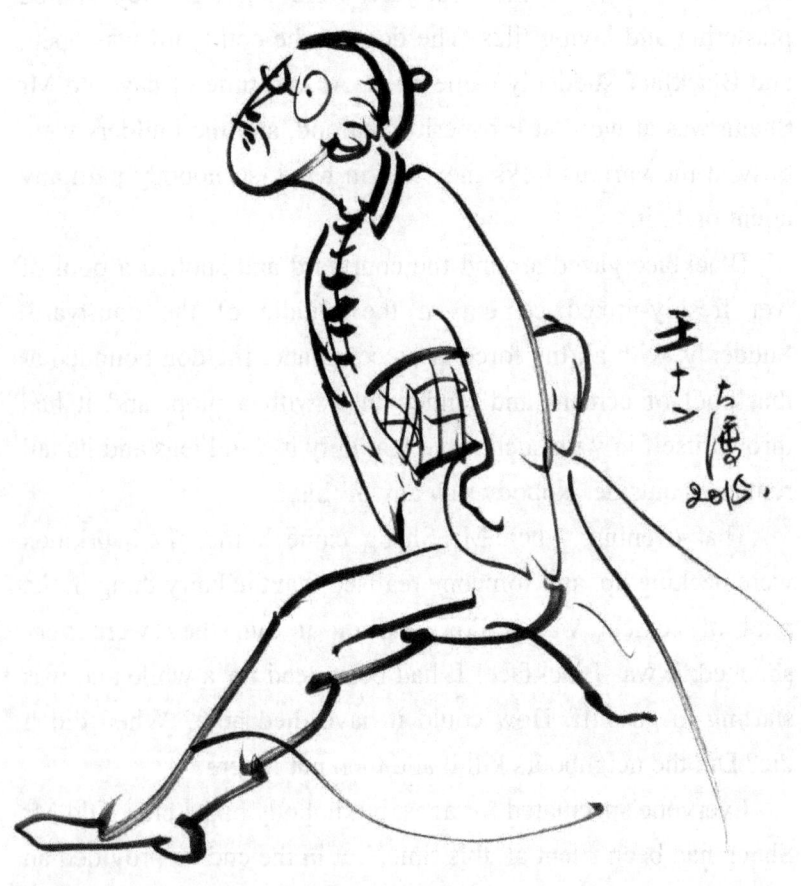

20
THE MIRACLE DOCTOR, WANG SHI'ER

TIANJIN IS A PORT CITY. In any port, the ground is going to be bumpy, and it is hard to find your footing – if you want to stand upright, you need to know what you are doing, and you have to have something you can rely on. What can you rely on? A skill of some kind? Well, no ordinary skill will work here – you need to have something very special up your sleeve. To put it another way: to be successful in Tianjin, regardless of what trade or profession you were in, you needed to be better than the rest. That was certainly true of the doctor Wang Shi'er.

When it comes to famous doctors, the sort where people say they can bring the dead back to life and what have you, there were more of them inside and outside the city walls than you could shake a stick at, but they were just famous and that's all – Wang Shi'er could work miracles. The difference between a miracle worker and a famous medic is like the difference between Heaven and Earth. The point about a miracle worker is that when you get sick, when you are critically ill, when you are going to die any moment now, other people don't know what to do, but he does. What he comes up with isn't a tried-and-tested remedy either; it is a flash of inspiration, a sudden instinct – he puts his hand in the right place and makes you well again.

There are lots of stories of that kind told about Wang Shi'er, so I will only give two here. One happened in the Foreign Concession, the other on Western Road in the old city. Let me give you the Foreign Concession story first.

One day, Wang Shi'er was walking along Kaifeng Avenue when he suddenly heard the sound of screaming. When he looked, he saw that a blacksmith making a stovepipe by the side of the road had both hands up to the left side of his face, and he was howling with pain. Wang Shi'er rushed over and asked him what the matter was. The blacksmith said: "A bit of iron slag hopped up into my eye... I am going to be blind!"

Wang Shi'er said: "Stop rubbing it. The more you rub, the deeper it goes in. Take your hands away and let me look at your eye."

The blacksmith put his hand down and forced the eye open. There was a tiny fragment of iron slag right there in his eyeball, along with tears and blood.

Wang Shi'er raised his head and looked up and down both sides of the street – there were shops selling all kinds of foreign goods lining the avenue. It so happened that Wang Shi'er was interested in foreign products and often came here window shopping. Suddenly, an idea flashed into his head – a moment of inspiration – and he said in a loud voice to the blacksmith: "Do not touch that eye! I will be right back and sort it out for you!" Then he ran into one of the shops.

When Wang Shi'er went in through the door, he grabbed

20

THE MIRACLE DOCTOR, WANG SHI'ER

TIANJIN IS A PORT CITY. In any port, the ground is going to be bumpy, and it is hard to find your footing – if you want to stand upright, you need to know what you are doing, and you have to have something you can rely on. What can you rely on? A skill of some kind? Well, no ordinary skill will work here – you need to have something very special up your sleeve. To put it another way: to be successful in Tianjin, regardless of what trade or profession you were in, you needed to be better than the rest. That was certainly true of the doctor Wang Shi'er.

When it comes to famous doctors, the sort where people say they can bring the dead back to life and what have you, there were more of them inside and outside the city walls than you could shake a stick at, but they were just famous and that's all – Wang Shi'er could work miracles. The difference between a miracle worker and a famous medic is like the difference between Heaven and Earth. The point about a miracle worker is that when you get sick, when you are critically ill, when you are going to die any moment now, other people don't know what to do, but he does. What he comes up with isn't a tried-and-tested remedy either; it is a flash of inspiration, a sudden instinct – he puts his hand in the right place and makes you well again.

There are lots of stories of that kind told about Wang Shi'er, so I will only give two here. One happened in the Foreign Concession, the other on Western Road in the old city. Let me give you the Foreign Concession story first.

One day, Wang Shi'er was walking along Kaifeng Avenue when he suddenly heard the sound of screaming. When he looked, he saw that a blacksmith making a stovepipe by the side of the road had both hands up to the left side of his face, and he was howling with pain. Wang Shi'er rushed over and asked him what the matter was. The blacksmith said: "A bit of iron slag hopped up into my eye... I am going to be blind!"

Wang Shi'er said: "Stop rubbing it. The more you rub, the deeper it goes in. Take your hands away and let me look at your eye."

The blacksmith put his hand down and forced the eye open. There was a tiny fragment of iron slag right there in his eyeball, along with tears and blood.

Wang Shi'er raised his head and looked up and down both sides of the street – there were shops selling all kinds of foreign goods lining the avenue. It so happened that Wang Shi'er was interested in foreign products and often came here window shopping. Suddenly, an idea flashed into his head – a moment of inspiration – and he said in a loud voice to the blacksmith: "Do not touch that eye! I will be right back and sort it out for you!" Then he ran into one of the shops.

When Wang Shi'er went in through the door, he grabbed

something off the wall with his right hand, and with his left hand he plonked down his green silk doctor's bag on the counter and said: "I am leaving this as a pledge. I am borrowing this thing for a minute. You can have it back once I am finished!"

Before he had even finished speaking, he was already halfway out of the door.

Wang Shi'er ran back to the blacksmith's side and said: "Open your eye as wide as you can!" The blacksmith strained to open his eye, and Wang Shi'er didn't even touch him; there was a "ping" sound, very light but perfectly audible, and then he heard Wang Shi'er say: "It's out. You'll be fine now. Try rolling your eye – does it still hurt?" The blacksmith moved his eye, and it didn't hurt at all – he felt just fine. When he looked up, Wang Shi'er was holding up a tiny sharp shard of iron in front of his face; that had been causing him agony in his eye just seconds before! Wang Shi'er didn't wait for his thanks; he headed back into the shop, and when he came out again, he had his green silk doctor's bag slung over his shoulder and was heading off down the road. The blacksmith shouted after him: "How did you cure my eye? You've got to let me kowtow my thanks!" Wang Shi'er didn't turn back; he just lifted his hand and waved.

The blacksmith was puzzled and went into the shop to enquire. The shop assistant pointed to the things hanging on the wall and said: "We don't understand either. He just said he wanted to borrow one and he brought it back a few minutes later."

The blacksmith raised his head – the things hanging on the wall looked like horseshoes, but they were too light. They were very carefully made too, lovely and shiny, and there was a strip of paint in the middle. Looking more closely he saw there were no holes for nails, so they couldn't be horseshoes. The blacksmith was now more baffled than ever, and asked the shop assistant: "Do foreigners use them for curing eyes?"

"Not that I've ever heard of!" the shop assistant said. "These things can attract metal – what foreigners call magnets." As the shop assistant spoke, he reached down one of these things from the wall and started to collect the various metal objects scattered across the table – a box, tweezers, nails, keys, even a pair of spectacles in a wire frame – all of them ended up stuck on the magnet. It seemed just like magic. The blacksmith had never seen such a thing before – he just stood there with his mouth hanging open.

Wang Shi'er had used this toy to pull the iron shard out of the blacksmith's eye.

But when it was all happening right in front of him, how did Wang Shi'er know that this was the right thing to do?

Isn't that amazing? The man was a miracle worker! And the next story is even better.

This story concerns events in the old city, and once again it took place out on the street.

What happened on this occasion was that something spooked the horse pulling a cartload of vegetables. It started careering down the road, and it didn't matter how hard the driver tugged at the reins or shouted – it had gone berserk. The people on both sides of the road were so scared they started running, and if they could find a side alley to slip into, they did. If there was no alley, they climbed trees to get out of the way, and in places where there were no trees, they rolled themselves into balls right by the walls. When the horse got to the crossroads, it met a big red-faced man coming the other way, his shirt hanging open to reveal a vast and pendulous stomach and a chest of black hair not unlike a furry caterpillar. Someone shouted at him: "Get out of the way! The horse has gone berserk!"

Who could have imagined the man's reaction? He shouted back: "Well, come and get me if you've got the balls!" Clearly, he was completely drunk.

The driver was very worried and shouted from his perch on the cart: "It'll kill you!"

The next thing that happened was there was the most almighty crash, as if something had hit a brick wall. The man was sent flying and landed hard against the wall on the other side of the road: he was now spreadeagled there. The horse was still galloping down the road. Although the man hadn't been killed, he was stretched out on the wall, making no attempt to get off. In fact, he was clutching the wall as hard as he could with his arms, completely motionless. Could there be something holding him fast there?

When everyone came forward to look, they realised that his ribs had been broken. The broken bones were now protruding out through the skin and had worked themselves into the gaps between the bricks. The force of the impact had been so strong that the broken bones had been driven deep into the brickwork, so it was impossible to pull them out. The man was in agony and was screaming with pain.

One person shouted: "Get your bones pulled out! Otherwise, when you run out of energy, you'll just die there!"

Another person called out: "Don't do anything of the kind! You've fractured your ribs – it'll kill you!"

Nobody had seen anything like this before, and nobody had a clue what to do.

The man was screaming: "Help! I don't want to die here!" His voice was thunderous. A couple of people started rolling up their sleeves to wrench him off.

Just at that moment, not far away, they heard someone shouting: "Don't move! I'm on my way."

Everyone turned around to look; not far away, a little elderly man was running towards them. His head was bare, he was wearing a grey robe, and his feet were moving as fast as they could go. Someone recognised this new arrival as the miracle doctor, Wang Shi'er, and said: "He'll know what to do!"

First, Wang Shi'er turned left and went over to a barber's stall, just a couple of paces away. He pressed his green silk doctor's bag into the hands of the barber and said: "This is my pledge." Then he plucked a white towel off the rack next to the stall and dipped it in the bronze bowl of hot water standing beside it, and only then came running forward. He was very quick on his feet, so he hadn't wasted any time; the white towel in his hands was still dripping with water and piping hot when he arrived at the scene.

Wang Shi'er rushed over to stand by the man, and with his left arm he supported his waist, while with his right hand he wrapped the hot and steaming towel over his face so that his nose and mouth were both covered. The big man was suffocating and started to shout and fight back, but Wang Shi'er kept him from breathing with all his might and refused to let go. The man must have been cursing him as hard as he could, but all that could be heard were a few muffled croaks. His face was now red and inflamed, and since his breath could not escape through either his nose or his mouth, his chest was expanding, becoming drum-like, shockingly swollen… and then with a "ping" sound, the broken bones embedded in the wall retracted. Wang Shi'er then let go, the man relaxed and flopped onto the ground. He said only one thing: "I'm going to live."

Wang Shi'er said: "Get this man to a doctor straight away to have those bones set." He turned around and gave the towel back to the barber, collected his green silk doctor's bag, and set off walking, as if nothing in the world had happened.

Those present just watched with their eyes wide and their mouths agape. Only one old man realised what exactly it was that he had done. He said: "Wang Shi'er used the man's own strength to pull his ribs out of the wall. If other people had tugged at him, it would only have done more damage – using his own strength saved him." Following that thought, the old man said: "But who else would have thought of such a thing?"

Miracles involve doing things that nobody else would have thought of, and that is why people in Tianjin called him the miracle doctor, Wang Shi'er.

21
BIGMOUTH PI

How do you know whether a place is rich or not? Do you look at the food and drink on sale there, or at what people do for fun? That's all on the surface; if you actually want to know how a place is doing, you need to see how many banks there are, and how many shops where you can buy gold or silver – and the number of gold shops is the most important. After all, the people going in and out of the banks aren't necessarily rich, and the truly rich have more money than they could possibly spend. If you have too much money, what do you do? Only a fool would stuff it under the mattress. Just think about it: are you trying to please the next burglar you meet? What happens if your house catches fire? Or your banknotes rot and fall to pieces? Or they get nibbled by insects, or termites, or rats? Or the value of the currency plummets and your notes end up worthless? Buying gold is always the best policy. Gold doesn't rot, nothing bites holes in it, and you can't burn it. Gold is gold.

Gold is so much more valuable than paper money could ever be.

If you have a lot of people buying gold bars, you have a lot of gold shops. Tianjin has an awful lot of gold shops, so you can be quite sure that Tianjin is a wealthy city.

But the gold-shop owners all wanted to be number one, and they fought each other relentlessly. As with the Eight Immortals crossing the sea, each one brought their own speciality to bear; and again, like when heroes go into battle, every one of them had a killer move to show off.

The Fountain of Honours gold shop by the North Gate was the first to come up with a real selling point. They had a gilded ingot, the size of a soup bowl, standing out on display in the main showroom, with the words "Touching the Ingot Will Improve Your Luck" engraved on it in large clerical script characters. That meant that plenty of people who weren't buying gold would still make a point of coming in through the door just to touch it in the hope of getting richer. In business, you have to think about your footfall – the more people in through the door the better, and the Fountain of Honours got famous on the back of this. However, with hands rubbing the thing day in and day out, the thin layer of gilding on the ingot pretty soon wore off, revealing the copper underneath. When the copper appeared on the surface, people didn't want to touch it any more. As with any has-been, it was up like a rocket and down like a stick. Once the place was deemed passé, the customers didn't come any more, and the feeling was that they might as well not have bothered with this stunt in the first place.

Shortly after this, the Treasures Complete gold shop came up with their own idea, and this worked an awful lot better. If you went and bought a gold bar from them, they'd throw in a set of real gold spectacle frames. That was much more successful than rubbing an ingot, because touching is just an empty gesture, while gold spectacle frames are a real benefit – the gold is right there glittering away on your face: just think how grand that would make you look! Of course, the Treasures Complete gold shop wasn't giving away the spectacle frames for free. If you wanted the frames, you had to buy a gold bar first. The boss was doing very well out of it all: this is what they mean when they talk about "the seller pulling the wool over the buyer's eyes". Pretty soon, there was a copycat in the Japanese Concession: the Flourishing Hall. If one shop was handing out gold spectacle frames, the other was giving away gold teeth. In fact, the Flourishing Hall even invited a dentist to set up in front of the till to put gold teeth into the toothless mouths of anyone who bought a gold bar. At that time, it was very fashionable to have gold teeth, to the point where some people would have perfectly good teeth pulled in order to have a gold one. As more and more customers of this type started turning up, it became something of a problem. The Flourishing Hall might as well have been a dentist's pure and simple – whichever way you looked there were people opening up their mouths wide to bare their teeth, waiting for a tooth to be removed to make room for a golden one. Even if you don't mind one way or the other about this spectacle, the smell was most unpleasant.

The Triple Honours gold shop at Majiakou pulled off an even greater coup; it was based in the Foreign Concession, and the boss was a bright guy with an eye for the very latest thing, who had learned a few tricks from foreigners. He had seen how successful the adverts foreigners put out were – it didn't cost much money, and if you got it right, absolutely everyone would know all about it. He found someone in the Foreign Concession to draw him a fashionable image, and then found an educated gentleman to write a challenging slogan: "It's better to buy gold than land or houses – and who has the purest gold? Triple Honours gold." He had three thousand copies of his advert printed by the Flourishing Lithography Press, and then he had his staff spend the next ten days plastering every wall, entranceway, lamppost, tree, train hoarding and tramway in Tianjin, just like the Boxers' posters in the year 1900. His adverts went up from the Foreign Concession to Beidaguan, from the old city to the outer city, from east to west, and all along the Gongnan-Gongbei Avenue – anywhere that could catch the eye. The problem is that you can't keep on putting adverts up, but after five days they get old, and after ten days they are getting tatty, and then after two weeks the colours have faded in the sun. A downpour ruins them, and a storm blows them away. This was not really a success.

In those days, there was a Tianjin storyteller called Bigmouth Pi, who was really quite entertaining-looking. He was tall and thin, with tiny hands and feet, and a small head. His round little head looked like a lantern perched on the end of a bamboo pole. But there was another oddity – his huge mouth. With this enormous mouth in such a small face, from a distance it was all you could see, and so people started to call him Bigmouth Pi.

When Bigmouth Pi was telling his tales, he could bring the dead back to life. He started performing the moment he opened his mouth, and was always "on", whatever the circumstances. Very quickly he was recognised as the finest solo performer in the southern part of the city. Any decent storyteller can produce his own material; but Bigmouth Pi's stories were the ones that went from mouth to mouth. He did well enough for himself as a storyteller in Tianjin, but nobody understood quite how desperate he was to get rich. There were lots of rich men in Tianjin, and he was terribly jealous. To begin with, he was hoping to get rich by alternating storytelling and selling candies – he'd tell a tale and then pause to make his sales of sweets. To listen to a storyteller while sucking a sweet was an enjoyable way to pass the time, and the two activities didn't interfere with one another, but he wasn't going to earn a lot of money this way. Then he tried a new idea: he would tell a story and then sell the padded stools he'd sourced from the Foreign Concession. The padded stools were a foreign novelty, and they were lovely and soft. Having sat on one of these stools while listening to a storyteller meant that you were comfortable and entertained all at the same time, and when the performance was over, people would find themselves buying the stools they'd been sitting on to take away.

Bigmouth Pi was a clever man, and the cleverer you are, the better you are at business. On rainy days, he sold umbrellas; on sunny days, he sold sunhats. At that time, there would be people to buy any imported product, and gradually he started to get rich. Once he had the capital, he opened a restaurant, and the restaurant made him even more money. Diners would be eating as they listened to him perform. With Bigmouth Pi's mouth and with his brains, he made money at everything he turned his hand to. Within three years, he'd opened a gold shop in the northeast corner of the city. In those days, there were eighty-one gold shops in Tianjin as it was, and they were all locked in the struggle to become number one. With someone wet behind the ears getting in on the act – what could he possibly hope to achieve?

When Bigmouth Pi was decorating his store, he pulled off a real coup with his so-called Gold-All-Over shop. Apparently, every single thing in his shop was gold. The door handles, the locks, the chain on the door, the lamp shades and the lamp pulls, the railings, the curtain hooks, the abacus, the brush handles, the flowerpots, even the taps and the washbasin in the lavatory were gold, and so was the western-style lavatory pan in which you peed or shat. Some people said that these things weren't solid gold, they were gilded, but they still shone so dazzlingly bright as to startle and amaze all who saw them.

Bigmouth Pi had no trouble picking out a name for his gold shop: it was the Gold-All-Over. The Gold-All-Over was indeed completely covered in gold. Before it was even open for business, everyone had heard of it – the place was famous! Some people believed everything they heard about it, while others shook their heads in doubt.

On the day the place opened its doors, there were brightly coloured lanterns hanging outside the door, and there was a banquet laid on in the main courtyard. Bigmouth Pi was there in a suit of new clothes, looking unusually cheerful. He'd hired an orchestra in from the Foreign Concession, and there they were with their western drums and trumpets, thundering away for all they were worth. The huge, shining tubas really assaulted the ears.

There were more onlookers than invited guests – everyone wanted to see whether Bigmouth Pi's Gold-All-Over lived up to its billing. Soon there was a joke about it:

The boss of a silk shop on Guyi Street came to offer

congratulations, but in actual fact he was there to check up on whether this Gold-All-Over story was true or not. He looked the whole place over and was completely stunned: it was all true! There was gold glittering everywhere you looked. He was blinded... overwhelmed by it. At lunchtime, there were a whole host of friends eating and having fun, and the more they enjoyed themselves, the more they drank, until he was feeling positively feverish and his face was bright red. He stumbled and swayed into the lavatory and peed all over the gold pan. Heading out of the door, he then called for a rickshaw to take him home. When he got in, he keeled straight over and slept like the dead, not opening his eyes until the following morning. "So did you have a good look at the Gold-All-Over yesterday?" his wife asked. "Is it for real?"

"Oh, it's all true! Absolutely everything is made out of gold," said the man. "Even the lavatory pan is made out of gold. I peed all over it!"

"You peed on something made of solid gold?" his wife said. "I don't believe it."

"If you don't believe me, go and see for yourself," the man said.

Afterwards, his wife still didn't believe him, and in fact the more she thought about it, the less she liked his story. So she rushed round to the Gold-All-Over to see for herself, and the handle was just as golden as he'd said, and when she opened the door, everything inside just shone. She asked one of the members of staff: "My husband says that even the lavatory pan in your shop is made of gold. I said that he was having me on, and he then said that he'd peed all over it!"

The member of staff heard her out in stunned silence, staring at her wide-eyed. Then he turned round and ran over to Bigmouth Pi and said: "Boss, I have just found out who peed all over the tuba at lunch yesterday!"

Everyone who heard this story would burst out laughing.

When this joke started making the rounds, it turned out to have legs. People told it to everyone they knew, and pretty soon the whole city had heard it. Whether they told it favourably or to denigrate the place, everyone in Tianjin had heard about the Gold-All-Over. That joke was very useful for Bigmouth Pi.

People in the profession realised at once that this was something that Bigmouth Pi had come up with. It wasn't really a joke; it was a comic storyteller's piece. There was the scene-setting, the build-up, the unexpected twist, and the punchline... really, you had to admire the man – he'd invented the story and then got everyone else to tell the tale for him, making him famous. He must have made a fortune out of it.

22
GOLDEN FINGERS

GOLDEN FINGERS WAS A VERY capable man, but he was jealous and small-minded and couldn't bear anyone else being more successful. If you did better than him, he'd find a way to get back at you, and it was always a horrible way, something that would make your life completely miserable.

There are some places where he might have got away with behaving like that, but in Tianjin he was asking for trouble. All kinds of people fetch up in a port city, and there are men with brilliant abilities everywhere you look – in fact, you soon realise that there are more things in Heaven and Earth than are dreamed of in your philosophy. Who knows what kind of person you might just have annoyed?

Golden Fingers was a scholar from the south that General Bai had invited to join his household to help keep him entertained. However, our story doesn't begin with Golden Fingers; it starts with General Bai.

General Bai was a military man, with the rank of major-general. The higher he was promoted, the more conscious he was of the dangers inherent in his official career. After he resigned his position, he decided he was best off moving to the Foreign Concession in Tianjin. Western-style buildings were so comfortable, what with the running water and electricity, and foreigners were in charge here, so local officials couldn't interfere. It was the perfect place for him to feel safe and sound, so he moved there with his entire family.

General Bai was a very wealthy man, but he had no interest in wine, women, or gambling. He had just one love – calligraphy and painting. In those days, if you were rich and powerful, you would quickly acquire a host of flatterers. If you liked to warble a bit of opera but were as hoarse as a crow, they would say you could rival Yu Shuyan; if you could write a line of wobbly characters, they'd say you were every bit as good as Hua Shikui – in fact, they might go so far as to say that Hua Shikui wasn't a patch on you. So when General Bai expressed an interest in calligraphy and painting, he quickly found himself boxed in. Thanks to someone introducing him, he soon got to know Golden Fingers, a painter from Lingnan.

As to what Golden Fingers was actually called, nobody knew. Everyone was too busy looking at his fingers. He didn't paint with a brush; he used his fingers. In those days, there was nobody in Tianjin who painted with his fingers. Fingers are like sausages after all – without hairs, what is there to paint with? But in spite of that, he could paint landscapes and flowers, plants and birds, horses and ladies with their faces, eyes, eyebrows and little cherry lips. When you have someone who can paint with their fingers, watching them at work is actually much more fun than seeing the final product. When General Bai invited him to move in and join his household, with everything he could eat and drink provided, he also gave him a soubriquet: Golden Fingers. He liked this name because it had a very good sound to it, and his original surname was Huang or "Yellow". So there it was, he was now called Golden Fingers, and if you called him by his real name, he wouldn't answer.

One day, General Bai said: "I have heard that there are some really great painters working in Tianjin."

Golden Fingers said: "I have heard that there is a figure painter in Tianjin called Shou Tao who took off his trousers and dipped his arse cheeks in his colours and painted that way."

General Bai took it as a joke. However, in any port city, ears are connected to mouths, and mouths to ears. Within three days, the story was known to everyone in Tianjin artistic circles. Not long afterwards, there was someone who passed the word to General Bai that a Tianjin painter would very much like to meet this Golden Fingers, who worked with his "claws". General Bai laughed and said: "What a charming idea! How about coming round one day to paint a picture at my place." He sent people to invite famous artists from the local region to join them on this occasion. Once he started sending out the invitations, he realised just how many famous painters there were in the city, and they all felt the need to play hard to get, to make a show of how special they were. In the end, he was only able to invite two guests, and neither of them was who he actually wanted to have: one was One Line Zhao's disciple, Second Master Qian; the other was the calligrapher, Huang Ernan's disciple, Fourth

Master Tang. (However, according to what some people said, Master Huang Ernan had never even met the man.)

Second Master Qian was famous for structuring his painting around a single long line, a couple of yards in length, drawn freehand in a single stroke, completely even and fluid, pulling the other elements of his picture into a coherent whole. Fourth Master Tang used neither brush nor hands to paint – he painted with his tongue. This was a technique introduced into Tianjin by Master Huang Ernan.

When Golden Fingers heard that, he was stunned, then cold sweat broke out on his forehead. One of these men could draw a perfect freehand line over a yard in length, a feat which was impossible for someone working with their fingers to achieve. As for painting with the tongue, he'd never even heard of such a thing before. If it was possible to paint well in this way, who would think that his finger technique was anything special?

Since he couldn't outclass them, he'd have to do them down by pulling some nasty trick. He began by sending his minions off to study how the two of them worked, what techniques they used and what tricks, and then he thought of ways to make them look bad, to ruin their paintings. Very quickly, he had a grasp of the two men's styles and started to come up with a plan for a neat way to get at them, so he could be sure that he would come out on top. Golden Fingers really was an extraordinary man in his own way.

On the day that everyone was going to convene at the Bai Mansion, the general decided to hold a party and invited a number of guests, all of them big bugs in their own different ways. An unusually large painting table, quite two yards long, was arranged right in the middle of the main room. The four treasures of the scholar's study – brushes, ink, paper, and an inkstone – were also all placed in readiness, each one exceptionally fine in quality, not to mention valuable. When the two artists, Qian and Tang, arrived, they sat down with a cup of tea and chatted for a while first, and then they got up and headed for the painting table to get to work. All of this was part of the competition: they were determining who was in charge, which one would dominate, and who would go on to wipe out the others.

A length of double-layered top-quality Xuan paper had already been laid out on the painting table – the preparations and materials for this art contest had all been arranged by Golden Fingers. From the way that he had set this up, it was clear that the other two artists were going to be put to the sword first, and then he would come forward to show off his skills.

When Second Master Qian saw the long scroll, he knew that he was supposed to be the first to paint, so he stepped right up to the table. Second Master Qian was a thin man with long arms, and the first thing he did was to spread wide his white hands and lightly feel the paper from one side to the other. People who paint with very fine lines need to know whether the table is solid and the paper even. They need to be prepared for every lump and bump. However, Golden Fingers had not expected him to do this. As Second Master Qian felt his way along, his heart suddenly began to pound. He realised that Golden Fingers had played a nasty trick on him and that this was nothing but a trap. There were at least three places where a stone had been placed under the painting mat. Even though these stones were about the size of mung beans, if his brush were to hit one of them, it would jump, and that would make his calligraphic line go wrong. He didn't say anything, and his expression didn't change, but he made a note of it. However, he didn't want Golden Fingers to realise that he'd spotted the trap that had been laid for him.

Second Master Qian always used his long line to join two elements in his painting that he had already put in at opposite ends of the paper – the line would link them together. For example, at one end he might draw a boy and at the other end a cart full of gold ingots, and then between the two he'd draw a rope to create the traditional auspicious image: *A Baby Boy Brings Treasure*. Or he might draw an old fisherman with a bamboo pole here and a huge red carp leaping out of the water there, and then between the two would be the fishing line hauling it out for another lucky image: *May You Enjoy Abundance Year After Year*. Today, Second Master Qian began by using a big brush to paint a child with a spool in one upraised hand, and at the opposite corner of the paper he painted a kite that had been caught by the wind. If he now joined the two together by a string, you should have the classic *Spring Winds Bring Happiness*.

Second Master Qian picked out a goat-hair brush with a long handle from the selection in the brush pot and then dipped it in the ink from the inkstone. He then breathed in deeply, taking air right down into his diaphragm, and allowed the brush to touch the paper. He began by drawing several loops round the spool held in the child's hand, and then started to spin out his line, the thin thread of ink following the brush, the brush following his movements as he gradually walked from left to right, the line bowing in the wind – he was painting the line as it caught the wind and the wind as it caught the line. The crowd of people surrounding him all held their breath too, since they would not want to disturb Second Master Qian as he drew this magnificent freehand line. Second Master Qian knew exactly where the little stones were, but he wasn't about to avoid them. No, every time he arrived at one of the places where a stone was lying in wait, he would gather his wits and concentrate even more on his brush, moving across the surface smoothly and without the slightest hesitation, without leaving any sign of the presence of an obstacle until he had connected up the spool with the kite. Then he put down his brush and said: "I have shown you all what one of my humble abilities can do." Immediately, everyone burst out in a roar of applause. Second Master Qian responded politely, but he did not forget to turn his head and say to Golden Fingers: "In a moment, I do hope that we will see you drawing a freehand line with your fingers?"

Golden Fingers didn't respond to this challenge. It seemed as though he'd already lost the first half of this contest. He just said: "Let's wait and see what happens when Fourth Master Tang has finished painting." There was just the shadow of an ugly expression on his face. He still felt sure that he could destroy this Fourth Master Tang who painted with his tongue.

Golden Fingers called for someone to take Second Master Qian's *Spring Winds Bring Happiness* away and place a fresh piece of Xuan paper, eight feet in length, on the table.

Everyone in Tianjin knew all about tongue painting, but people who'd come from the Foreign Concession or from some other part of China were seeing this for the very first time. Plump Fourth Master Tang was quite red in the face, but there was absolutely nothing wrong with his brains or his eyesight. He sucked up a small saucer of ink just as if he were drinking soup and then stuck out his bright red tongue and licked some of the really thick ink from the heart of the inkstone. After that, he bent over until his face was nearly touching the paper, then licking a tiny spot on the paper, a round plum blossom petal appeared... dark here and light there, fresh and clear. He licked the paper five times, and there was a small plum flower sitting on the paper. As they watched, the tip of his tongue flickered back and forth, and flower after flower bloomed across the paper. It wasn't just the guests that were amazed – even Golden Fingers was stunned. General Bai couldn't help himself. "Amazing!" he cried. That almost made Golden Fingers explode with rage. However, he hoped that his trap would shortly be sprung and the man would get his comeuppance.

Just as Fourth Master Tang was in the middle of his painting, he started to feel that there was something wrong with the taste of the ink. As he was contemplating what might be wrong, he realised that the problem wasn't in his mouth, but in his nose. When you are using your tongue to paint, you bend over and compress your chest. Furthermore, since your mouth is full of ink, you have to use your nose to breathe in and out. As time went by, his breathing became more and more laboured, and he realised that what he could smell was pepper; keeping his eye on the paper, he spotted some white flecks on the surface – ground white pepper. He immediately grasped that someone wanted to see him fail. As quickly as he could, he swallowed the ink, but when he straightened up, his nose and eyes were smarting painfully, as if a host of ants were crawling all over them. He knew that he was in trouble; no matter what he did it was already too late... Atishoo... As he sneezed, a whole cloud of black specks settled across his paper, ruining his painting. Clearly, it was an utter disaster. Golden Fingers was delighted.

The onlookers were struck dumb. The only person who seemed entirely unconcerned was Fourth Master Tang himself. He called for a bowl of water and rinsed his mouth with it. Then he took a mouthful of the pure water and spat it from his mouth in a fine mist, so it fell like rain across the paper. The black ink spots covering the paper now gradually became lighter, softer, as if flowers were unfurling their petals across his canvas. Fourth Master Tang now slowly mixed up a saucer of ink, neither thick nor thin, and then dipping his tongue in his ink, he hunched his back, moving first his torso and then his legs, as a thicket of branches and a gnarled old tree trunk appeared. An ancient plum tree covered in beautiful blossom now leapt up from the paper. The onlookers exclaimed in admiration. The best of all was the poem Fourth Master Tang had written as the colophon to his painting – he'd chosen to make use of Wang Mian's famous poem about plum blossoms, dating to the Yuan dynasty:

> *There is a tree by my inkstone pool,*
> *Each of its flowers blooms inky-cool.*
> *There is no need to praise colours bright,*
> *Just enjoy the pure scent that fills the light.*

General Bai seemed to be in ecstasy. "That sneeze of yours almost scared me to death, Fourth Master Tang," he said. "I had no idea that such a masterpiece could come from a sneeze."

"When you sneeze on a tongue painting, it's called splashing ink," Fourth Master Tang said with a smile.

General Bai had heard the expression "splashing ink", and

having admired the painting all over again, he turned to look for Golden Fingers, only to find that he was long gone.

After this, Golden Fingers was not to be seen around the Bai Mansion any more, but there were now two new artists-in-residence – one of them was tall and thin, the other short and fat: Second Master Qian and Fourth Master Tang.

23
FORTY-EIGHT VARIETIES

PEOPLE IN TIANJIN are always really quick on the uptake, so they put medicinal herbs in sweets in order that they would be both delicious *and* cure diseases – these sweets were called medicinal candies.

Medicinal candies first became popular at the end of the Qing dynasty and the beginning of the Republican period; they were retailed as far afield as Beijing, and they sold very well. Buying and selling is the seed and the fruit – if people eat them then people make them; if people buy them then people sell them. Because of this, there were plenty of people in the Tianjin-Beijing corridor who made these kinds of things. First, they worked out how to insert all kinds of different medicinal herbs into the sweets so that there were various sorts of pretty and delicious medicinal candies; then they had to be sharp on the selling side too... you need to be there singing the praises of your product or lauding it to the skies, or using some other kind of technique to puff it to make sure that your customers are happy and content, so that they would be glad to put your medicinal candies in their mouths.

The people you find in Tianjin are quite different from the inhabitants of Beijing, and you have to use completely different techniques to sell medicinal candies in these two markets. Beijing is full of government officials, so the only thing people think about are the various officials who live there, and they like to know the latest scandals that have overtaken them. Therefore, Soldier Huang, who sold medicinal candies over on Tianqiao Street, did very well for himself by cursing officials. He would stand there cursing and swearing, first about the warlord Duan Qirui and then about General Zhang Xun, before moving on to President Yuan Shikai – in fact, he'd curse any official who was important enough, and the more other people feared them, the more he dared to say. Of course, his candies sold like hot cakes.

Tianjin is an ordinary city, and the people who live there care most about their daily round – eating and drinking and having fun, and so anything that is extra delicious or particularly good to drink or exceptionally amusing or enjoyable is sure to pique their interest. They also like to see people exercising an unusual skill, and so when it came to selling medicinal candies, people pulled all kinds of amazing tricks. There were people who told jokes, there were people who put on a comic crosstalk, some did magic shows, while others did martial arts or puppet shows or bicycle acrobatics or bat-and-ball displays or archery, so that even calling out to passers-by came to be a matter of great skill and judgment in tone and volume.

There was a man called Yu Liu, originally from Baodi County, who had his pitch selling medicinal candies right outside the Drum Tower. He was a pretty bright guy and terribly good with his hands. Unlike everyone else, he didn't make any particular efforts on the selling side; he worked at his candies. When he set up his stall outside his house selling medicinal candies, he wasn't shouting or singing or bellowing at passers-by. Instead, he had a table with a couple of long glass-lidded boxes set in a wooden frame, made to open in the middle. Each one had a different candy inside. Since the lids were made of glass, you could look in to see the different colours of the medicinal candies. If you wanted to buy one, he would open up the box and then pick up a few cubes with tongs, which he would put in a paper bag and hand to you – no performance, no pandering to the whims of his customers and trying to please them... but his candies were so good. They were brightly coloured, flavourful, and beautifully made. You could really taste the herbs that went into them. He didn't just use regular medicinal plants like tea, osmanthus, ginger, safflower, rose, cardamom, orange peel, amomum seed, lotus seed, almond, and mint; he would also put in delicious fruit flavours like pear, peach, plum, persimmon, loquat, banana, cherry, sour plum, sour jujube, watermelon and so on. However, in business, you cannot rely purely on the quality of your product – you also have to know how to sell it. Although he made by far the most different kinds of medicinal candy – at his height he was making forty-eight different flavours – he set up his stall right outside his house, so how many people in the city were going to know about it? If you mentioned sellers of medicinal candies in Tianjin, most people would say Wang Baoshan was number one, Idiot Li number two, and Lian Huaqing would be number three. They would carry on listing until their mouths ran dry, and yet none of them would so much as mention Yu Liu.

Second Master Liu, living in the same ward, was a fine gentleman, who'd got a good education but never gone in for an official career. Having made his pile in business, he'd retired years ago to enjoy a good life in the bosom of his family. One day, he happened to bump into Yu Liu and said: "You're good at making candies, but you have no idea how to sell them. You simply cannot make a living out of a stall by your own front door."

"I'd be happy to move around," Yu Liu said, "but I can't work up any kind of patter, and I don't know how to sing. I couldn't put on any kind of performance that people would enjoy."

"They've already got that kind of thing covered," Second Master Liu said, "and you won't necessarily ever be any better than them. Besides which, he who follows is always behind. Since you are not a local, you wouldn't know, but people in Tianjin like to see real skill on display, and it has to be something unique."

"Where could I find a unique skill?" Yu Liu asked.

"You don't find them," Second Master Liu said. "First you have to think of something, and then you have to practise it."

"How do I think of something? How do I practise it?" Yu Liu still hadn't got the point.

Second Master Liu laughed and said: "Let me explain. When you are pondering the subject, you need to think of some new and fresh way of making people aware of your forty-eight flavours. When you are practising, you draw in the customers by using the technique that you thought of earlier. So for example, how about you don't use tongs? Every single person in Tianjin who sells medicinal candies uses them all the time."

Yu Liu was far from stupid. These words were like firing a train. Not long afterwards, Yu Liu invited Second Master Liu to come round to his house and have a cup of tea while nibbling a few medicinal candies. Then he took Second Master Liu out to the courtyard at the back, at which point his eyes immediately lit up. In the middle of the courtyard, there was a carrying pole with tins at each end, and in each there was a layer of square boxes for medicinal candies, one kind to each box. Each of the boxes had a lid on top, with hinges, so it could be opened with a flick of the wrist. The two tins could each contain twenty-four boxes, so in total there would be forty-eight varieties.

The decoration on the carrying poles for the tins was something he'd never seen before. On each half of the pole, there was a dragon's head, meeting in the middle, with glaring eyes and gnashing teeth, and right in the centre there was a shining golden orb: so it represented two dragons fighting over a pearl. There were two springs sticking up from each of the dragons' heads, with a red pompom attached to the end, so that when he picked up the whole contraption and set off walking, the pompoms would bob with each step. He did not know where Yu Liu had found a decent lacquer worker, but he'd japanned both tins in a lovely shiny black lacquer and then written "Yu Family Medicinal Candies: Forty-Eight Varieties" on them in gold paint. Each of the individual candy boxes had its name written in red paint on the glass lid, and the medicinal candies looked bright and colourful underneath. Going out onto the street with equipment like that to sell candies was guaranteed to be a sensation! Second Master Liu was very happy to see it, and he praised his efforts: "Really, this stuff could all have come from the imperial palace."

At the same time, Yu Liu had been practising his sales technique. He grabbed a paper bag with his left hand and took hold of a small bronze spoon with his right hand, between the thumb and index finger – clearly he wasn't going to be using tongs any more. He would walk round the two tins in a circle, flicking open the lid of first this box and then that with the ring finger of his right hand, scooping out a single candy with his bronze spoon and popping it into a paper bag. He had got very fast at opening the box lids, and the action of scooping up a candy was really smooth – he was every bit as good as Fingering Liu when he was working the shell game. It would be worth spending the money just to watch his sales technique, even if you weren't going to eat the candies.

Second Master Liu could see how much care and attention (not to mention effort) Yu Liu had put into all of this, and he said happily: "You'll do! It's time for you to put this into practice, and I am sure that your forty-eight varieties are going to be famous."

The very next day, Yu Liu picked up his carrying pole and headed out of the door. He went to the old city and the new, east and west, Gongnan and Gongbei Avenue, and visited each of the nine foreign concessions in turn – immediately he was famous the length and breadth of Tianjin. He had also put some thought into how he would be dressed: blue trousers and a white jacket, with cloth shoes and clean socks. He picked up his uniquely decorated tins on his carrying pole and moved out along the streets halting at every second step – there were even some foreigners who wanted a photograph of him with all his equipment.

However, Yu Liu wasn't all on his own for very long. Soon

he heard that over on the east side of the city there was someone selling medicinal candies who also used lacquered tins with a dragon theme, and who also claimed to have forty-eight varieties. This meant his own forty-eight varieties were no longer anything special. He was furious and upset, and he rushed off to find Second Master Liu to ask him for his advice. "You may not copy other people, but you can't prevent other people from copying you," Second Master Liu said. "You have to find something that they can't copy, which can be your unique selling point."

Within three months, Yu Liu had come up with a new trick: his split step. Originally, when he was collecting the candies out of his tins, he held the spoon in his right hand, so he was always facing inwards. This didn't look very good. Now he was doing his split walk, so he'd circle one tin facing left and then switch round so he circled the second tin facing right. As he changed direction, he'd swap what he held in each hand, just like the boys serving tea at the Queen of Heaven Festival would swap from one shoulder to the other. With this change, his split step and his two hands changing jobs, there was a performance taking place. And don't forget – at the end of all this you could eat one of Yu Liu's forty-eight varieties of delicious medicinal candies! Who wouldn't be happy to pay for that?

However, it was not long before he was told that someone was working up his own split step routine. Yu Liu kept this information to himself for a few days as he thought of a new wrinkle… he was going to add a few more boxes of candies in each tin, which would contain half cubes. He thought that he would sell half cubes in addition to the regular forty-eight flavours. These half cubes could be selected by the purchaser in any combination; whatever they wanted, he would open the box and scoop up for them.

He went to see Second Master Liu to tell him about his new idea.

Second Master Liu laughed his head off. Then he explained: "Sooner or later someone else is going to copy your technique. I'll tell you what you have to do." Having said that, he wrote out a few lines on a piece of paper and handed it to Yu Liu. "You don't need to sing this – you just need to learn it off by heart. When you are making your moves, you should recite it. That should hold them."

Yu Liu looked – there were six lines on the page:

> *Tianjin medicinal candies are famously good,*
> *But the forty-eight varieties are the best in this 'hood.*
> *Each colour, each flavour is better than the last,*
> *Or take some half-candies to break your fast.*
> *The skills of the Yu family will be kept in-house*
> *If anyone copies me, well, he's a louse!*

Yu Liu wasn't a native of Tianjin, and he didn't understand their sense of humour, the way that their jokes contained insults – the locals were very tough. He was still feeling a bit concerned. Second Master Liu could see that he wasn't happy, so he said: "Just do what I say. Nobody will ever dare copy you again."

Yu Liu said: "You've racked your brains about how to help me out so many times. If this works, I'm going to pay you back with a lifetime supply of medicinal candies."

The following day, when Yu Liu was selling his candies and

doing his split step routine, he recited the mantra that Second Master Liu had composed for him. The first time didn't go too well, but by the second recitation he had it off by heart, and as he became more familiar with it, he gradually started to use it to pace himself. His steps were quickened, and he kicked out dramatically, like in the Peking opera *Xu Ce Runs the Gauntlet*. His customers and the other onlookers all burst out laughing. Someone said: "If anyone dared to steal your patter, he really would be a louse." Everyone hooted at that.

Yu Liu now understood that he had found his unique skill. He also realised the art with which Tianjin people spoke – they would crack a joke with underlying menace, or make threats with underlying humour. Nobody would pay attention if he just complained, but taking it all with a laugh wouldn't work either. After this, nobody ever copied him again. He was terribly grateful to Second Master Liu and sent him candies every single day. He gave him six different pieces a day, so that every eight days he ate all forty-eight varieties. It went on like this year after year.

Yu Liu was married, but he and his wife never had any children. When he died, there was nobody to carry on his skill. However, he was long outlived by Second Master Liu. People said that Second Master Liu lived to be so very old because he ate so many of Yu Liu's medicinal candies.

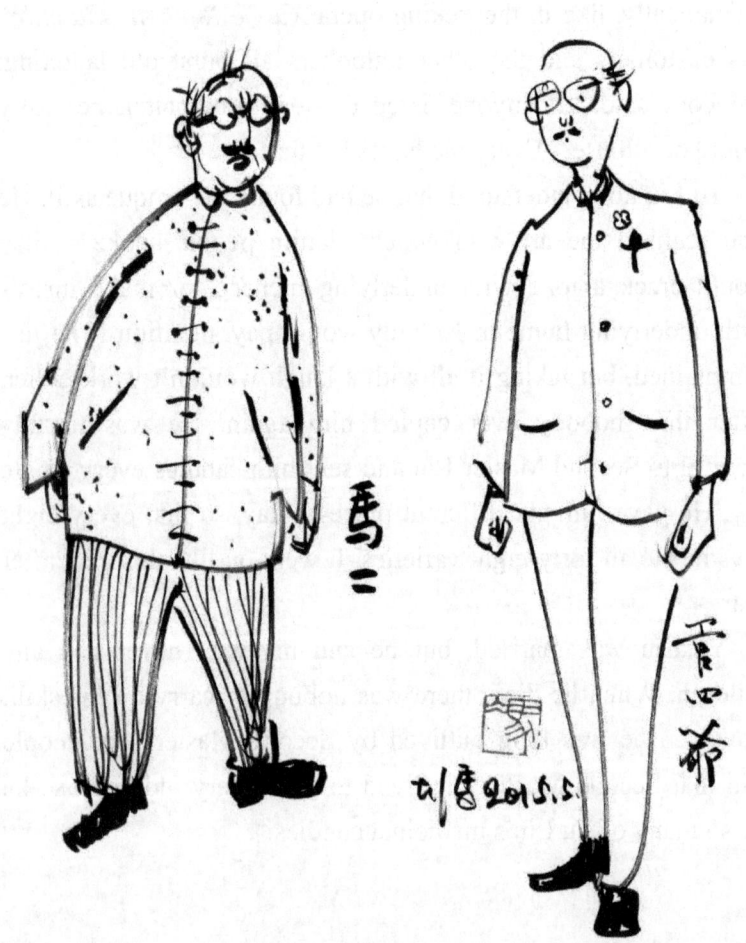

24
MA ER

BEING REAL ISN'T DIFFICULT, but acting so as to give people the impression that they are looking at the real thing is very difficult indeed. For example, should Ma Lianliang open his mouth to sing, then it is Ma Lianliang singing – that's not hard, is it? But if you start singing and everyone who hears you says it is Ma Lianliang... well, that's practically impossible. So people in Tianjin really admired anyone who could do a good impression. When talking about someone like that, they would never say that he was "taking someone off" or anything like that – they would praise him for "getting it right". Getting it right was a sign of real skill.

During the Republican era, the old city in Tianjin produced a very clever man who was terribly good at doing impressions – his name was Ma Er. His father had started out life by pulling a rickshaw, and ended up owning his own dock for water and land transport out on the Grand Canal served by more than one hundred dockers. Having made a pile of money at that, he went into trade with the south, and that made him really rich. At this stage, he started buying up properties in both the old city and the Foreign Concession, and opened up shops; he ended up with good connections in all sorts of unlikely places. Of course, Tianjin is full of smart crooks, and there are plenty of people who are ready and waiting to stab you in the back – if you aren't careful, it is really easy to annoy someone dangerous. They will get you for it, make no mistake about that, and you will lose everything. Ma Er's father lost all his money that way, but that's another story. This is about Ma Er.

Ma Er was brought up in luxury and wasn't required to learn any kind of special skill, but when his family went bankrupt, he found himself unable to go and do any kind of coolie labour. He spent all day in idleness, having fun; if he left the bars it was only to head for the teahouses, and time hung heavy on his hands. He wasn't a noticeably intelligent man, but he had a few tricks up his sleeve, and his greatest talent was his ability to imitate others. Ma Er could give you a wonderful impression of seven or eight different people, including the mayor, a couple of important guys in Tianjin, a few of the famous businessmen, and some well-known gangsters. He worked up his impressions of a couple of these important and famous figures into skits, and whether it was walking or standing, smiling, waving his hands, or grinding his teeth, he was perfect – he wasn't doing an impression of them anymore, he *was* that person. It got so that you might really imagine you were looking at the genuine individual concerned. When the impressionist gets it right, it is a source for endless jokes, for the very perfection of his performance will make you laugh until you can barely stand;

such a person is even more amusing than the great comic Chang Lian'an himself.

Ma Er's very best impression was of Fourth Master Guan, the official in charge of education over in the Foreign Concession. There was a slight resemblance between the two men in that they both had a pale round face, but other than that they didn't look like each other at all. Fourth Master Guan was a senior government official (and looked it), while Ma Er didn't even have a job; Fourth Master Guan went everywhere by car, while Ma Er walked on his own two legs; Fourth Master Guan had his hair slicked back with oil and a carefully washed face, where Ma Er was filthy; Fourth Master Guan was always to be seen elegantly turned out in a suit, while Ma Er had never done up the top button on his jacket in his life; Fourth Master Guan would pull out a western handkerchief and cover his mouth every time he coughed, whereas Ma Er would follow any coughing fit by spitting a lump of phlegm out onto the ground. But none of that really mattered. When he wanted to pretend to be Fourth Master Guan, you could swear it was the man himself!

Ma Er went regularly to the Foreign Concession, and Fourth Master Guan was a public figure – it wasn't difficult to find him out and about. Most people who lived in the old city never went to the Foreign Concession, so quite half his audience had never clapped eyes on Fourth Master Guan and had no idea how good the impression was; they just enjoyed his performance. However, there was one occasion when Fourth Master Guan came to the north part of the city to give a speech at a cultural event organised by the Chamber of Commerce. Lots of people went to attend, and they were amazed; Ma Er had done a wonderful job! Afterwards, when they got to see Ma Er's new and improved impression, they were even more impressed: Ma Er was absolutely perfect in his part!

After this, Ma Er was famous in the old city. When people met him, they would call him Fourth Master Guan for fun. However, Ma Er was quite clever enough to know that it was dangerous to annoy a famous or important figure, so no matter what other people said to him, he never called himself Fourth Master Guan.

Gradually, he got to be famous in Tianjin. He was welcome wherever he went, since everyone loved his impressions.

Tianjin is a commercial centre, so everyone is trying to make some money or get something for nothing. After Ma Er became famous for his impressions, from time to time people would ask him out for dinner or to attend a banquet on the back of it. Some of these people didn't have a clue who Fourth Master Guan was, but they still invited him for a joke to bring a bit of excitement to their meal. He didn't care in the slightest since he got to eat and drink for free, and a penny saved is a penny earned. So when a wedding was being held or there was a hundred days celebration for a baby, a sixtieth birthday or a party to celebrate a business deal, he would be sent an invitation.

Tianjin isn't that big, so when Ma Er became famous in the old city, news gradually filtered round to the ears of Fourth Master Guan in the Foreign Concession. Fourth Master Guan was no ordinary man – he didn't show any overt interest but secretly he sent one of his own people, Ge Shitou, over to the old city to find out the truth and see what Ma Er was up to and whether he had indeed worked up so fine an impression as to fool people they were one and the same.

Ge Shitou was pretty lucky; when he arrived at the old city, he soon found his opportunity. The Great Peace brush shop over on Guyi Street was celebrating sixty years in business, and they were having a banquet to celebrate at the Optimus on Da Hutong, and Ma Er was invited. Ge Shitou found someone who could wangle him an invitation, so on the appointed day he arrived at the Optimus and quickly picked Ma Er out from the crowd. He could see at first glance that Ma Er bore a slight facial resemblance to Fourth Master Guan, but other than that the two didn't look at all similar. Fourth Master Guan was an important man – and who was this? He was obviously barely scraping by.

But shortly after the banquet started, someone shouted: "Let our Fourth Master Guan say a few words!" Everyone bellowed their approval. Ma Er stood up from his place at a table across the way, and as he did so, he seemed to turn into someone else. His body was the same, but he moved it in a totally different way. His left hand went back to pat himself on the small of the back... Fourth Master Guan had just that habit when he was giving a speech; at the same time his stomach puffed out... again Fourth Master Guan's stomach would puff out too when he was patting his back. Before he'd even opened his mouth, he'd managed to win the audience over with his impression. "It's Fourth Master Guan to the life!" someone cried. "How amazing!"

"Today, the Great Peace brush shop is celebrating its sixtieth anniversary," Ma Er said happily, "and we've all come here to wish Mr Zhu well. It is a wonderful opportunity for everyone to get together, so let us all eat and drink our fill – let my department foot the bill!"

Ge Shitou was stunned. In tone, in accent... it might as well have been Fourth Master Guan standing there in front of him.

When he looked again, Ma Er was lifting up his glass with the words: "Let's drink to that!" When he lifted his glass, his arm was as straight as a ruler – he didn't bend it at all... That was exactly how Fourth Master Guan lifted his glass!

Ge Shitou now had his eyes out on stalks; Ma Er was eating and drinking, chatting to people and laughing, and whatever he did, he looked for all the world just like Fourth Master Guan. Not only the guests at his own table, but even the ones on either side, were now roaring with laughter. It wasn't only that Ge Shitou couldn't see the slightest mistake – in fact, he felt the more he looked, the more lifelike the man seemed to be. Later on, Ma Er got a bit drunk, but even the way he wobbled about added to the impression – it was already very hard to say that he was merely "imitating" Fourth Master Guan. He looked just like Fourth Master Guan did every time there was a banquet at the education division.

But Ge Shitou also noticed that as he was giving his impression, he didn't forget to eat and drink. He was popping first the chicken and fish, then the shrimp and the pork into his mouth, making sure he came out with a full belly. Think about this little bastard eating and drinking on Fourth Master Guan's account, and at the same time making a joke of him for the assembled company to laugh at – it really was too bad of him!

When the banquet was at its height, Ma Er bent forward to dig his chopsticks into a dish of succulent sea cucumbers placed at some distance away, and as he swung forward he farted. This was a real fart, and it didn't half stink. The person sitting beside him immediately said: "The Fourth Master's farts smell worse than any chamber pot!" Everyone fell about laughing. "If it doesn't stink, can it be a fart?" Ma Er replied in Fourth Master

Guan's tones. The company laughed again. They kept on laughing right until the party broke up.

Ge Shitou headed back to the Foreign Concession and reported everything that he had seen and heard to Fourth Master Guan. He concluded by saying: "There really isn't anything we can do to stop him. Ma Er never said that he was doing an impression of you, sir, and it was always other people who mentioned your name."

Ge Shitou had imagined that Fourth Master Guan would be absolutely furious, but in fact he didn't say a word. He just smiled.

Within a couple of days, the reason was known to the entire old city: Fourth Master Guan was a cultured gentleman and held high status within the Foreign Concession – it was inconceivable he would fart in front of anyone else. If Ma Er was doing an impression of Fourth Master Guan, he should have realised that farting would ruin it. However, Ma Er was nothing but an ignorant yokel – now everyone could see his failings! This was all capped off with a very cutting slogan: a single fart blew Ma Er's rice bowl away!

In a commercial centre, rumours count. People who live in a port city like to tell each other jokes – it is a way to amuse themselves. After this, nobody ever invited Ma Er to dinner again, but Ma Er's fart was a joke told at many a dinner table.

25
STONY FACE

OUTSIDE THE SOUTH GATE, there was a blacksmith, some forty or more years old, who was most strange in his behaviour. He never smiled, and his expression was always dark, so people called him Stony Face.

It wasn't because he had a nasty temper that he never smiled – even as a child, he'd never been amused. Whatever happened, no matter how many people were laughing their heads off around him, even if they were clutching their stomachs having practically giggled themselves sick, he wouldn't even smile. His face could have been beaten out of cast iron; it was that dark and hard.

Stony Face had come originally from Baoding Prefecture, but by this time he'd lived in Tianjin for at least twenty years. He was a stubborn man, with a depressed air about him, someone who was difficult to befriend, and so nobody knew very much about him. Later on, a story sprang up from god knows where to explain the reason that he never smiled: supposedly his father was a farrier, and when he was four or five years old, he'd been standing right next to his father watching while he was shoeing a horse. Suddenly the horse had been spooked by something or other and kicked out like a wild thing, its back hooves catching him on the head. He lay down not moving with his eyes shut, not taking any sustenance, and when the doctor was called and felt his pulse, he announced that the child was dying, that within three days he'd have gone to see Yama, King of the Underworld. However, three days later he hadn't yet died, and he was still breathing. Seven days after that, he opened his eyes and was clearly conscious, then he got up and could walk and talk, eat, drink, and shit just like before, but there was one small difference – he couldn't smile. People said that Yama had kept back any capacity for enjoyment after his visit to the Underworld.

This story seemed to explain everything, don't you think? But nobody dared to ask him if it was true or not.

The year that he first came to Tianjin, there were some tiresome young hoodlums who refused to believe that he couldn't smile. One day after it got dark, they got together and pinned him down somewhere, and set about tickling him, in the hope that he would laugh. No matter how much they tickled him, he didn't even smile, and they kept on going until he was crying and had wet himself. He was begging and screaming for mercy, but he still hadn't laughed. The young men gave up at that point and agreed that he wouldn't ever be able to smile in this life.

It was strange that he couldn't smile, but there was something even more peculiar about him, which is that he was a fan of comic dialogues. Don't you find this odd? People go to hear a comic performance in order to laugh – since that was impossible for him, why did he go? Was he practising being amused? Nobody could understand.

Stony Face never gambled or went with whores, nor was he the kind of person to enjoy a good drink. When he finished work, if he had a bit of free time, he would go to a theatre where pairs of comedians were performing their dialogues, find a free stool and take in a couple of performances. Everyone in the theatre recognised his stony and expressionless face, which seemed designed to render the comics giving their performance nervous. Comics hate it when their audience doesn't find their jokes funny. The fact that you have not been amused is a heavy burden to them; they haven't done their job properly, and that means that they lose face. In Tianjin, if you wanted to annoy comics, you could just find a couple of people and go and sit in the theatre looking unamused – that would drive them to the brink of distraction! Stony Face was an immense challenge to the comics performing their routines. As it was said in Tianjin, there were as many fine comedians there as there were trees in the forest. People started to go on purpose to the theatre outside the South Gate to see who could make Stony Face laugh, but every single one of them failed utterly and had to return humiliated. As a result, there was a saying in that part of the city: "A comedian wanting to amuse Stony Face is asking for trouble."

Stony Face himself was the only person who didn't know this saying.

Beijing is pretty close to Tianjin, and this bizarre individual and his strange story were known to comics in the capital too. There are some very fine performers in Beijing, and they were quite sure that there wasn't anyone that was genuinely unamusable. This challenge was therefore taken up by a comedian and his straight man. They had already made their name in the theatres in Guangdian and Tianqiao. Even before you consider how superb their crosstalk and singing was, their appearance was very unusual. The comic was tall and thin, and somewhat simian in appearance – his surname was Hou. Meanwhile, the straight man was short and fat, looking not unlike a kitten – he was called Mao. Everyone in the business called them Mao-Hou, pronounced as if it were one word. Isn't there a kind of cute toy made out of cicada skins that people in Beijing call a "mao hou"? Their name quickly became famous in the capital city.

When Mao-Hou arrived in Tianjin, they started their tour at the Happiness Theatre outside the South Gate. On the first day, every seat in the house was filled. Stony Face had heard the news and was there too. There were plenty of people who knew that Mao-Hou had come to see what they could do with him, but Stony Face himself was completely in the dark. Once he sat down, they began their attack.

Mao-Hou came on and stood on the stage: one was tall and one was short; one was thin and the other was fat; one was clever and the other stupid – this immediately had the whole place in fits of laughter. Mao-Hou looked about them, and their hearts thumped – some seventy or eighty faces in the place were alight with laughter, but there was one face that might have been made from cast iron, so cold and dark and expressionless was it. They didn't need to ask – it had to be Stony Face. The pair of them wondered: had they really met their match? But Mao-Hou had been in the business for more than twenty years, and they'd seen everything there was to see, so they began by ignoring that face. Just as everyone was giggling at their comic patter, they put in a bit of business – this was unexpected but beautifully done, it really had the place in an uproar, and everyone was in stitches. Nevertheless, Stony Face wasn't laughing. Mao-Hou's eyes swept round, and then they glanced at each other. They carried on as if nothing were wrong, cracking one joke after another, and then yet again they threw in another bit of business at a totally unexpected moment – this was even better, even more finely judged, and you could really see the skill of the two men in the way that they carried it out. Again the whole place hooted with laughter, but Stony Face didn't even smile. Mao-Hou saw this but refused to give up; they were determined to carry on. The next bit of business was Mao-Hou's best routine: it worked every time. Mao-Hou threw it in, and the theatre rocked with laughter; in fact, they nearly raised the roof with the racket they made. But when Mao-Hou checked his reaction, he looked just like a corpse that had been propped up with its eyes open.

Mao-Hou knew that they were in trouble – if they didn't handle this well, they'd fail in Tianjin. Since they felt out of their depth, they knew that whatever they could pull out of the hat would have to do. They did a few old routines and a couple of new ones; some were refined while others were vulgar, and they kept on adding new spur-of-the-moment embellishments in until their voices were hoarse and their foreheads beaded with sweat. However, Stony Face still sat there, stony faced. In the end, after his final-throw-of-the-dice bit of business, the tall, thin, simian comedian faced Stony Face straight on and said: "Excuse me, sir. If you don't laugh at whatever we do, we're going to have to do a strip routine next."

The whole theatre erupted in laughter at that. Suddenly Stony Face stood up and put his hands up to his face in a gesture of respect. Then he said: "The two of you gave a wonderful performance today, so thank you. I will now leave the theatre." Having said his piece, he turned round and walked away. From start to finish, he hadn't laughed once.

Mao-Hou just stood there, with no idea what to do next. They had completely failed, and might as well go back to Beijing right away.

Having got rid of Mao-Hou, nobody dared to perform a comic dialogue at the South Gate again. The more the story made the rounds, the more amazing people made Stony Face sound, as if he were a natural-born destroyer of comedians' careers. But the strange thing was that from that day on, nobody ever saw Stony Face in the theatre by the South Gate again, or in any of the other comedy theatres in Tianjin. Some people said that he'd moved away, but other people said that he hadn't gone anywhere at all, that he was still a blacksmith working by the South Gate but he didn't go and listen to comic routines any more.

This is worth thinking about. If he really thought that Mao-Hou was wonderful, why didn't he laugh? If he genuinely couldn't laugh, why did he insist on going to listen to comics perform dialogues? If it was true that he loved this form of performance, why did he stop going to the theatre after this?

Nobody ever answered these questions. They didn't find an answer then, and there still isn't an answer now.

26
PINWHEEL

OVER BY THE junction of the Three Rivers, you can find every kind of food, every possible item of dress, things for the house, and also all sorts of different entertainments – this is a place where you can satisfy all your cravings. In a port city, half of what you see is local goods, and the other half are new products being hauled in by boat from every point of the compass. It is these strange products that attract the locals, while the local products draw customers from elsewhere. As a result, people with any kind of training in the performing arts came rushing over to earn a bit of cash and put food on their tables. However, it was not exactly easy to make a name for yourself in such a competitive environment. Who knew when an even better performer with even greater skills would suddenly appear? You could find your act ruined overnight.

In 1912, the first year of the Republican period, there was a wrestler from Shandong who could take on all comers. He was a mountain of a man, with shoulders the size of a haunch of beef

and arms as thick as most people's thighs. His head was shaved, and his round face was quite puce – when he exerted himself, his muscles seemed to form themselves into lumps which rippled up and down his body. His finest skills were seen in lifting his opponent. He would use both hands to take hold of his shoulders, get a good grip, and then with a muscular effort, he would straighten his back and lift his opponent into the air. When your feet leave the ground, you can't brace yourself; his arms were so long that you couldn't kick him; and whatever skill you had in wrestling wasn't any use. And him? He would just hold you up there motionless, since no matter how heavy you were it didn't make any difference to him. When you'd wriggled enough, he'd put you down on the ground as you might put down a puppy or a kitten that you'd got bored of playing with.

Apparently, he had studied an unusual technique from a very young age: lifting jars. His father was a potter, and to begin with he had instructed him to lift little jars, so that every day he would take a turn round the courtyard holding up a jar. When he could hold it up with no more effort than if he'd been lifting a chicken coop, he switched to a larger jar. Over time, the jars got bigger and bigger, until he was lifting a jar big enough to grow water lilies in with the same effort as you or I might hold up a bucket. Then he started putting water inside it, adding another scoop every ten days, until he could lift a huge jar full of water with the same insouciance as if he were just going for a leisurely walk. That was how he learned this most remarkable technique.

There were many fine wrestlers in Tianjin, but none of them could think of a way to deal with him.

However, do not imagine that this brute from Shandong with his jar-lifting act was able to make a living at the Three

Rivers! One day, a tough guy turned up from Cangzhou in Hebei, who had learned Shaolin Iron Palm kungfu. He was very dark-skinned, and since he wore a little summer jacket, he looked quite black. He had a huge straggly beard and a very nasty glint in his eye – you could tell immediately that this was someone you wanted to give a wide berth to. Nobody had ever seen him before; he stood in front of the wrestler from Shandong and didn't say a word. He just took off his cotton jacket and tossed it aside, showing a torso as dark as bronze and curiously shiny skin... how could skin possibly be so shiny? The jar lifter from Shandong didn't take this challenge at all seriously. He put out his hands to grab him by the shoulders, but as he did so, a strange thing happened. He simply couldn't get hold of the man. He tried a second time and failed again; the dark man's shoulders were far too slippery to get a grip on – they were like glass. The wrestler from Shandong had never come across such a thing before: he tried to grab him three times, but each time it was like trying to keep hold of a fish. Suddenly he realised he was in trouble – the dark man had smeared a thick layer of grease all over his torso, so no wonder it was so shiny and slippery! But if he couldn't grab his opponent by the shoulders, he couldn't lift him off his feet, and in that case his technique was useless. Caught between alarm and anxiety, the dark man suddenly punched him in the chest with both hands, lightning quick. It all happened far too fast for him to realise what had occurred; he just thought his chest was feeling hot, but he had to pick himself up off the ground a full five yards from where he'd been standing before. As he did so, he could hear the crowd of onlookers shouting and applauding.

After that, the dark man from Cangzhou was a boss out by the Three Rivers.

There was always someone trying to take him on, though, and every time the dark man beat them to a pulp. His two-handed technique allowed him to hit hard and fast, and if he connected, only someone really strong would be able to hold up against it.

However, in less than a couple of weeks, a truly remarkable individual had appeared.

He looked like a scholar: a thin young geezer, wearing a fine eggshell-blue silk gown. He looked very refined standing there, and the corners of his mouth curled up in a smile. Without waiting for the dark man to even open his mouth, he told his servant boy to help him remove his long gown and then to put it back on again. However, when he put his long robe back on, he didn't put his arms into the sleeves. That meant that the two long sleeves were hanging empty from his shoulders, like streamers of cloth. The dark man asked: "How are you going to fight me like that?"

The young geezer smiled gently and said: "A gentleman shouldn't use violence, and so I never fight with my hands." His tone revealed his arrogance.

"You aren't going to use your hands?" the dark man said. "Let's get this clear – it's not me who is refusing to allow you to use your hands, and I can use whatever technique I like."

"If you've got the guts, then go ahead and fight me," the young geezer said.

"Let's get on with it," the dark man said, and he came forward with his palms slapping away at the smaller man. If any one of those slaps had connected, it would have really hurt. But somehow or other not a single slap touched him because the young geezer moved to avoid them. The dark-skinned man was putting in a lot of effort to make sure that his slaps were delivered as fast as possible, but the quicker he moved his hands, the more neatly the young geezer stepped aside. One of them was attacking here and hitting out there, while the other was spinning about to avoid him, jumping and twisting, looking even more sprightly than an acrobat bouncing across the stage. The dark man fought him for ages, but it seemed as though he were punching empty space. The thing about any fist-based martial arts technique is that the blow needs to connect in order to have any effect; if you don't touch your opponent, the effort is wasted. After some time, the dark man was so tired he was puffing and blowing. It was all made worse by the young geezer's empty sleeves, dancing around him, blinding and dazzling the dark-skinned man until gradually he came to feel that he was fighting half a dozen opponents. However, he carried on until he was absolutely exhausted and completely coated in sweat. Then he stopped and said: "You win."

The young geezer stood there looking just the same as he had at the beginning. His two empty sleeves hung down limply as he stood there and laughed – he appeared entirely relaxed and at ease. He hadn't launched a single attack, he hadn't fought back at all, and yet he defeated the dark-skinned man. As to who this young geezer was or where he'd come from, nobody had a clue. But from this day onwards, there was a new boss in the Three Rivers district, and it was the young geezer who was in charge. There was always someone trying to take him on, issuing a challenge, but the young geezer never fought back. Instead, he relied on the speed of his movements and the two empty sleeves dancing in the air to confuse his opponents and give them no opportunity to strike, keeping it up until they had exhausted themselves.

It seemed as though the young geezer was going to be in charge for a while, but in less than two weeks, a new martial arts master had appeared.

Nobody noticed him: for the first few days this master was hidden in the crowd, admiring the young geezer's technique in never hitting back, and thinking about the skill involved, looking for mistakes. This man was young and vigorous, dressed in a white cotton shirt and black cotton trousers. Where his trousers were rolled up, you could see his shins like huge hard lumps of stone. You could see men dressed exactly like this all over the Three Rivers district – they were boatmen. They could take a hand at the oars, or pull the boat by hauling on cables, or raise the sails, all of which served to make them nimble and agile – when the wind was roaring and the waves foaming, they could shin up and down the mast as fast as any monkey. But when it came to challenging someone trained in martial arts – particularly someone like the young geezer – it would be very hard to know who would win and who would lose.

Right, let's see which one would put the other to the sword.

The boatman began by balling up his fists, and he came out punching. The young geezer twisted and turned as usual, so that the boatman couldn't touch him. The young geezer's two empty sleeves were very useful at this point since they danced around confusing his opponents, who then wouldn't know where to aim their blows. The sleeves were empty so hitting them was no good at all. However, though nobody anticipated this, the boatman had his eye on these long sleeves. Suddenly, he reached out a hand

and grabbed hold of the left-hand sleeve and then spun around behind the young geezer. He then grabbed hold of the right-hand sleeve and again, quick as a flash, twirled round behind him, so that he could tie the two of them in a knot. What is more, he used a "living" knot. Anyone in the know could tell at a glance that this was the kind of knot that is used for anchoring a boat. Although it is called a living knot, the more you fight against it, the tighter it locks. When the sleeves were knotted as tight as they could be, the young geezer was standing there like a stick that had been planted in the ground. The boatman got a foothold on the young geezer, and then in a trice his two feet were planted on his shoulders. The young geezer knew that things were going badly for him, so he wriggled and shook his shoulders, trying to shake the boatman off. However, no matter how he jerked from one side to the other, it didn't make the blindest bit of difference; the boatman just giggled as he balanced himself with outstretched arms, standing firm and unmoving. A boatman who spends all his time on deck, amidst storm winds and towering waves, is hardly going to be bothered by a bit of shaking. He waited until the young geezer didn't have the energy to move and was standing quiet as a lamb. Then he jumped down and untied his sleeves. After that, he turned around and walked off.

The young geezer disappeared completely, and the boatman too was never seen again. Who was this boatman? How had he learned this technique? Where did he come from?

Gradually, word got round that he came from Beitang, and that nobody there had ever heard that he'd learned martial arts. His neighbours just knew him as a fine boatman, who'd travelled up and down the Bai River many times over the last two decades. He was supposed to be a good swimmer and very agile, who was known by the nickname Pinwheel. Someone said that they'd bumped into him a few days before in Dazhigu, and they'd asked him why he didn't try and make a go of showing off his physical prowess over by the Three Rivers and earn a bit of money. Pinwheel had said that the port was just too big, and there were too many different kinds of people there; he could never be sure what he might find himself up against. It was much more relaxing being on a boat.

27

OLD ZHANG GUO

IF ONE OF a set of antique objects gets lost, it isn't a set any more, and the item that has gone missing is now a singleton. Finding a singleton is always upsetting, and of course it is worth much less money than it would otherwise have been. But once such an object arrived in the Tianjin antiques market, it could still be worth an awful lot. What... you don't believe me?

Today, the weather was lovely. Suo Qi arrived at Guyi Street, where he walked round his favourite antiques store, the Beholder's Treasures. He was in luck: at first glance, he spotted a set of five-coloured porcelain figures standing on the wooden display case in the window facing out on the street. He knew a great deal about porcelains, and when these figures swam into his ken, he immediately recognised them as a set of Eight Immortals in five colours, produced by the government kilns during the reign of the Jiaqing Emperor.

Having made his way inside, he went straight up to them. The closer he got, the more he could see the quality; the colours were lovely, the glaze was clear, the figures were beautifully sculpted, and each of them was individually differentiated. At nearly a foot high, they were unusually large. The whole set seemed flawless. It is very easy to break the fingers on a porcelain figure, but not one of these had so much as lost a digit. They were so beautiful, so calm, so rich, so carefully-done, and to top it all off, they came from an official kiln during the Jiaqing reign era!

But as he looked more closely, he saw a problem. If you have a set of the Eight Immortals, there should be eight of them – why were there only six here? He stared at them: all present and correct were Zhongli Quan of the Han dynasty, Iron-Crutch Li, Imperial Brother-in-Law Cao, Lü Dongbin, Immortal Lady He, and Lan Caihe. Missing were Han Xiangzi playing his flute and Old Zhang Guo riding on his donkey.

Before he'd even had time to find the boss and ask him about it, he heard a voice in his ear: "I know it's lost some pieces, but that means you'll have to pay less for it." Looking round, he saw that the manager, Xin Juren, was standing right beside him, grinning away. Manager Xin was a short man, with a few greying hairs forming a moustache on his upper lip. Raising his head, he smiled up at him and said: "If this set of Jiaqing era Eight Immortals from an official kiln was complete, given that they are such wonderful quality, they would be worth at least eight gold bars. One gold bar a figure! However, as it is, you would only have to pay half price..." He sketched out a "four" with his hand, and then laughed and said: "Half price! We are practically giving it away... Where could you find such a thing for sale anywhere else? I can tell you, Mr Suo, you are very lucky indeed. The seller needs the money and has to dispose of them!"

Antiques are dead, but people who sell antiques can talk until they bring them back to life again.

"Where did they come from?" Suo Qi asked.

"Look at you! How could people in our line of business possibly tell you where our things come from? Though in this case, they do come from a very important collection – everyone in Tianjin knows all about it… but I simply can't give you a name and address. Besides which, the pieces are so wonderful, so why would you concern yourself with the provenance?"

Suo Qi looked carefully at the six porcelain figures again. They really were terribly tempting. The porcelain figures were completely handmade: each one of them was beautifully sculpted, the paintwork was lovely, the firing was excellent – they were amazing works of art! If the set had been complete, he would have had to bite the bullet and pay the price, even if it were ten gold bars. However, with pieces missing from the set, it would be a lot less expensive.

Manager Xin seemed to know exactly what he was thinking and said: "Sets of Jiaqing era porcelain always have bits missing, don't they? If you want to have them on display at home, you don't have to put them all out – you could just have one or two on show. If you put them on display one at a time, it would look very elegant and refined, and then if you feel the need for a change you can refresh yourself by putting a different one out."

Suo Qi was deeply tempted.

In business, you have to be even better at looking at your customer's slightest reactions than a doctor does. "I'll tell you what," Manager Xin said, "if you don't buy them now, you won't see their like again. We've only had them on display since this morning, so that's why they're still here. They are such good quality and so cheap, I wouldn't be surprised if they're gone by this afternoon."

Suo Qi then went home and got the money, and came back to settle the account. While Manager Xin was wrapping up the figures for him, he said: "You are very lucky, Mr Suo, and I am sure that things will continue to go well for you. Who knows, maybe you'll even come across the two missing figures as singletons – in that case, you'll have done very well out of this."

That was a deeply pleasing thought for Suo Qi, and he was very happy as he carried his six Immortals back home.

From that day on, Suo Qi visited antique shops virtually every day. Tianjin is a commercial hub; lots of rich men come to Tianjin to do business, and there are also lots of foreigners there, so naturally there are plenty of antique shops. In fact, from the Foreign Concession to Majiakou, and in and outside the old city, there were several dozen antique shops of various sizes. Every five days, Suo Qi visited every single one of these antique shops at least once.

There were plenty of people in Tianjin like Suo Qi. He had rich ancestors, but he himself could not hold down a job. Other than eating and drinking, his main interest was antiques – every day he was wandering round the city in search of a bargain.

A month later, Suo Qi headed back to the Beholder's Treasures on Guyi Street – this was his third visit in the space of a month. On his previous visits, there had been no joy, but this time he was in luck. At first glance, he spotted a single five-coloured porcelain figure standing on the wooden display case in the window facing out on the street. At the same moment, he spotted Manager Xin bowing and waving to him, his eyes alight with laughter.

He rushed through the door as quickly as he could, and Manager Xin came forward to greet him. "I told you Heaven was on your side!" he said. "Look, one of your missing pieces has come to find you."

Suo Qi narrowed his eyes – he was absolutely right! Here was another of the Jiaqing era five-coloured porcelain figures from the same set as his six, but this was Han Xiangzi holding a flute in his two hands, each of the ten fingers placed in an entirely naturalistic way on the holes of the flute, his little face turned to one side, his lips pouting – for all the world like a flautist caught in the middle of playing a tune. This figure seemed to be even finer than the six he already owned. It was now just a question of handing over the cash.

At this point, Manager Xin said: "Don't be in so much of a hurry, we haven't even discussed the price yet. Last time you got the six figures really cheap, but this time, you're going to have to pay." His opening price was two gold bars.

"Why am I now paying for one figure what I paid for three last time?" Suo Qi asked.

Manager Xin responded: "Don't imagine you can bargain it down! Even at this price, we can sell it in three days. When it comes to selling a singleton it's the quality that counts. As you said yourself, even though the six figures you already own are lovely, this one is better than all the rest of them put together. Out of all the Eight Immortals, this one is the finest! It is the very best you'll ever see!"

The two men bargained for ages, and then in the end Manager Xin threw in an incense burner made in the reign of

Emperor Xuande in the Ming dynasty, but kept to his opening price of two gold bars.

Finally, Suo Qi agreed to this so he could take the Han Xiangzi away with him. He asked whether this figure came from the same collection as the others.

"Who on earth would split up a set like that?" Manager Xin asked. "This particular Han Xiangzi figure was bought from a stall beside the moat in 1900 after the Allied Army had massacred the Boxers and put the city to the sword. The owner loved it and kept it until he needed the money and had to sell it. I can tell you for free that the moment we put that figure out on the shelf we had two buyers for it. I wouldn't sell it to them because I was waiting for you to come – I wouldn't want this piece to stay as a singleton. It might be decades before another chance came along to complete the set."

"I'm still missing the Old Zhang Guo figure," Suo Qi said. "You've got to keep an eye out for it."

When Manager Xin heard that, he smiled and said cheerfully: "Well, if that's what you want, you'd better spend every day in prayer at the temple. I've never heard of such a thing happening before in the antiques business."

Suo Qi took his Han Xiangzi home and put it in a row with the other figures he'd purchased. They all looked wonderful, but they also made him feel really uncomfortable. Before he had the Han Xiangzi, he had a set of figures that happened to have some pieces missing; now he had the Han Xiangzi, he had a damaged and incomplete set. One of Suo Qi's friends told him that the Eight Immortals represented the Eight Trigrams, and that one missing ruined the whole thing. Suo Qi, like a lunatic, searched the whole city for his Old Zhang Guo. Every three days, he went to the Beholder's Treasures on Guiyi Street, outside the North Gate, but every time he drew a blank. He was in such a state about the whole thing that he began to wonder whether he shouldn't just buy a donkey and ride it himself.

One afternoon on his way home, walking along Taiping Street in the northeast corner of the city – his regular route home – he noticed a dozen people standing by the main junction, and they were all excited about something. Walking over and craning his neck, he saw that someone was holding an object up in one hand and trying to sell it. When he looked more closely, he nearly fainted. He forced himself to calm down and looked again – it was the porcelain figure of Old Zhang Guo he'd been searching for! It seemed like Heaven's will. Someone had brought it right to his door. He looked at the man trying to sell the object: about fifty years of age, dressed like a small shopkeeper or something of that ilk in quite good clothes, but with a face suggestive of a long struggle with grinding poverty.

Suo Qi stepped up and asked: "Where did you get that from?"

He was not expecting that his words would see the other man explode in anger: "Are you buying this figure or what? Do you think I stole it or something?"

Suo Qi hurried to explain his interest, but the longer he spoke, the more irritated the man became. In the end, he pulled a handkerchief out and started to wrap up the Old Zhang Guo, after which he put it under his arm and made as if to leave, as if he wasn't interested in selling it after all. Suo Qi rushed after him to stop him, apologising and saying every nice thing he could think of, insisting that he really wanted to buy the figure. When the man heard this, he said crossly: "If you really want it, it'll cost you six gold bars!"

That was an enormous price, far more than the figure was actually worth, but Suo Qi didn't dare refuse outright. He tried his best to bargain it down, but the more he tried to argue, the more the man dug his heels in, until in the end he came right out and said: "Don't bother wagging your tongue any more – if you don't pay my price I'll break the bloody thing rather than sell it for less."

There was nothing that Suo Qi could do. He went home, collected the money, and came back to buy it.

The onlookers were baffled: why on earth would you pay the price asked by someone who was obviously trying to be annoying and awkward by asking for a fortune? Was this some kind of family treasure or what? Surely it couldn't possibly be worth so much money?

When Old Zhang Guo arrived in his house, the Eight Immortals were finally reunited, and each showed off their own special attribute.

One day, a friend of Suo Qi's from Shanghai was visiting Tianjin and came round to his house. He happened to notice the set of Jiaqing era Eight Immortals in five-coloured porcelain from the government kiln displayed together on a table. This friend was another connoisseur of porcelains and knew exactly what he was talking about. He admired them highly. "This set must be worth six gold bars at least," he said. "How much did you pay for them? Did you get them very cheap?"

Suo Qi reckoned it up in his head, and by buying it bit by bit, his set had cost him twelve gold bars. How on earth could he have spent so much money? Now he thought about how he had come to buy these Eight Immortals and suddenly understood what must have happened – he'd fallen into the trap that had been set for him! However, he couldn't possibly tell anyone else about how he had been done down, so he said: "Oh, I didn't pay much, not much at all." But he felt that the Eight Immortals standing lined up on the table were all grinning at him for having been such a fool.

28
HE JUST IGNORES YOU

TIANJIN PEOPLE LIKE to talk about food, and they like to talk about entertainments, but they couldn't care less about clothes – if you want to talk about who is wearing what then find someone from Shanghai. In Shanghai, they care about your appearance, but Tianjin people care about the finer things in life. Having enough to eat is the most important thing in life. As Tianjin people are wont to say, you wear clothes for other people to look at, but food you eat for yourself. On the other hand, Shanghai people say that wearing silk twill, gauze, brocade, and satin is all to make yourself beautiful, but that eating fine foods is just showing off. A Tianjin person would reply: "Have you ever seen a dog pass up a meat bun? Who is it impressing by eating that? The only one who enjoys the experience is the dog itself."

The food and entertainments favoured by the inhabitants of Tianjin are not expensive at all; it is a matter of eating your fill and having as much fun as possible. Tianjin people liked to eat three particular snack foods: Eighteenth Street fried sesame twists, Earlobe red bean stuffed rice cakes, and He Just Ignores You steamed buns. That's some dough, plus a sweet, plus a bit of meat. They also enjoyed three particular entertainments: the work of Master Zhang the figure maker, Master Wei the kite maker, and Yangliuqing's New Year pictures. That's clay, plus paper, plus paint. You won't find gold or silver, jade or ivory here – what counts is the skill that is brought to bear and not the cost of the materials. We are talking about an art form; for those people who are genuine artists, it doesn't matter whether they are using clay or flour, paper or grass or cloth – once it has passed through their hands, they can make it into a real treasure.

The Whelp, who sold stuffed steamed buns by the side of the Grand Canal, had originally come to Tianjin with his father from the nearby village of Wuqing. His real name was Gao Guiyou but only his father knew that. Everyone else knew him by his nickname, Whelp, which is what his father always called him. In those days the children of poor parents often didn't live very long, so the parents would give their offspring an unlucky or ugly kind of name, like Whelp, or Pup, Idiot, Fool, or Pockmark, so that Yama, King of the Underworld, would imagine that they wouldn't amount to much. If he despised them and forgot all about them, he wouldn't carry them off. People didn't treat this kind of whelp or pup very kindly either, but if there was a job of work to be done, they would make him do it. Nobody knew his father's full name either; they just knew that his surname was Gao, so they addressed him as Old Gao. Everyone ignored the Whelp and so he never spoke, but just because he didn't say anything, it didn't mean he was stupid.

Old Gao didn't have any kind of special skill or talent. The steamed buns he sold were just a lump of dough around a meatball. There was an awful lot of dough and very little filling, and what filling there was consisted mostly of vegetables with a very small amount of meat – this was the kind of bun that got sold round the wharfs for dockers to eat. People who lift heavy loads for a living need a bit of meat, and the huge lump of dough that went with it served to give them endurance. Anyway, since people were prepared to eat this, he earned a bit of money, and he didn't really care how much he got; providing he could feed his own family, he was grateful enough.

As long as Old Gao was alive, as far as his bun business went, he called the shots, but once Old Gao died, it was the Whelp who made all the decisions. Ever since childhood, he'd admired the delicate flavour of belly-of-pork soup made by one of the restaurants over on Houjiahou Street; this got him started on trying to put a bit of either belly-of-pork or spare-rib soup into the filling of his buns. He'd also discovered the wonderful possibilities of adding a lump of lard into the meat filling thanks to a little mixed-grill place over on Da Hutong. This gave him the idea of putting lard into his steamed buns; it would give them a better texture, make them smell nice, and make them more satisfying and filling. As a result, he started dropping a little cube of lard into each meatball he used as stuffing. Apart from that, he decided to change the shape of his buns to make this a feature – he pinched the dough more tightly, and put in more pleats, until there were eighteen pleats on the top of each of his buns and they looked like a flower. When you bit into them, they were so delicious and light; so when these new and improved buns hit the market, they were famous overnight. There were even more people who wanted to eat steamed buns than there were people who wanted to see the fun.

The Whelp was now incredibly busy – in fact, his whole family were rushed off their feet. He didn't want to hire in people from outside because he was afraid they would copy his methods. At peak times, there was heap after heap of soup bowls outside his front door and a basket of chopsticks. Anyone who wanted to buy buns would put the necessary coins in their bowl and then take it to where the Whelp could scoop them into the money box at his side and then shovel however many buns it was you'd paid for into your bowl. That was it; he wouldn't say a word. If you asked him something, he wouldn't reply – how could he possibly have time to talk to anyone? This gave rise to the saying: "When the Whelp is working, he pays no attention to anyone!"

Other bun shops complained and criticised him, saying: "He just ignores you." They were hoping to discourage his customers from buying his buns.

The Whelp's bun business originally didn't have a name, but now it did. When people mentioned his steamed buns, they said: "You know the one – he just ignores you." It was supposed to be a complaint, but it made him famous.

In Tianjin, there are two different worlds: officialdom and business. If you want to become really famous, it is going to depend on whether you make it with either the world of business or officialdom.

Let us start by considering the world of business. If you want to become famous there, what matters is whether you have a selling point or not. As the saying goes, good news gets ignored while bad news gets spread far and wide. Who cares if someone says something nice about you? It is a criticism that is going to make people curious. "He just ignores you" was meant as a complaint: it seemed interesting and amusing and memorable and something that you might want to tell other people about – there was sure to be some kind of story behind a name like that. Since the Whelp made delicious steamed buns, the moaning about how "He just ignores you" served to make him famous in the trade!

Now let us consider officialdom. There were a couple of army bases where Ziya River meets the Hai River and the Grand Canal in the middle of the city, and the soldiers all liked to eat He Just Ignores You buns. That was the year that Yuan Shikai, the viceroy of Zhili Province, visited Tianjin and the various officials in the army bases were summoned to meet His Excellency. They were quite sure that His Excellency ate all kind of rarities every day of his life and that he must be bored sick of them, so they provided two steamers of He Just Ignores You buns instead. They instructed the Whelp to put in extra lard and more meat than usual and to make sure that the buns were exceptionally finely worked, and then he produced two steamers for lunch, just ready to eat. The Whelp was no fool and made sure that money went to the right people in the yamen so that his He Just Ignores You buns were served first. When people are eating, the first mouthful is always the best. His Excellency Yuan Shikai bit into his bun, and the delicious flavour burst against his tongue, and his whole mouth filled with delightful aromas. He was very pleased and said: "These are the best steamed buns I have ever eaten." The officers who'd come up with this idea were naturally rewarded generously.

A few days later, His Excellency was due to return to the capital and was wondering what on earth he could possibly take back as a gift for Her Majesty the Dowager Empress Cixi. As everyone knows, officials all think alike. The way His Excellency thought about it, Her Majesty was surrounded by rarities all day every day; she dined on shark fins and swallow nests; and since she had all the money in the world at her disposal, there was really nothing that she would find fresh and new, so why not give her some of those He Just Ignores You buns that he'd had the other day in Tianjin? He sent a couple of sharp-as-knives underlings off to arrange this, so they brought the buns safe and sound to Beijing, then he spent a bit of money bribing the people in charge of the imperial kitchens to make sure that they got served first to Dowager Empress Cixi at lunch, piping hot and fresh from the steamer. Her Majesty was also informed: "These were brought specially from Tianjin as a gift from His Excellency Yuan Shikai." When Dowager Empress Cixi bit into them, the delicious smell and taste burst against her tongue and she started to wolf them down. Having eaten six in a row, Her Majesty decided that she didn't want anything else. Then she said: "If God on High ate some of these, I am sure he'd enjoy them!"

Her pronouncement was quickly known throughout the palace and then to everyone in the capital, and the news soon made its way from Beijing to Tianjin. For Her Majesty to praise these steamed buns was the very best advertisement, and He Just Ignores You was soon famous throughout the empire, and indeed is still famous today.

29

FISHING FOR CHICKEN

IN 1927, the sixteenth year of the Republic, a man of remarkable abilities appeared in Tianjin. Nobody ever saw him, and as to what he was called or what he looked like, well, nobody could say. However, since he was a person of remarkable abilities, he had amazing qualities. He was a fisherman, but he didn't catch fish, he fished for chickens. How do you fish for chickens, you may ask? Don't be in so much of a hurry – let me explain.

In those days, every family in Tianjin kept chickens, dogs, and cats. They kept chickens in order to be able to eat eggs; they kept a dog to guard the front door; and they kept cats in order to keep down the rats and mice. The dog would be out in the front courtyard, and the cats were kept inside, while the chickens were free range and went wherever they felt like around and about the house. In the evening when it was time for them to return to roost, you could go out and stand by the door and call them, or bang on their food dish, and they would all come running home – you never heard of one going astray. But in the sixteenth year

of the Republic, people in Tianjin started to lose their chickens. To begin with, they thought there was a weasel about, but when a weasel catches a chicken, there would definitely be feathers left behind. This time, when people lost chickens, there were no feathers out at all. In the end, everyone decided that a person must be catching their chickens, but even when there was someone right there at the scene when the bird was snatched, they didn't hear it call, and normally you should be able to at least hear the chickens clucking away.

Pretty soon, a wily old character called Liu who lived over on Liangdianhou Street realised what was going on. He noticed that the chickens never went missing from exactly the same place: today it was over on the east side, tomorrow it would be north a bit, and then in two days' time it would be over in Yangzhuangzi. The area where chickens were going missing wasn't particularly large, a couple of lanes and a few alleys, but several dozen chickens had been snatched – they seemed to have gone with the wind, leaving nothing behind. It was absolutely impossible that a weasel could think like this – it had to be a person that was responsible. This is what they call a hit and run. The chicken thief was pretty bright, but how come he didn't make a sound? Why didn't the chickens squawk? How could anyone remove a couple of dozen chickens that were running about all over without leaving the slightest trace of activity?

Old Liu started going for long walks, keeping his ear close to the ground. He heard many times about chickens having gone missing, but he never heard that the thief had been arrested. He was told that whoever it was had acquired the nickname Our Shi Qian after the robber in *All Men Are Brothers*. That had a nice ring to it. Before anyone had even identified the man, they'd already named him.

A couple of weeks later, a local hoodlum told him something about Our Shi Qian, which gave him a terrible shock.

Supposedly, Our Shi Qian didn't snatch the chickens with his bare hands – he fished for them. He would take a yellow bean and drill a hole in it, then he would run a fine fishing-line through it and tie it off, so that the bean was sitting at the end. Then he would get the metal cap from a fountain pen and drill a hole in that, and then thread the fishing line through it too, so that it could slide up and down smoothly like a bead on a string. With the bean, the line, and the cap from a pen up his sleeve, the thief's preparations for stealing a bunch of chickens were made.

When Our Shi Qian found a good spot, he would squat down in one corner, smoking a cigarette or pretending to enjoy the sunshine. When a chicken came over, he would play out the line with the bean on the end of it, with the cap of the pen held back in his hand. If the chicken pecked at the bean, he would wait until it had gone down and then pull on his fishing line, and when it was taut, he would push the cap down. The cap would go flying down the line as fast as it could go, right until it hit the chicken's beak, fitting in over the top of it. The more the chicken struggled, the tighter the line would be. Why? The bean was stuck in the chicken's beak and the cap of the pen fitted over it, and the two of them worked together in concert to make sure that it couldn't open its trap and make any kind of noise. Our Shi Qian could now reel his chicken in.

The young hoodlum said that Our Shi Qian normally did most of his fishing for chicken in the winter. He would wear a black padded coat, and when he caught a chicken, he could put it inside, and nobody would notice a thing – particularly since nobody could possibly imagine he was stealing chickens using such a technique. The hoodlum also said that he ate three chickens a day, but the rest he sold in the market.

Old Liu asked if this was true. The young hoodlum said that he'd seen him with his own eyes a couple of days before near the Guajia Temple.

Old Liu considered the matter over the course of a day and a night and came up with a plan of action. Where he lived on Liangdianhou Street there were plenty of people who kept chickens, and the whole neighbourhood was very higgledy-piggledy – sooner or later Our Shi Qian would turn up there to steal some chickens. He kept chickens himself, so he'd stay comfortably at home and wait for the thief to come to him. As he said: he fishes for chickens, but I'll set a trap for him.

In the last lunar month, suddenly he and his neighbour, Chen San, found that they lost a dozen or more chickens: there wasn't a single one left. Old Liu said: "Great, we got him."

He knew exactly where to go to find Our Shi Qian. He took a turn round several of the nearby markets for live birds, and as he moved around, he spotted a fat man with a red face and shining skin, with little piggy eyes like shining black glass beads. He was squatting down, dressed in a thick coat, and in the bamboo cage behind him there were five or six live birds. Old Liu went up and said to the fat man: "You must eat a lot of chicken meat. I can practically see the juices dripping from your mouth."

The fat man was so surprised that he overbalanced and sat down on the roadway. Old Liu was now quite sure that he'd found Our Shi Qian.

Our Shi Qian put his hand down on the ground and pushed

himself back up into a squatting position. He smiled at Old Liu and said: "How could I possibly be lucky enough to eat such fat chickens?"

Old Liu could hear from his accent that he wasn't a local, but he wasn't here to bandy words about with the man. Pointing at the chickens in the cage, he said: "Can you get that white cockerel out of there for me to have a look?"

Our Shi Qian stretched out a hand and grabbed the white cockerel out from the group of clucking chickens, and handed it to Old Liu. It was a fine bird, with beautiful white feathers and a bright red comb. "This cockerel weighs about ten *jin*," Our Shi Qian said. "It's a young bird too, so it's very plump and tender. It would be delicious either steamed or fried."

Old Liu picked up the chicken and asked: "How much?"

Our Shi Qian said: "It's not expensive, but then it's not that cheap either. Ten coppers."

"Fine," said Old Liu. "You give me ten coppers for this one. There are another five chickens in that cage back there – that'll be sixty coppers in total."

"What the hell is this?" Our Shi Qian said. "You eat my chicken, and you want me to pay for it?"

"What do you mean, what the hell is this?" Old Liu responded. "You snatch my chickens and then demand money from me!"

Our Shi Qian felt that a screw had worked loose from this conversation somehow, so he looked severe and said: "Right, you need to explain yourself! How can this chicken possibly be yours?"

Old Liu laughed and said: "You say this is your chicken – can you prove it?"

Our Shi Qian was now feeling that he'd been caught on the back foot. "You didn't bring the chicken here," he said, "it came out of my coop. I don't mark my chickens in any way, do you?"

"There'll be a red circle on the stomach," Old Liu said.

Our Shi Qian grabbed the chicken and turned it upside down. He showed it to all the circle of onlookers: "You see, everyone? There's no red circle here!" It was perfectly true – there was just a thick layer of soft white feathers.

Old Liu smiled coldly, and with his left hand he grabbed hold of the chicken, while with his right he parted the feathers on the chicken's stomach. The red circle appeared, painted on the skin of the living bird. "I put that red circle on before it even fledged," he said.

Our Shi Qian understood: this trick is finished – the guy put that red circle on the bird ages ago and waited for me to walk straight into his trap. Well, he's certainly put one over on me this time. People in port cities are just as tough as they come, and all that's left for me to do is beg for mercy.

Old Liu was a wily character, and like so many of his ilk, he wasn't out to make enemies. He told Our Shi Qian to tie up the chickens he had in his coop and then took hold of them all, hanging in bunches, head down. He just had one last thing to tell him: "A little trick like that won't see you out, and if you're not careful, you'll get yourself killed. It's time to give it a rest."

After that, nobody in Tianjin talked about having lost chickens again. However, everyone knew that over on Liangdianhou Street there was an old Mr Liu, who was now called Shi Qian's Nemesis.

30
DRAGON-ROBE ZHENG

THERE IS a story about every single famous person that Tianjin has ever produced, and sometimes the story touches upon some very important people. In the case of the old man nicknamed Dragon-robe Zheng, he owed his fame to the single most important man in the world – the emperor of China.

Old Zheng was a fisherman who worked the Hai River; he was all by himself on his one little boat, and if he felt like it, he would busy himself pulling in the nets, but if he was being lazy, he would get out a rod and fish that way. He ate some of the fish he caught and sold the rest, and that was how he made his living. He wasn't very clever, but he had a happy life.

When the Qianlong Emperor was on a tour of the south, he sailed passed Tianjin. He was amazed to see the masts of the boats along the river standing as thickly as trees in a forest, and the goods piled up like mountains on the banks. Although the imperial palace was stuffed with treasures of every kind, he had never before seen this kind of lively commercial scene. The

emperor was delighted and wanted to go for a stroll along the bank, but he was afraid of attracting too much attention and did not dare to make a parade of his presence. Therefore, he covered up his dragon robe with a thick coat and had his boat brought close to the bank so he could get off, attended by only two servants. He walked along looking from side to side. The more he saw, the more interesting he found it all, and so he walked further than he intended.

As he was looking about, one particular scene caught His Majesty's attention. Not far from where he was standing, a boat was anchored in the middle of the river. This boat had an awning over the middle, and a man was sitting underneath it with a rod in his hand. The boat and the man were reflected in the water – it looked just like a painting. If you are watching someone fishing, you are waiting to see them pull a fish out of the water; this old man caught one fish after another on his hook. The emperor gazed at all of this in fascination. Turning his head, he said to his servants: "When I get back to the palace, I want to go fishing in the imperial gardens."

His servants said: "Your Majesty will fish much better than he ever could, since it will be goldfish that you catch."

Not long afterwards, the old man packed up his rod and line and rowed his boat to the riverbank. This fisherman was none other than Old Zheng. His Majesty walked over and asked him: "The fish were biting so why have you packed up?"

Old Zheng stood on the dock and pointed to the west: "Haven't you noticed the clouds? It's going to rain."

The emperor looked towards the west, and black clouds were indeed gathering there. The cloud formations were most unusual, since at the edges they looked as if they had been slashed with a knife. There was still some blue sky to be seen ahead of the clouds, and this made it look as if a black sheet were rolling out across the heavens. "That's mackerel sky, and it's coming on fast," Old Zheng said. "It is going to rain any moment now. Where are you going? If you don't run, you're going to get soaked."

"Oh dear, oh dear," His Majesty said. "I got off my boat to go for a walk, but I seem to have gone much further than I intended."

"Well, if you don't object, you could always get on my boat and take shelter there," Old Zheng said. "It really is going to pour."

His Majesty looked up, and now half the sky was black, and an icy-cold wind was rising, slicing into his flesh where it was exposed at the collars and cuffs. His servants bundled the emperor onto the boat. It wasn't particularly big, but it was large enough, and there was room enough for His Majesty and his little entourage. This was the very first time the emperor had ever been on a fisherman's boat, and he found everything he saw fresh and interesting. Old Zheng took out a couple of bowls and made tea. All you could say about this tea was that it had a bit more flavour than if he'd just put the leaves of some ordinary tree in, but the emperor thought it was delicious. While they were drinking their tea, the rain started hammering down on the roof, as if someone were throwing handful after handful of dried beans down on it. Then His Majesty said: "Do you have anything here to eat? I am feeling a bit hungry."

Old Zheng laughed and said: "I guessed you might be hungry so just sit there while I fry you up a mess of whitebait! Everyone loves my fried whitebait. People who go fishing out here often come round with a calabash of wine to have a taste of it." As he said this, the smell of the frying fish had already reached the emperor's nose and he was entranced.

When Old Zheng served his fried fish, the emperor ate a couple of mouthfuls and then exclaimed about how delicious they were. Fried whitebait was far too common and meagre a dish to ever be served by the imperial kitchens, and so His Majesty had never tried it before. However, fried whitebait are fresh and delicate and don't have any bones, so it was no wonder that the emperor enjoyed them the first time he got to eat them. The imperial kitchens send up all their dishes covered in fancy sauces, but ordinary people rely on the original flavour of the ingredients. The emperor had managed to find shelter in a downpour, and he was eating and drinking and enjoying himself, so in an expansive moment, he took off his thick coat and removed his dragon robe and gave it to Old Zheng. The old man could never have imagined in a thousand years that such luck would come to him and that he would entertain the emperor of China on his little boat. His legs buckled and his knees went weak. With a thud, he knelt down and began to knock his head against the floor over and over again. When the wind died down and the rain stopped, His Majesty went away, but all this time he was still knocking his head against the planks of his boat with a resounding bang.

Even after thinking about it all night, Old Zheng couldn't make up his mind if it was true or not. Nobody would ever believe that the emperor had come on board his boat and eaten fish and drunk tea... but the dragon robe was right there glittering away in his hands. At the time, he felt as if he were dreaming – even he could not believe that it had happened.

The morning of the next day, Old Zheng didn't leave his boat. At the prow, he arranged a table and a chair. The dragon robe was laid on the table, and he was sitting on the chair. This soon attracted a few curious bystanders, and then more and more people came to look. In the blink of an eye, the news that the Qianlong Emperor had been on board Old Zheng's boat, had eaten his fried whitebait and loved it, and awarded him a dragon robe was known to the entire city. A few years earlier, the emperor had visited Tianjin and attended the festival at the Mazu Temple. On that occasion, he'd bestowed two imperial yellow magua jackets, and the whole city had gone wild with the news. A dragon robe was obviously much more impressive than a magua jacket; seeing a dragon robe was like seeing the emperor in person, and so people rushed round to kowtow to the robe. The whole place was thronging with every scholar, rich businessman, official and expectant official in the city: you might have imagined that the emperor was still there. In such circumstances, officials are always worried about not being seen to be present, so apparently even the prefect rushed to the scene.

Old Zheng was now famous, and everyone called him Dragon-robe Zheng. All sorts of stories were now in circulation about him. However, when some people become famous overnight, they have delightful stories told about them, while others are the subject of foul rumours. A single nice story can end up being completely overwhelmed by a mountain of evil gossip – this is jealousy and envy in action. Some unpleasant individuals who were just trying to get him into trouble proclaimed that Dragon-robe Zheng secretly wore his robe every evening, sitting out on his boat and pretending to be the emperor. When this story got out, it had the most terrifying consequences:

when the prefect was told this, he went off in a fit of rage and ordered Dragon-robe Zheng's arrest and the removal of this garment from his possession. He intended to punish him for the serious crime of lèse-majesté. After that, the stories just got worse and worse.

All of this served to scare Dragon-robe Zheng off. Three days later, he and his boat and his dragon robe had all vanished. He must have been absolutely terrified, and so he sailed away somewhere else.

No matter how much fuss is made over something at the time in the port, once it is all over, it pretty soon gets forgotten. Gradually, people ceased to talk about Dragon-robe Zheng, though from time to time someone would moor his boat where the old man had always had his berth, baiting a hook on his fishing line, in the hope that he too would get to meet the emperor.

Over on Guyi Street, there was an itinerant betel-nut salesman, sharp as a knife, who was desperate to get rich but had never come across the slightest opportunity for doing so. His surname was Zheng too, and he was the third son of his family, so he was called Zheng San. One day, someone happened to say to him: "You're called Zheng just like that 'dragon-robe' man – just think how lucky he was with the emperor coming to visit him. However, he couldn't make anything out of such an opportunity... he clearly didn't have the luck. Such a wonderful thing happened to him, and he ended up nearly getting himself killed."

When Zheng San heard that, a flash of inspiration came to him. With glittering eyes, he said: "I have an idea." Within a couple of days, he'd sold the family home at the foot of the city wall and bought a new house out by the Hai River, where he opened a fried whitebait shop. He claimed that he was a relative of Dragon-robe Zheng's and that he'd learned his technique for frying fish – that was why his whitebait shop had a sign hanging outside saying "Dragon-robe Zheng".

A good signboard can give a real lift to your business. Who wouldn't want to try the dish that the emperor had enjoyed? Zheng San's crisp-fried whitebait became one of Tianjin's most famous snack foods. The real Dragon-robe Zheng had vanished to some far corner of the earth, but the fake one raked in the cash. As time went by, Zheng San gradually became known as Dragon-robe Zheng, and this story was told in his shop every day.

31
CHEN SI GIVES A GIFT

THERE ARE four ways to make sure you are successful in this world: either you need money, or power, or a father, or good looks. If you have money, you can get away with murder; if you have power, it's even more useful than having money; if you've got a good father behind you, there is always someone you can rely on; and good looks will make you welcome everywhere you go. But these things all by themselves won't make you successful. It is great to be rich and powerful, it is also fine if you've got a father behind you and are terribly good looking, but there is another quality that you need, and that is knowing your way about.

For example, you might need to give a gift to someone, such as an official. Although it is said that officials never look a gift horse in the mouth, you can't just roll up at one of their front doors with a chest full of gold bars, now can you? If you are going to give a gift, you need to do it right. In the whole of Tianjin, the very best person at giving gifts to officials was

Chen Si, and he had many friends in that world. Although he wasn't educated at all, he managed to get himself promoted to the position of deputy director of the Post Office at an unusually young age. People said that every step in his path was carefully prepared with gifts of one kind or another. Chen Si himself said that the road to officialdom was exceptionally rocky and giving presents here and there served to flatten the bumps – without gifts, it would have been impossible for him to get anywhere.

The key to Chen Si's technique was giving gifts in secret so that absolutely nobody knew anything about it. The gift itself had to be hidden, but the giving needed to be public, and that took an awful lot of doing. The person receiving the present had to know exactly what was going on, but everyone else needed to be kept in the dark. Now how exactly do you do that?

One day, Mr Ge, a friend of Chen Si's who worked in the jewellery business, wanted to invite Governor Jia of Zhili Province to dinner at the Peace Hotel in the French Concession. Chen Si had never so much as clapped eyes on Governor Jia before, but he had long hoped for an opportunity to offer the governor a gift and build up a connection with him. This was a great opportunity for him, and he was working on Mr Ge to take him with him and introduce him to the provincial governor.

"You'd better not give the man a present right there in front of me," Mr Ge said. "The provincial governor is a man who cares about his position; he's not going to take a gift in front of other people. It would really embarrass me and ruin any chances for my business."

Chen Si laughed and said: "Do you think I am still wet behind the ears? If I were indeed to give him a gift, I can guarantee that you wouldn't see a thing."

On the day of the dinner, Mr Ge did indeed introduce Chen Si to the provincial governor – but the position of governor was so much superior to that of the deputy director that he pretty much ignored him. Among businessmen, whoever is the richest gets to speak; while among officials, it is the most senior figure that gets to lay down the law, so under no circumstances whatsoever was Chen Si supposed to open his mouth. He waited patiently for ages until the conversation finally hung fire, and then he suddenly pointed to the painting of birds and flowers hanging on the wall and said: "That picture is quite hideous." Chen Si had been informed long ago that Governor Jia was interested in art and had a fine collection of calligraphy and paintings by famous artists. He was hoping to use this gambit to attract Governor Jia's attention.

It worked. "What, are you interested in painting too?" Governor Jia asked.

Chen Si waggled the chopsticks he was holding. "Oh, I don't know anything about art, and I'm not really interested, but my father was a connoisseur of painting and calligraphy. He died earlier this year and left me with a mountain of artworks. If he'd invested in land or property, I'd be a rich man today, but he spent every penny of his money on art. I've got a ton of these things lying about which are no good to me – they are a complete waste of space as far as I'm concerned. I am trying to get rid of them."

When Governor Jia heard that his eyebrows lifted. Clearly, he was becoming fascinated. "Who are these paintings by?" he asked.

Chen Si gave his talented impression of being a complete fool and said: "How would I know? People tell me that they are by famous artists so I suppose they must be. Do you know about art, Governor?"

Governor Jia hesitated and then said: "I know a little bit about it, but mainly I like to look. Can you remember the names of any of the painters who produced these pictures?"

"I think there was one with 'Shi' in his name, and there were a few lines of characters written on the painting," Chen Si said.

Immediately Governor Jia asked: "Would that be Qi Baishi?"

"Qi Baishi I know," Chen Si said. "Wasn't he the man who painted all of those crabs and shrimps and what have you? I didn't like them; after all, you can't eat them. We had several scrolls of his work at home, but I've given all of them away already. This definitely wasn't Qi Baishi, though the same 'Shi' character was in the name… Something something Shi… I just can't call it to mind. A very dark painting, you can't really make anything out, it's all fuzzy. When the dustman calls round next time, he can take it away!"

Governor Jia thought a bit more, and his eyes glittered: "How about Fu Baoshi?"

Chen Si thought it over and then suddenly said: "Right… yes, that's right! Baoshi, Baoshi… I always thought it was a really weird name that the painter had. Very odd indeed. Is he famous?"

Governor Jia thought about that and then said: "Well, he's made a name for himself. And his paintings are quite nice."

Chen Si picked up on the final remark: "With his picture being all dark and smudged, how can anyone say that it is 'nice'? But what would I know? If you want to see it, Governor Jia, I'll bring it round for you to look at one of these days. If you hadn't happened to mention it today, I swear I would have given it to the dustman tomorrow." From the way that he was carrying on, you might have imagined that he was a matchmaker palming off a hideous girl on a hapless husband and that he was quite desperate to get rid of her.

Everyone laughed at that and carried on eating, and the governor and Chen Si got on like a house on fire.

Even though Mr Ge was sitting right there at the table, he hadn't really understood all that was going on. He wasn't an educated man, and it was only after he'd got back home and found someone to ask that he realised that Fu Baoshi was a very famous artist indeed, who'd recently held a very successful exhibition of his paintings in Nanjing which had amazed the entire city. Thinking about it in the light of this information, he came to understand just how refined, how elevated, Chen Si's technique in giving gifts really was. About six months later, Mr Ge heard that Chen Si had been promoted and was now a director at the Post Office. He couldn't help saying: "When Chen Si gives a gift, even if you see it done, you don't notice at all. I am sure he is going to go on to even greater heights as an official!"

32

THE SWALLOW, LI SAN

IN THE LAST years of the reign of the Guangxu Emperor, at the beginning of the twentieth century, a truly remarkable man appeared in Tianjin – they called him the Swallow, Li San. His name was Li San, and the Swallow was his nickname. He was a truly remarkable cat burglar who made a speciality of robbing the very rich. Every time he stole something, he would draw a swallow somewhere nearby as a sign, so that everyone would know that the famous Swallow, Li San, had struck again. Given that the crime always involved a rich and noble household, the yamen would have to make serious efforts to arrest him, but Li San was unusually skilled in martial arts, and he could vault walls and climb over roofs as if there were nothing there. If he had to cross water he would seem to dance across the waves on the tips of his toes – first he was on this side of the bank, and now he was on the other. This was known as "Dragonfly Touches Water". If he hadn't been truly exceptionally skilled, he could never have learned such a technique.

Within the first six months of the appearance of the Swallow, Li San, a dozen or more wealthy households in and around the city had been robbed of all their treasures, and the only thing that was left behind was that drawing of a bird. The yamen runners had come up with all kinds of ideas for how to arrest him, but they'd never even so much as caught a glimpse of Li San. Some people said he looked just like Shi Qian – a character in *All Men Are Brothers* – and wore tight-fitting black clothes with soft shoes on his feet, and that he carried out his robberies in the dead of night, so that he could fade away into the darkness and you would never see him. Some people said that he looked like Yang Xiangwu from the opera *Judge Peng*, with the little black moustache on his upper lip brushed upwards to look like two wings; supposedly that was how he got his nickname of the Swallow. For a while, men with little moustaches walking along the road found themselves the objects of an awful lot of staring. Later on, people said that he didn't look anything like Shi Qing or Yang Xiangwu – that was the kind of idiocy that only a bookworm or a mad-keen opera fan could possibly have come up with. He must look completely ordinary and attract no attention at all. His only unusual characteristic would be sleeping during the day and going out at night, like a bat.

Why did Li San suddenly appear in this way? Why had nobody ever heard of him before? He must have recently come from somewhere else. Tianjin was full of rich people, and where you have rich people you have treasures which would attract someone of Li San's calibre. Supposedly, he was originally from Hebei Province... many people from that part of China had good martial-arts training. Sometimes, the story was even more specific, and he was said to come from Wuqiao. Wuqiao people are supposed to be good at acrobatics, they learn techniques like pole climbing and tightrope walking, and they are often highly skilled. Although there were lots of tales told about him, nobody had ever clapped eyes on him. The more time went by with nobody seeing him, the more wild guesses were made, and the more wild guesses were made, the more mysterious and dangerous they made him out to be. There were even some people who claimed that Li San was really the new magistrate of Tianjin, who'd been appointed just a couple of months before. The magistrate was a native of Hebei Province, thin and bony, highly intelligent and very corrupt. As to whether there was any truth in these rumours, who can say, but it made a good story; as time went by, it got more and more amusing. People in Tianjin do like to waggle their tongues, whether it is in eating or in having a good gossip – they enjoy both equally.

The legend of the cat burglar Li San lives on thanks to the stories people told about him. Besides which, he never robbed the poor. He only stole from the rich, and he would use his ill-gotten gains to help the needy. There was one wretchedly poor family living by the East Gate that owed their landlord money for the rent that they simply couldn't pay, and they were at the end of their tether with his demands. One evening as they were sitting there crying, suddenly they heard a thump as someone threw a bag in through the window. Opening it up, it was full of silver, and the even more amazing thing was that one corner of the bag had a little swallow drawn on it. The family rushed out to thank their mystery benefactor, but when they got out of the door, it was pitch black – whoever it was had disappeared completely. Supposedly, the person who got closest to ever being able to see Li San was the beggar, Pei Shiyi, who had his pitch squatting by one of the city gates. Li San put a paper bag filled with cash into his hand, but Pei Shiyi was blind and only felt his hand. He said that the hand wasn't big, but it was very hard. Even though they were there face-to-face, he couldn't see a thing.

With all of this, Li San became an even more mysterious figure in the tales told about him.

One day, the Swallow, Li San, committed a crime that shook the city to its foundations – he robbed the home of the most senior official in Tianjin, the Manchu viceroy of Zhili Province, Gūwalgiya Ronglu.

That morning, Ronglu's wife got up early and started to do her make-up, whereupon she noticed that a pearl pin that should have been on her dressing table had gone missing. This was the greatest treasure that she owned – the pearl was the size of a grape, more or less, with a brilliant sheen. To grow a pearl of such a size, it would have to be formed in the clam over the space of some five hundred years. Previously, Ronglu had wanted to give it as a gift to the Dowager Empress, but his wife had resolutely refused. As far as she was concerned, that pearl would leave her possession only over her dead body. The most infuriating thing was that the silk pad where she kept her pearl pin was now adorned with a little drawing of a swallow – the cat burglar was clearly trying to show up the viceroy! This was so irritating that Ronglu ground his teeth and cracked a rear molar.

Gūwalgiya Ronglu was also a remarkable man in his own way, and he came up with an original method of getting his own back: he had an octagonal table placed right in the middle of the main room, and he put his official seal as viceroy in the centre of the table, covered with a glass jar. Then he put out the word that overnight he would have all the doors closed, but that no soldiers or bodyguards would be allowed inside. He intended to sit up all night watching over his official seal, right through till dawn, and if the Swallow, Li San, had the guts he could come and try and take the seal away!

This was a test for Li San, and it was one that the viceroy was guaranteed to win. Think about it: even if there weren't any soldiers or bodyguards inside the room, there would be plenty outside. The doors would all be shut, and the seal would be held under a glass jar with the viceroy sitting there on guard and staring at it – no matter how skilled Li San was as a cat burglar, how could he possibly operate under these conditions? Besides which, if all the doors and windows were closed and fastened, how was he meant to get in? He could hardly be expected to introduce himself through a mouse hole, now could he?

That night, the viceroy made exactly the preparations that he had described. The table was put in the middle of the room, the official seal was placed in the centre of the table, and a glass jar covered it. Then he ordered all the yamen runners to leave, and the windows and doors were all locked and bolted. The viceroy took up his seat in front of his desk, lit the lamp and started to read a book, waiting patiently for the arrival of the cat burglar.

The viceroy sat up from dusk until dawn the following day, and it was only in the early hours of the morning that he was overcome with exhaustion and had a short nap – however, it seemed the moment he closed his eyes, he jerked awake again. The whole night, he didn't notice the slightest movement. After it got light, he opened all the doors and windows, and the light streamed in. His servants arrived, and they could see that the official seal was still sitting there untouched. The viceroy smiled and said: "I am afraid that this Li San didn't live up to his billing."

Then he raised his arms and stretched, rinsed his mouth with tea and spat it out on the ground, and prepared to go back to his bedroom to rest.

It was just at this moment, when the servant was lifting the glass jar to get the official seal, that he suddenly noticed that there seemed to be an insect crawling up one side of it. Looking more closely, he saw that it was a little black swallow that had been drawn on there with a brush! The Swallow, Li San, had struck!

The viceroy sat there with his mouth gaping and his eyes out on stalks. He guessed that it must have been his little nap in the early hours of the morning that gave Li San his opportunity. However, the doors and windows were all bolted – how on earth could he possibly have got in? Nobody in the yamen had the slightest idea.

In any society, you will find all sorts of people in the know, and very soon someone provided an explanation of what had happened. The story was that Li San came in long before the doors and windows were closed, and he hid behind the wooden placard hanging in the main hall that read "Upright and Enlightened". He waited there until the viceroy was exhausted and had to take a nap, and then he crept down and did the necessary. Then he climbed back and hid behind the placard again, and at dawn when the doors and windows were opened, he fled at some point when everyone's backs were turned.

This seemed to explain everything. But the viceroy was still puzzled: why hadn't he stolen the seal? Why had he just drawn the little swallow on top?

People laughed and said: "An official seal? Li San could have stolen it, but he didn't, because he wanted to tell you that this might be a treasure to you, but nobody else would want it!"

33
DRUMMING A PRINT

THE PEOPLE OF YANGLIUQING VILLAGE, within the purlieus of Tianjin, were highly sensitive, and every single person in every single household was good at art; the older people drew the designs, the men cut the blocks, the women coloured them, and the children made sure the paint pots were kept topped up. Each generation passed on their skills to the next, and many fine artists were produced this way. Every winter in the last month in the run-up to the New Year, each family would bring out their prints and put them up for sale. There would be endless heaps of new motifs and new colourways, as far as the eye could see, forming a dazzling spectacle. However, it did not matter how many new designs were produced for that season; as time went on, there would always be one print that got "drummed" and outsold all the rest. The people in Yangliuqing always said that whichever one got drummed was the one that seemed to come to life – it was the one that people liked the moment they saw it, that was the one they wanted to have, and they would fight each other

for it. That print seemed magical: it would just sell and sell and sell.

Every year, the people of Yangliuqing would wait to see which print would come to the fore, and they all hoped that it would be one of their own that got drummed – they would put their very best prints out and see what happened. At this time, the New Year's prints produced in this village were each finer than the last.

How does a print get drummed? That was hard to say. Nobody went about making a fuss over it, nobody screamed or shouted, nobody made any particular effort at all... it was as if, without anyone really noticing, the print would drum itself until it stood out from the thousands of others offered for sale. But how could the print drum itself? That was hard to say too. The two biggest shops, Dai Lianzeng and Qi Jialong's, employed several dozen printers at each, and they had a huge number of artists whose job it was to provide them with new designs – they put out a couple of hundred new prints every year, but that didn't mean one of them would be drummed. Gao Tongxuan did very delicate high-quality prints, so you could see the window behind the tree in his image, and then the person standing framed in that window. His prints sold very well, but he never had one that got drummed. It is just the same in opera; you may be a very fine singer, but that doesn't necessarily mean you'll become a star. People would talk about it and agreed that the gods would choose: whichever print the deities picked would be the one that got drummed, but they definitely wouldn't pick a whole bunch, and because of that, there was only ever one picture that sold that well. As a result, there was an old saying that remained current in Yangliuqing: every year there is one New Year's print that gets drummed, but it is impossible to know in advance which one.

There was one print maker in the village, Bai Xiaobao, whose ancestors had been in the business for many generations, and they'd taught him everything they knew about drawing the design, carving the blocks, and then running off the prints – he was good at every aspect of the trade, but he didn't have what it takes to come up with a new and original motif, so he was stuck with carrying on with the same ones that his family had always used. There were several of these: *May You Enjoy Abundance Year After Year*, *General Lu Wenlong with His Double Spears* and various other one-liners. He also did a perfectly nice *May the God of Wealth Shine on You*. These old designs sold pretty well, so he earned enough to keep a roof over his head and put food on the table, but the fact remains that they were too traditional, and were never going to come into fashion again. Since these prints could not possibly become the must-have item that year, he wasn't ever going to be able to earn big money from them. This was depressing, but there really wasn't anything he could do about it.

At the beginning of winter in the year 1869, in the eighth year of the reign of the Tongzhi Emperor, he set up his printing table, put out the old blocks, and rolled up his sleeves to start running off a few pictures. He began by printing his *General Lu Wenlong with His Double Spears* – each time he did a run of one thousand prints from each block. Then he went on to do his *May You Enjoy Abundance Year After Year*; that print showed a fat little baby boy hugging a huge red carp, against a background of green lotus leaves and pink buds. The word for "lotus" is pronounced the same as "year after year", and the word for "fish" is pronounced the same as that for "abundance", so the whole thing goes to make up a really auspicious image. This was a design that his family had always found some demand for. As a matter of fact, pretty much every print shop in the village could sell you a *May You Enjoy Abundance Year After Year*, and the designs were virtually identical, but the Bai family had a very cheerful and sweet baby and a lively-looking carp. They could sell anything up to two thousand prints of this particular design a year, and an awful lot of them were taken up by traders who would pack them up and sell them on in Wuqiang and Dongfengtai, both of which were also big centres for New Year's woodblock print production.

One afternoon, Bai Xiaobao was tired of printing, and so he hung up the last one on the line and went to a little restaurant down the road for a drink of wine. An older man was sitting at the same table drinking with him. Yangliuqing isn't such a big place, and everyone in the village would know everyone else by sight. This older man was called Gao; when younger, he'd worked as an accountant in a shop, and he was very chatty, so the two men were soon gossiping away as they sipped their drinks. As their conversation proceeded, naturally the subject turned to prints, and they began to discuss this year's output and which would be drummed. Mr Gao had drunk a little bit too much, and he said: "My friend, you need to find a new design. As long as you're just putting out your ancestors' work, you aren't going to get drummed." This was like a kick in the guts for Bai Xiaobao. He couldn't sit there any longer, so he tipped the last of the wine down his throat and headed for home.

As he walked along, he thought about what Mr Gao had said, and he got angrier and angrier. He wasn't annoyed by what he had said; he was furious with himself... furious that he hadn't been able to do better. The moment he got in through the door, he caught sight of one of the old blocks sitting on his printing table, and his rage seemed to become unstoppable. He picked up one of the carving knives that was lying on the table and started to hack away at the old block. He could hear his wife screaming: "You're going to ruin us if you do that! We'll all starve!" Afterwards, in a complete daze, he was helped to bed by his family and slept like a dead pig.

The next day when he woke up, he looked carefully at it... Oh, damn! The old block of *May You Enjoy Abundance Year After Year*, which was a family heirloom, was now damaged – he'd broken off one corner with its piece of the design. Looking more closely, he realised he was lucky: the face of the baby hadn't been injured at all, but the peony flower on one side of the head, just where the hair was drawn up into a cute little bunch, had been broken off. That wouldn't do... the image was supposed to be symmetrical, with two bunches of hair and a peony tucked behind each: it didn't look right at all now. However, it was far too late: a broken block is like a chopped-off finger, you can't just put it back. Within the next few days, his New Year's prints would have to go on sale. Fortunately, he'd already printed off a thousand, and if he now printed another thousand, he could sell them all together. If he could sell any at all, it would be a bonus, and if people refused to buy them, he'd just have to lump it.

When he put his New Year's prints on sale, something strange happened. Not only did the customers not mind that the child was missing one flower and was no longer symmetrical, they laughed and said that the plump baby looked really naughty

– he must have wrenched the flower off from behind his ear and thrown it away somewhere, such a loveable little fellow! And with that, it really did seem as if the baby in the print came to life. First one person wanted a print, and then another one did too, and then it was each person wanting a couple of prints, and within three days, a thousand copies had just flown off, and there wasn't a single one left. Since Bai Xiaobao didn't have any more, he had to take out the original print with the two bunches and the two flowers, but the customers just said: "Have you sold all of the ones you had yesterday?" He was flabbergasted; why did everyone want the one with the missing flower?

He wasn't completely stupid, though, and that evening he rushed home to print off some more as fast as he could, and then next day he put them on sale. When this print was put out, they sold every single sheet in the blink of an eye. When something has become what everyone has decided they want, there is nothing you can do to dampen demand. The whole family was put to work: his wife was at the market selling the prints, he was at home running off new copies, and his son was running back and forward between the two of them with the finished prints. He printed even more overnight, but simply couldn't keep up with demand. After a few days of this, someone suddenly came running round to his house and said: "Mr Bai, everyone in the whole village is talking about it – this year, your print has got drummed!" Afterwards, he asked in a low voice: "Your family has been doing this one print for generations now – why didn't it get drummed before? How come that this year it has suddenly been so successful?"

Bai Xiaobao just smiled. He didn't say anything, but he felt he understood. But when he turned the matter over in his mind, he didn't understand it at all. Why did a missing flower mean that his print got drummed?

On the evening of the thirtieth, Bai Xiaobao counted up his cash. He had made what amounted to a small fortune. Immediately after New Year, his family built themselves an extension to their house and made a number of other big purchases. Their lives really improved from this point on.

He was hoping that the fashion would continue to the following year, but instead it changed to a completely different direction. Although his print still sold quite well, the one that really rushed of the shelves was a new design put out by a tiny shop called the Virtue and Harmony. It was entitled *The Family at Peace with Itself*. It showed six girls banging away together at a huge drum. There was nothing about this print that marked it out as particularly special, but it sold like you wouldn't believe. Every day, long before the sky got light, there would be a huge queue of people lined up outside the door to the Virtue and Harmony waiting in the cold to buy one of these prints.

34
APING A FOREIGNER

FROM THE MOMENT that foreigners arrived to do business, establishing the Foreign Concession and moving in, all kinds of novelties came to Tianjin. Nobody had even heard the words "Foreign Concession" before, they'd never seen people with golden hair or green eyes, and the people in the old city were deeply curious about what was going on there.

The first thing was that when the skies started to get dark, people would go to Majiakou to see the electric lights – they really were amazing for the people of Tianjin. The foreigners had put up poles outside the church at Majiakou and hung up empty glass balls there. There was an iron plate on top of each of the balls, which would protect them from the rain. Whether old or young, the onlookers standing around each pole would gaze upwards with their mouths hanging open, watching these mysterious glass balls and waiting for the foreigners to work their magic. Once it got dark, the glass balls would suddenly light up. The light was extraordinarily bright, so that all the faces

below were lit up too, and a circle of light was thrown upon the ground. Everyone would exclaim in amazement, as if they had seen a miracle performed by the gods. What trick did the foreigners use to make these glass balls light up?

Another fun thing was that in the winter you could watch the foreigners ice-skating. Beyond the South Gate, there was a series of levees and canals, so if it got cold enough, you'd get ice forming in a thick, glistening mass. Foreigners with big moustaches, little moustaches, and sometimes with no moustaches at all would come running out of the Foreign Concession with knives strapped to the soles of their boots, and then go sliding about on the ice, turning here and twirling there, very pleased with themselves. When they saw that Chinese people were lined up on the banks watching them, they were even more self-satisfied, and they would spin about on the spot, for all the world like spinning tops. Sometimes, things didn't go so well, and they would end up falling on their bottoms or sliding spreadeagled across the ice, which made the onlookers all roar with laughter. A scholarly gentleman at the time wrote a poem about this:

> *With knives on their feet they fly through the air,*
> *Happy and glorious they are without pair.*
> *But falling over before others is really a 'mare,*
> *With head, arms, and legs forming a square!*

Shortly afterwards, some of the young men went over to the Foreign Concession to see if they could buy any foreign goods, and they brought them back to show them off round the old city. One day, a young man took an alarm clock to the Jade Spring teahouse over on Da Hutong in the northeast corner of the city. He put it out on the table and set the alarm, and then he called everyone round to have a look and wait to hear it chime. When the alarm went off, the sound was deeply pleasing. This toy had everyone in Tianjin fascinated, and the teahouse was packed to the rafters from morning until night. The boss of the Jade Spring was so pleased that he simply couldn't stop smiling – in fact he said that the young man could have his tea and food for free for bringing along his alarm clock.

However, just over a week later, a middle-aged man came into the Jade Spring. He was extremely smartly dressed and carried a beautiful brocade silk bag with him, which he put down on the table. When he opened it up, there was a foreign gilded box inside, but nobody knew what it could possibly be for, though it was very pretty indeed. They watched him wind it up, but this time it didn't set an alarm – the box started to emit the most delightful tinkling music from somewhere inside. People called these magical little boxes "eight note boxes". This time, twice as many people came to the Jade Spring to drink their tea and enjoy the fun, and there were so many people crammed in that it was standing room only.

Not long after this, a strange person suddenly appeared on the main avenue leading through to the East Gate of the old city – he looked like a foreigner, but at the same time not like a foreigner. He was of middling height and aged about thirty, wearing a short western-style jacket. Underneath, he was wearing a little western shirt tied with a black silk bow-tie at the collar, and he was wearing western-style shoes, and a western-style hat on his head. He also had on smoked glasses, which made sure you couldn't see what he really looked like. His face could have been foreign, but looking again, his nose was too small. Foreigners have huge, high noses, which might even be hooked – the ones people called "eagle noses" in those days. This person's nose was small and bulbous, like a head of garlic.

This strange creature stood for a while by the side of the road and then suddenly took out a small paper box from his waist. He took out a little wooden stick about an inch long from inside – one end of this little stick was white. He held this wooden stick and swiped it from side to side, and the white bit suddenly caught light. When the wooden stick started burning, it really gave all the people on the street a turn – they had no idea what this weird object held by the strange person could possibly be. When it was about half burned, the strange person tossed his little wooden stick on the ground. He then took out another from his box and swiped it again; it caught fire and burned, and then he threw it away. Having been through this performance more than a dozen times, it was all over. He walked away without saying a word.

After this, Tianjin people referred to these "one swipe and they're lit" sticks as "playing with fire".

Ten days or so after the first appearance of this strange creature, he reappeared on the main road leading out of the East Gate, in a different costume, and this time his bow tie was golden. Yet again he played with fire, swiping away, but this time he didn't just toss the sticks away. He fished out yet another paper box from a pocket, but this time the paper box was bigger than the one that the playing-with-fire things came out of, and there were some foreign words printed on top in bright colours. He took out another stick from his box, but it wasn't made of wood – it was a white paper stick about the size of a little finger.

He put it in his face and then played with fire to light it. People on both sides of the road were so scared they covered their ears: they thought he was about to set off a firecracker or something. However, having lit his thing, it didn't explode; it just smoked. He sucked in a few mouthfuls, and what came out of his mouth when he opened it again was still smoke. People had no idea what on earth he was doing; those who were standing nearby could smell something like burning leaves, but there was also another kind of unidentifiable scent as well. People who'd been to the Foreign Concession before were able to inform them that he was smoking a cigarette, as westerners did. It appeared that westerners didn't smoke pipes; they wrapped their tobacco in paper tubes and kept them in boxes in their clothing, rather than in a bag hanging from their waist.

After this, Tianjin people called western tobacco products "pocket tubes".

For a while, some people gathered every day at the East Gate to the old city in the hope of seeing this strange person and his weird belongings. He didn't appear every day, but whenever he did, he caused an uproar. One day, there he was with a dog on a lead. This dog was white with black spots, and it was big but thin, with its two ears hanging down to its shoulders and its long tongue hanging down to the ground. It had a very nasty expression in its eyes, and when it walked down the road, the local strays didn't dare even to bark at it. In fact, they were so scared they disappeared for the next few days.

Having caused such a sensation, it prompted people to think. Who could this strange person possibly be? Was he a genuine foreigner or was he a fake? Pretty soon, there were two competing explanations in circulation. One said that he lived over on the west side of the city, and his father was in the salt business. The family was loaded, and the last few years his father was always off in the south, trading in this or that, and so nobody took any interest in what he was up to. He'd got obsessed with foreigners and spent all of his time in the Foreign Concession, until he behaved just like one of them. The other story was that this man was a genuine foreigner who'd been living in the Foreign Concession for a year now, but found the old city more interesting, and he liked to walk around there and have a look – supposedly he could also manage a word or two of Chinese. Then someone said that this strange person was actually English, and was called Bobby.

At this time, residents of Tianjin were interested in modernisation and being at the cutting edge, and people often came to give lectures on these subjects. There was a lot of discussion about what it meant to be modern, how to overturn old-fashioned customs, and develop our culture. These lectures were held at the Chamber of Commerce, opposite the Ever-Increasing Blessings teahouse on Guyi Street, and they were organised by people at the Hall of Widening Knowledge. One day, there was going to be a lecture at the Chamber of Commerce. The lecturer was the first to step onto the stage, and he introduced an honoured guest from the Foreign Concession to the audience gathered below. The strange creature then emerged, dressed as usual, but this time his bow tie was green stripes on a white ground. He bowed and then shook hands with him, quite in the foreign fashion, and then said a few words in some weird language.

One of the students said: "What language is he speaking? It doesn't sound like English. I've been learning English myself."

That opened the floodgates.

Suddenly someone asked: "Are you really called Bobby?"

The strange person seemed worried that his audience might be getting the wrong idea about him, and so he immediately replied: "I am Bobby."

Then someone else asked: "Where did you learn Chinese? How come you have a Tianjin accent?"

With that question out in the open, everyone started to think – the strange person had indeed just spoken with a slight Tianjin accent.

The strange creature was silent; this was not an easy question to answer. Now another query came: "What's your father called?"

The strange person blenched, but he replied immediately: "Mister Bobby."

Now the questioner really started yelling: "Hey, you, have a good look at who you're talking to! I'm your father! I've just got back from Guangdong! Bobby? What the hell is this? Get those disgusting rags off you and come home. I've had enough of you going about aping a foreigner!"

From this day onwards, people in Tianjin called studying western ways or wearing western clothes "aping a foreigner".

Even today, people talk about "aping a foreigner", and the expression comes from this story.

35
THE YELLOW LOTUS DIVINE MATRIARCH

IN THE YEAR 1900, Tianjin was ripped apart by the uprising of the Fists of Righteous Harmony, otherwise known as the Boxers. As a result, the city gates were no longer closed as it got dark, fires were kept burning all night, nobody slept, and the streets were in uproar. Wave after wave of Boxers poured into the city from Hebei or Shandong Provinces, and they all wore distinguishing Eight Trigrams badges on their chests and the backs of their jackets. They wore turbans of different colours and carried flags, with swords by their sides, and held either cudgels or spears. However, their attitudes were very different: some of them screamed and shouted wildly, some of them marched in unison, and some of them looked dark, saying not a word, and with a murderous expression on their faces, grinding their teeth with a horrible gritting noise that made your hair stand on end. After entering the city, they began by setting up an altar which they draped with their flags and hung with talismans and red lanterns. Immediately, the ordinary people of the city rushed to

bring them bread and steamed buns, pickled vegetables, onions, and fragrant deep-fried dough twists. They had heard that the Boxers planned to fight the people in the Foreign Concession straight away. They could already see the light of the fires burning in Majiakou and Laolongtou, and black smoke was rising over the city, accompanied by sporadic bursts of gunfire. The Boxers were burning the foreigner's "rats' nests" over there.

The population of the old city was about one hundred thousand, but they were now joined by at least two hundred thousand Boxers. There were plenty of battles between the people of Tianjin and the foreigners in those days, but win, lose or draw, they were never afraid.

One day at the beginning of the sixth lunar month, all the Boxer divisions in the city rushed out of the North Gate and lined up in battle formation on either side of the Grand Canal. Their glittering swords were drawn; their flaming torches blazed, and all this was reflected in the waters. Everything took place without anyone saying a word – it was amazingly silent… scarily silent. Supposedly, the Yellow Lotus Divine Matriarch was on her way from the south at the head of a flotilla of Red Lantern boats and would arrive at any moment.

Over the course of the next few days, stories about the amazing exploits performed by the Red Lanterns militia circulated throughout Tianjin. A poster appeared all over the city, and the wording was very frightening:

> *Men should study to become Boxers;*
> *Women should learn to become Red Lanterns.*
> *Let us leap across Zizhulin and chop every*
>   *foreigner into pieces.*

The word "foreigner" on the poster had been crossed out with a thick line of red ink, just like how the names of the dead are written on official notices concerning the execution of criminals. Supposedly, when these posters were put up around Zizhulin, the foreigners were so scared they didn't dare be seen on the streets; they stayed at home with the curtains drawn as tightly as they could.

Although the poster mentioned Red Lanterns, nobody had ever seen one. Everyone said that they were unmarried girls or young wives who wore red and were as beautiful as fairies, and they knew a special incantation that killed foreigners. Their leader, known as the Yellow Lotus Divine Matriarch, was supposed to be as lovely as a goddess, quite as beautiful as the statue of the Queen of Heaven in the temple. When it came to martial arts or knowledge of magical incantations, she was also much better than any of the male Boxer leaders.

As they watched, a flotilla of huge boats sailed up the Grand Canal with red lanterns hanging from the masts. They travelled as far as Jiajia Hutong and then stopped, and here the Red Lanterns disembarked. Each one of them was wearing red trousers and a red jacket, with a shining silver sword carried on her back, and they each held a red silk fan in one hand and a red gauze lantern in the other. As the light shone on their faces, they really did look more beautiful and powerful than the Women Generals of the Yang Clan in the opera of that name.

The Boxers standing on the bank had been very well trained; when they caught sight of the Red Lanterns, they all put their one hand up to their chest in a gesture of respect, simultaneously bowing their heads. Not one looked straight ahead. The Yellow Lotus Divine Matriarch didn't get off the boat and never even showed her face – the leaders of each group of Boxers were summoned to the boat to meet her. The senior commanders, Zhang Decheng, Cao Futian, Liu Chengxiang and so on, lined up and boarded the boat in single file, looking very serious and formal, as if they were entering a temple to pray to a god.

With this, the inhabitants of Tianjin were left to speculate wildly about the identity and appearance of the Yellow Lotus Divine Matriarch. Some people said that her real name was Lin Hei'er and that she was a local girl who'd grown up where the river met the sea. Her father had taught her martial arts, and they'd worked together as acrobats and performers, but somehow or other her father had angered a foreigner who'd had him thrown into prison where he died, and she was determined on revenge. Other people said that she wasn't human at all – she was the Queen Mother of the West born into human form, who could call up a magical fire to burn up Zizhulin and make the seas run dry so that no foreign boats could sail. Of course, there were all sorts of people who worked at the Tianjin docks: some of them said that she was a shaman from the other side of the river who could summon the really important gods, but even more said that she was a local whore with a terrible temper who had worked in one of the brothels in Houjiahou. Naturally, it was the most unpleasant of these stories that everyone believed.

Early one morning three days later, the Red Lanterns suddenly all left their boats and lined up on the bank. In a very short space of time, three thousand Red Lanterns were standing in rows, their steel swords strapped to their backs, with lanterns in their right hands and fans in their left hands.

The Yellow Lotus Divine Matriarch still didn't appear, so it was a young woman dressed as the goddess Sanxiangu, with her hair combed up into a high bun on top of her head, who led the militia into the city. The Boxers who were already there had lined up along each road and avenue to stand guard for the Red Lanterns.

As the Red Lanterns marched in through the gate to the city, they stamped their feet in unison. The sound of several thousand people stamping their feet like that is truly shocking; it shakes the earth and resounds through the sky. The Red Lanterns were famous for this manoeuvre; they called it "stamping a city". They did this to suppress evil spirits and terrify foreigners.

The Red Lanterns began by stamping their way around the city, and then they went to the church over on the western side of Tianjin. Five hundred Red Lanterns were lined up outside, and then suddenly a palanquin appeared, carried by four people. It appeared so unexpectedly in front of the church, it might as well have dropped from the sky. Even though the curtains were open, it was impossible to see who was inside. In spite of that, everyone knew that the Yellow Lotus Divine Matriarch was sitting right there in the palanquin. Nobody had a clue what spell she cast from inside, but they saw Sanxiangu run from her position beside the palanquin to the door of the church, which she kicked open with one foot. Then she turned round and screamed: "Burn it!"

The five hundred Red Lanterns threw the lanterns they'd been holding into the church, and in an instant it was a mass of flames, and thick black smoke was coiling up into the sky. The five hundred Red Lanterns now raised their left hands and began fanning the flames. The little fans seemed magical – before their very eyes, the flames began to roar, burning ever hotter and more fiercely.

As the onlookers shrieked and called out, the church was burned to a blackened skeleton, and then collapsed into a ruin.

News of the Yellow Lotus Divine Matriarch's awe-inspiring powers soon reached the ears of the viceroy, Hitara-Hala Yulu. Three days after these events, Yulu invited the Yellow Lotus Divine Matriarch and the senior Boxer leaders like Zhang Decheng and Cao Futain to visit the vice-regal yamen at the Three Rivers Crossing to discuss an attack on the foreigners in Zizhulin.

As to what happened when Yulu met the Divine Matriarch, or what the two of them spoke about, nobody ever knew. However, one of the men who carried her palanquin heard the viceroy ask the Divine Matriarch: "Will the foreigners attack Tianjin?" The Divine Matriarch was sitting inside the palanquin with the curtains down, and she just said: "Don't worry about that." It seemed a throwaway remark, but thinking about it carefully, it was full of self-confidence – there must be a reason why she spoke that way. If she was prepared to treat such a serious matter as unimportant, Yulu felt reassured and broke out in smiles. He immediately made the Divine Matriarch a gift of yellow cloth suitable for making flags.

When the Yellow Lotus Divine Matriarch got back, she used the yellow cloth to make a huge battle standard, quite two yards in length, with four black velvet characters appliquéd onto it: Yellow Lotus Divine Matriarch. Her standard was bordered with gold tassels, and when it was suspended from the mast on the main boat, two lines of red lanterns hung down on either side. This was a very impressive sight, and when it was lit up at night, it was even more eye-catching. Every evening, the ordinary people in Tianjin rushed round to Jiajia Hutong to set up tables of offerings and burn incense in front of the main boat. They really did treat her like she was some kind of goddess, and they begged her to keep them safe. Now all the evil gossip of days gone by were swept away and forgotten.

Every seven days, the Red Lanterns went and stamped the city – this was to show off their might, to embolden the men in the Boxer units, and to encourage the ordinary people of Tianjin in the coming fight. Within a very few days, battle was joined, and their role in stamping the city became even more important. Every time they stamped the city, the people of Tianjin felt so much more encouraged, and their morale redoubled. Because of this, it became so that they stamped the city every three days, and then eventually they were doing it every day.

The girls in the militia were so busy they couldn't comb their hair or do their make-up... their hair was all over the place, and their clothes were put on anyhow. In the heat of battle, nobody cares how you are dressed – what matters is morale. As they stamped the city, they would sing as they crashed their boots in unison:

> *Women don't comb their hair; they cut off*
> *foreigners' heads!*
> *Women don't bind their feet; they laugh to see the*
> *foreigners dead!*

When the time came to fight, the Red Lanterns were always right there on the front line. They would move around setting fires, and they burned the Foreign Concession to the ground. Every time they successfully set a fire in the Foreign Concession, one of the Red Lanterns would set off at a run to report the good news, holding up high a triangular yellow victory flag. When it was all over, the flags were taken back on board the boat.

At this time, there were many stories and many mysteries made about the Yellow Lotus Divine Matriarch, in spite of the fact that nobody had ever seen her face. But how could she fail to be extraordinary? She was a woman, in command of several thousand female warriors, who had struck awe into the entire city, and who could make even the most senior official in the entire country obey her commands, who killed people without turning a hair and defied the foreigners' weapons. And if she was just a mere mortal, was that not even more impressive?

The Boxers were defeated in 1900, and the Red Lanterns disappeared from the face of the earth. Before their final victory, the foreigners were so scared of the Red Lanterns that they would wet their pants at the mere thought of them. When they burst through the Tianjin defences, they shot any woman they saw who was dressed in red, but the fact is that the women they shot dead for wearing red clothes were not necessarily Red Lanterns. People in Tianjin always wore red for celebrations, and young women in the city were often dressed in this colour. Because of this, for the next twenty years or more, you didn't see the girls of Tianjin wearing red.

As to what became of the Yellow Lotus Divine Matriarch, nobody quite knew: some people said she was killed in battle, others that she went into hiding, and yet others that she was taken prisoner – there were all kinds of stories. Supposedly, the foreigners arrested the Yellow Lotus Divine Matriarch and Sanxiangu at the Three Rivers, and they were imprisoned in the jail attached to the vice-regal yamen. The foreigners took pictures of the two of them, and they were afterwards exhibited all over the world as part of their spoils of war. As to whether this was true or not, who knows? There was never any further evidence or news about them.

Tianjin people never accepted this explanation. As they pointed out, the two female prisoners in the photographs were obviously women from ordinary families; the whole thing was faked by foreigners trying to show off their military might. There wasn't anyone in Tianjin who so much as caught a glimpse of the Yellow Lotus Divine Matriarch – how could the foreigners be so sure that it was her? All you could say was that they might have won, but they were still afraid of the woman.

36
ZHEN THE GULLET

When it came to necking alcohol, nobody could out-drink Zhen the Gullet.

He could drink like there was no tomorrow; he could cope with any combination, no problem; and when it came to drinking shots, he could slam them down his throat as hard and fast as he could, and he never, ever choked. When he was drinking beer, he would just raise his head and upend the bottle into his mouth; he wasn't holding the bottle at all – he just supported it in his mouth, and the beer rolled straight into his stomach. He seemed to have what they call an "open" throat, so the liquid never went down the wrong way. If he was the kind to choke up, he'd have been dead long ago. Who else could drink like that? In one evening he could put away two cases of beer – that's twenty-four bottles – necking them one after another. That's how he got his nickname Zhen the Gullet.

Some people complained about him, pointing out that he was the magistrate and wasn't paying for all this drink himself.

Since he was drinking on the public dollar, naturally he wanted to put away as much as he could, and as for his technique, anyone could learn it if they put in as much practice as he did. While it was perfectly true that technique is a matter of practice, drinking all that alcohol and never getting drunk speaks of a natural aptitude. Zhen the Gullet never got drunk. As he said himself: "My mother told me that if I ever got really drunk, it would kill me."

Other people thought it was a joke, but his mother's pronouncements were something that clearly couldn't be ignored. However, let us turn first to another part of the story.

Someone asked: when he tipped a couple of dozen bottles of beer down his throat, where did it all go? It was a good question, and it cut right to the very heart of his technique for drinking. When people drink alcohol, it enters their body and has to come out somehow – the stomach is only so big, so how can it possibly cope with twenty or thirty bottles of liquid? The booze has to get out of you somehow, by some process of expulsion. If you can drink, you can dispose of it as well, though there are various different methods of doing so. Some people pee, and get rid of it that way; some people throw up, which works too; and some people sweat, removing the liquid through their pores. There was one director of the Customs Bureau that always had a towel by his table when he was drinking; when he finished, the towel was sopping wet from the alcohol.

Zhen the Gullet had his own technique – he expelled the alcohol through his feet.

When he wasn't drinking, his feet were dry; when he drank, his feet were covered in beads of sweat.

The beads of "sweat" all over his feet weren't sweat at all – it was the alcohol. The more he poured into his mouth, the more seeped out of his feet. When attending a banquet, he never wore silk socks or leather shoes; it had to be cotton socks and cloth shoes, since leather would keep the liquid in where cloth would let it out. His staff had the task of making sure a nice thick mat went down on the floor in front of his chair, just where he would put his feet, which would also mop up some of the booze. Every time the drinking was over and everyone went home, he took his feet out of a puddle of alcohol. When he got home, the very first thing he would do was to have a footbath in hot water – that would expel the last of the wine. Otherwise, he would have been as drunk as a lord. Because of all of this, Zhen the Gullet's feet never smelt the way some men's do; they were beautifully soft and white, more like women's feet.

One day, Zhen the Gullet was in a meeting with his superiors, and when the time came to go home, one of them insisted that he stay behind for dinner to discuss matters further. This was his immediate superior, who would determine any future promotions, so he couldn't refuse. He agreed with the best grace possible. His staff reminded him: "If you start drinking, sir, you need to be careful. You aren't wearing cloth shoes, and we didn't bring your little mat." Zhen the Gullet just said: "I know what I am doing." But when he got to the dinner table and the wine was being poured, it was quite another matter. To begin with, Zhen the Gullet was being careful and refused the drinks that were pressed on him. However, when it was his superior who was encouraging him to have a glass, he simply could not say no. The first few cups went straight to his superior's head – he was elated and happy; then the next few cups went down and he was in an even better mood. He now went straight to the point: "I've heard that they call you Zhen the Gullet, and that when you drink beer you put the whole bottle straight into your mouth. Well, seeing is believing, and I'd like to take this opportunity to see what you can do. If you refuse, it will show that you don't really respect me."

Zhen the Gullet was now in real trouble: he couldn't possibly refuse to drink, and in fact he didn't dare to say no. A case of beer was now carried in and opened, and the caps removed. The two men agreed: Zhen the Gullet would drink a bottle of beer, while his boss would down a cup of spirits. At least half of the cup that his superior held up ended up being tossed somewhere other than down his throat, but Zhen the Gullet was really drinking. He lifted the bottle up above his head, tilted his noggin back and upended the bottle with a flick of his wrist so that its neck was in his mouth. Neither his mouth nor his chin moved, his neck was straight as an arrow, and a whole bottle of beer was tipped into his stomach. With another flick of his wrist, the empty bottle was placed back on the table. His technique for drinking really was unique.

His superior was immensely impressed and kept shouting: "Wow, that's amazing!" He slapped another bottle of beer down in front of Zhen the Gullet with a thump and screamed: "Do it again!" It was intended as praise, but it was also an order – he wanted to see what the man could do. So one bottle after another was tipped down his throat.

Very soon, Zhen the Gullet could feel his feet getting hotter and hotter, burning in fact – he was in such pain with his feet. He realised that he was in trouble, he needed his feet to get rid of the alcohol, but leather shoes would hold it back... What on earth was he to do? Long before he had come up with an answer, he was in no fit state to think at all.

Afterwards, Zhen the Gullet's servant said that when he took off the magistrate's leather shoes, he poured a whole bottle of beer out of each one.

Zhen the Gullet collapsed and proved the truth of what his mother had said: if he ever got really drunk it would kill him.

But how could his mother have known?

37
THE BEIDAGUAN DING

TIANJIN IS the single most important entrepôt in the whole of northern China, so all the best food ends up here sooner or later, and all kinds of entertainment are available too. This spoils the local rich young men. These playboys can eat before going out to have their fun, then having had their fun they can eat all over again. And when they are not doing that, they can talk about eating and discuss what entertainments are on offer. Each one of these activities has its own pleasure. Ding Boyu, the eldest young master of the Ding family of Beidaguan, was just such a one.

These people were actually a branch of the Ding family of Shaoxing in Zhejiang Province. Back when the future Yongle Emperor was just the King of Yan, he arrived at Tianjin on his northern campaign, and the ancestor of these Dings managed to wangle a really plum post out by the Grand Canal, north of the big city – chief inspector of customs! His job was to sit by the river, and all the ships coming north had to hand over money to

him to pay the customs duties. He didn't have to work: he just sat there collecting money, and in the blink of an eye a mountain of silver and gold piled up by his side, while the copper coins tossed in his direction were such that he could never spend in a million years.

The Ding family were in charge of the customs post north of the city: that is Beidaguan. They managed to make this a hereditary position, handed down from one generation to the next. They kept this in the family, never allowing any outsiders to take over. Tianjin folk called them the Beidaguan Dings.

Although the Beidaguan Dings were rich and powerful, Ding Boyu, the eldest young master of the family, was far from being an ordinary playboy. He wasn't just some guzzler of food and wine; he was a connoisseur of entertainment and a gourmet of no mean order.

Let's start with the world of entertainment. Ding Boyu didn't play cards or collect rare birds or fancy dogs, nor was he interested in drinking games or pretty girls with bound feet – in fact, those kinds of things were all old hat to him. Even when he still had a pigtail hanging down from the back of his head, he went out riding on a foreign bicycle, weaving in and out of the city, until everyone in Tianjin had their eyes out on stalks.

Supposedly, Li Hongzhang had heard ages ago that foreigners overseas all rode about on this kind of contraption, zipping back and forward along the streets. Later, when Li Hongzhang visited the United States, he got to see this with his own eyes, and he exclaimed in amazement! He said that bicycles were the foreigners' very own "workhorses". The Americans gave him one, but he didn't have the courage to give it a try. Who would dare to give it a go if even Li Hongzhang wouldn't?

He brought it back with him, but it ended up being abandoned in a warehouse somewhere. When Ding Boyu heard about this, he was curious. He went to a friend in the Foreign Concession and spent a lot of money on importing one from the West. When he got it, he started to ride it, but to begin with he could not help but fall off all the time. But after a couple of weeks, there he was, making a fine impression, cycling around Guyi Street. That one appearance got the entire city talking. Six months later, everyone inside and outside of the city had got to see the tall and strongly built eldest young master of the Ding family riding his two-wheeled foreign bicycle, on both sides of the Grand Canal, up the main roads and down the small alleys. Here he was, free and easy, as light as a swallow, racing down the street. He was the first person from Tianjin to ride a bicycle, and for a while this was quite one of the sights of the city.

Who, other than the eldest young master of the Ding family, could do such a thing just for the hell of it? They might think about it… fine, but who else would actually do it?

Now let us turn to eating. Young Master Ding was no fan of the rich omelettes turned out by the Realm of the Immortals restaurant. Nor did he like the Korean silverfish served at the Gather All, the local purple crabs in their so-called "silver sand" sour sauce at the Garden of Heavenly Abundance, or the fried carp at the Ascending Virtue. Nor was he interested in eating any of the famous dishes turned out by the local Cantonese and Ningbonese restaurants, or the foreign restaurants over in Zizhulin. In the port city of Tianjin, you can find delicacies from the four corners of the earth, and all manner of delicious things. Sour, sweet, salty, savoury, sweet-and-sour, spicy, peppery, aromatic, pungent yet fragrant, sticky, crisp, crunchy, soft, flaky, slippery, floury, flame-grilled, well-done on the outside but tender on the inside, gummy and chewy... There are so many of these things that you simply cannot get round to eating them all; in fact, you won't even be able to see all of them. But Young Master Ding had his own special gourmandise, in that he liked to eat the same thing. It was something that he never got tired of and could never eat too much of, but was neither expensive nor rare; you could see it everywhere in the streets, and that is... candied hawthorn.

So what is so special about hawthorn fruit stuck on a stick like a kebab and dipped in sugar? This is something that the poor eat to alleviate their hunger; that children are given to eat to coax them into better behaviour; that cute young girls nibble away at... so why would one of the richest young men in the entire city want to eat this?

People laughed at him for having the tastes of a poor man for all his money, but he didn't care. When he was crossing Guyi Street in his rickshaw, if he happened to spot a hawker selling candied hawthorn on the corner, he'd immediately call for the driver to stop and send him to buy one. Then he'd sit in the rickshaw, munching away. Everyone in the northern part of the city had seen him do it. You mustn't think that the eldest young master of the Ding family was just saving his money; he said that even if candied hawthorn cost a tael of silver per kebab, he'd still eat them. From this, we can see that the rich can do whatever they damn well want. Young Master Ding owned mountains of gold and silver, but as far as he was concerned, this street snack was the most important thing in life. Who else would do something like that?

One day, a rich young gentleman from Beijing came to visit

him. Although Beijing and Tianjin are close neighbours, the people there are quite different in temperament, the cuisine is different and so is the lifestyle... even their manner of speech and what they like to talk about are not at all the same. Tianjin people liked to take their cue from the eight grand families there, while those in the capital were always talking about the old Empress Dowager; the rich families of Tianjin could trace their ancestors back two generations at most, but the Beijingers would crush you with their high official rank.

Now, when the conversation turned to candied hawthorn, the young gentleman from the capital said to Ding Boyu: "In Beijing, candied hawthorn is called candied calabash – because of the gourd-like shape, I guess. The old Empress Dowager enjoys eating candied calabash as well. Did you know that?"

Ding Boyu shook his head.

The young gentleman from the capital now lowered his voice and said with a smile: "The candied calabash the Empress Dowager gets to eat are really fabulous – infinitely better than anything you can buy out on the streets." Then he added: "Wang Laowu – right now, he's the head chef at the Nine Dragon Hermitage restaurant in front of the Beijing Drum Tower – used to work in the imperial kitchens. I'm told he made candied calabash for the Empress Dowager..."

The young gentleman from the capital was happy that he'd been able to put a provincial in his proper place, so he stopped talking about candied hawthorn and changed the subject. In fact, he'd shot his bolt on this topic.

However, as soon as the rich young gentleman from the capital was gone, Ding Boyu sent two capable men with a lot of money to the capital. They found the Nine Dragon Hermitage restaurant in front of the Drum Tower, and then they sought out Wang Laowu and invited the chef from the imperial kitchens (short of money ever since his retirement) to visit Tianjin. The things that you would need a senior government official to fix for you in the capital have always been done – and done well – in Tianjin with cold hard cash.

Wang Laowu was a short man, and a little bit plump, with small hands and feet, a small nose and small ears. He was in no way striking looking, nor was he particularly easy to talk to, but he did have a certain dignity about him. If you are not born into a famous family or do not have some unique skill, you cannot acquire such an air. Having taken his place in the middle of the main courtyard of the Ding mansion, he first set up a stove and then put an iron wok on top of it, after which he arranged a marble-topped table and a wooden table. Then he opened the two big bags he had brought from the capital and set out all kinds of tools that none of them had ever so much as seen before, as well as a whole pile of colourful and deliciously scented foodstuffs. One after another, they were arranged neatly and in order. This process amazed all the servants and maids who were standing around watching. Young Master Ding grinned cheerfully: this courtyard had now been turned into the imperial kitchens!

He watched carefully as Wang Laowu made each candied hawthorn skewer step by step. For the first time, he saw that the candied fruit could be so very bright and eye-catching, colourful and exquisite, like a string of tiny glowing lanterns. He ordered the servants to deliver freshly candied hawthorns to each of the other members of the household, and for himself he picked out a glistening new skewerful and opened his mouth to take a bite, imagining all the while that he was the old Empress Dowager.

What a delicious treat this would be for a monarch! But anything that an emperor could eat, he could have too... if he spent the money! After this, any time he wanted to eat the same candied calabash enjoyed by the Empress Dowager, he'd send a carriage to bring Wang Laowu out from the capital. On one occasion, he held a candied hawthorn banquet at his home and invited all the greatest gourmets and famous men that the city could provide. After that party, everyone who'd laughed at him for eating candied hawthorn was left with nothing to say. When you were talking about who knew how to have a good time in Tianjin and who was the greatest gourmet, the eldest young master of the Ding family of Beidaguan was undoubtedly number one.

Gradually, people stopped talking about this rich and powerful family as being the Dings of Beidaguan... and he became *the* Beidaguan Ding.

For better or worse, no one can expect their luck to last for an entire lifetime, and sooner or later, the tide will turn. In the year 1900, disaster struck – the court was riven by dissent, the Boxer Rebellion raged, and there was a terrible battle between the Chinese army and various foreign nations. This was followed by the Eight Nations Allied Army, stationed in the Foreign Concessions in Zizhulin, massacring the inhabitants of the old city of Tianjin. The Ding family of Beidaguan attracted attention just because they were so rich, and they suffered terrible pillage at the hands of the Allied forces. After that, they lost their sinecure – the customs post the family had managed for so long was pillaged and abandoned in its turn. In a very short space of time, Ding Boyu found himself ruined. That's the way the world goes: someone who's always lived a life of ease and who suddenly loses everything is soon in dire straits, but ordinary folk who've always struggled to make a living don't suffer reverses in the same way: they can still eat, sleep and go to work as if nothing had happened.

Not long after the Allied forces had put the city to the sword, the weather turned much colder. There were only a couple of rooms left in the Beidaguan Ding's mansion that hadn't been wrecked, and he had a huge household that were going hungry. They didn't even have blankets to cover them as they slept, and there was nothing in the house to sell. Neighbours suggested that he try and borrow some money, but he refused: he didn't want to go into debt. He knew that going into debt would tie him to a life-long burden, one that he wouldn't be able to put down until he was in the presence of the King of the Underworld himself.

One day, he saw a villager selling candied hawthorn fruit over on Guyi Street. He'd been eating these candied fruit for half his lifetime, so he couldn't help but be moved when he saw them. But this time, he wasn't just moved; he was also thinking furiously. He had just a handful of copper coins in his pocket, but that was enough to buy about fifty hawthorn fruit, and then he went into a grocery store to get a small bag of sugar. When he got home, he cut up the fruit, peeled and cored them, and boiled up the sugar syrup. Then he pulled out some canes from the reed curtain lying in a heap in the corner, stripped them to expose the white stalks, cut them into suitable lengths and sharpened one end. Then he skewered his fruit on the stalks and glazed them in the sugar syrup, before taking them out to sell them on the street. Everyone said they were quite delicious, and in a trice he'd sold out. Grabbing his money, he went off to buy more hawthorns and more sugar with which to make his candied fruit. He came and went, running hither and yon, and for all that it almost killed him, he rode through this crisis.

Two months later, Ding Boyu was to be seen selling candied hawthorn in an alley opposite the Jiangxi Guildhall on Guyi Street, and he was looking pretty good. It seemed that he'd been making some money. It was cold, and he was wearing a thick cotton-padded jacket, a felt skullcap, and he had a pair of felt boots lined with rabbit skin on his feet. A thick pad of straw was wrapped around the wooden pole he was holding, and that was then stuck full of skewers of deep red, glistening candied fruit. There are always a few candied fruit sellers out and about on Guyi Street, but people would always choose the best – and pretty soon everyone had worked out that the best was the Beidaguan Ding. His hawthorns were nice and big, really good quality. The sugar enrobing was thick and even, giving a crisp glaze that did not stick to the teeth. One of his skewers was worth two of anyone else's.

By the end of the year, the eldest young master of the Ding family had more money in hand and began to experiment with his candied hawthorns, putting a bean-paste stuffing inside, or a filling of black or white sesame paste, or inserting all kinds of dried or fresh fruit. The more he made, the better he got at them: he was endlessly inventive. Tianjin people had been eating candied fruit for many years, but they hadn't eaten anything like the exciting new candied hawthorns that the Beidaguan Ding was producing. And it was all most peculiar: he was just a rich young playboy, so where on earth could he have learned all this?

Even the other members of the Beidaguan Ding's family didn't know where the eldest young master had learned his skills. No one realised that it was from Wang Laowu, the former imperial chef – he'd watched every move he made when he was preparing candied hawthorn at his house. He'd noted exactly how to choose the fruit, remove the core, make the stuffing, boil the sugar syrup, add flavourings, cut the sticks, skewer the fruit, dip them in the enrobing and so on. At that time, he had no intention of using the art himself, and Wang Laowu was not shy about showing every detail of his technique to a rich young man. Ding Boyu was curious and asked all sorts of questions, which Wang Laowu answered in full. The highly skilled are always tight-lipped about their abilities, so Wang Laowu had no confidants in the capital. That meant that when he went to the senior young master's house out in Tianjin, he was ready to tell him everything – nothing was held back. The more Wang Laowu explained what he was doing, the prouder he became, until he'd told Ding Boyu every trick of the trade he'd taken an entire lifetime to learn. The eldest young master of the Ding family loved candied hawthorn, so of course he remembered everything he was told. Who could have imagined that Wang Laowu's slightest words all those years ago would now serve as weapons in the hands of the Beidaguan Ding?

The Beidaguan Ding used to eat candied fruit, but now he was making them. To eat them, all you need is a mouth, but to make them, you need a head on your shoulders. Once you start taking care, you can double your skill level. He began sourcing his hawthorns from Ji County up north, his jujubes from Zhangzhou and his skewers from Baiyangdian. Tianjin is a port city, so you can have whatever it is that you want. The Beidaguan Ding had eaten the kind of candied calabash enjoyed by the old Empress Dowager herself, and it is only because he knew exactly what they ought to taste like that he was able to produce them himself. Tianjin had a Foreign Concession, and you could buy foreign products there – and he knew exactly which things the foreigners made best. He started buying in white granulated sugar from Holland, which was not just deliciously sweet but also gave a really lovely translucent coating. It seemed as though each individual red fruit was suspended in a glass bubble. What would an ordinary hawker know about such refinements? During the Spring Festival, the Beidaguan Ding made unusually large candied hawthorn, and the fruit at the very top of the skewer was particularly big. In a nice touch, he used strips of candied peel, melon seeds and almonds to make this top fruit into a tiger's head, with a pair of grapes as eyes – it looked quite ferocious and was very cute. He called this kind of candied hawthorn a "Tiger Amid the Flowers". Tigers are powerful beasts, and they can ward off evil spirits in the New Year. People don't mind treating themselves to something expensive for New Year's. In a flash, Ding Boyu's candied fruit were famous throughout Tianjin. At first, Tiger Amid the Flowers were limited to three skewers per person. Later, it sold so well that anyone arriving late couldn't get even one.

The Beidaguan Ding was back on his feet again.

He grew up in and around the customs and knew how to behave. He would take the same route every day, starting from Zhenshi Street, passing through Guyi Street and Guodian Street in the east and Dahutong in the west. Every afternoon, he would appear at the same time. He would only fail to appear if it was windy, rainy or in the dog days of summer. Many rich people lived around the North Gate, and they were thinking of asking him to set up shop there, but he declined. He said he made a limited quantity every day, which was really just enough for his regular customers over on Guyi Street. His candied hawthorn had become famous when he was selling them on Guyi Street, and he would always be grateful to his regulars there.

As a result, you could find him every day on Guyi Street. When he got rich, his clothes got better too. His small skullcap was made to order from Russian cloth, and his jacket and trousers were scrupulously clean. His face was tanned, and his eyes glowed. He no longer had to tote about a wooden pole with the skewers stuck into it but hired someone to carry it for him. He strutted along in front with his chest puffed out, with a long-handled fly-whisk of speckled chicken feathers grasped in his right hand. Every time they arrived at the entrance to a small alleyway, he would shout down it: "Hawthorrrrrrrrrrrrrrrrrrn…!"

When Tianjin folk are hawking candied hawthorn, they never call out both words, just: "Hawthorrrrrrrrrrrrrrrrn…!"

Ding Boyu was a tall man with a rounded stomach, and he had a loud voice with lots of puff. With just one shout, his voice would go right to the end of the alley. If it was a dead end, his call of "Hawthorrrrrrrrrrrrrrrrn…!" would bounce off the wall at the end and come echoing back.

He always retained that bit of style from his days as *the* Beidaguan Ding.

Tianjin people were no longer in any position to despise him – they admired him instead. Individuals ought to be able to make a life for themselves, rich or poor. When you're rich, you should not waste your money, and when you're poor, you need to put your back into earning. If you can cope with being rich and with being poor, you're a real hero.

38
FOLLOWING THE PROCESSION

TODAY, just after dawn, Blockhead put two corn cakes under his arm and hurried off to the Temple of the Queen of Heaven outside the east city. In fact, he did not close his eyes all night, lying on the kang, waiting for dawn, the time passing ever more slowly the longer he waited. He was eighteen years old, and his father had finally agreed to let him go to the Imperial Festival. He'd never dared to agree before, for fear that Blockhead would just get himself into trouble. People were injured or killed every year in the festival crush. For this reason, the government had banned it many times. They would ban it, then allow it again, and having allowed it, they would then ban it for a bit. They banned it for fear of accidents and then allowed it again because they had to: having no festival at the Temple of the Queen of Heaven was like not being allowed to celebrate on New Year's Eve.

Tianjin is close to the sea, and many people there make a living on the ships, so they care more than somewhat about the

Queen of Heaven, who is also the Goddess of the Sea. The Goddess of the Sea can protect sailors. When out on those dark depths, lashed by the waves, it is all too easy for the boat to overturn. If that happens, everyone on board will be feeding the fishes. For this reason, when Tianjin folk eat fish, when they finish eating the top side and flip the fish over to eat the other, they will never speak of "turning it over". The expression "turning it over" is taboo. They will speak of "rowing it over" instead. The word "rowing" is used in the same sense as rowing your boat to shore. Ordinary men and women have their own way of dealing with the stresses that they face.

The birthday of the Goddess of the Sea is celebrated on the twenty-third day of the third lunar month every year, and Tianjin residents will hold a festival dedicated to the Queen of Heaven for this occasion. They burn incense and kowtow to the goddess for several days in a row, as well as take the statue of the goddess out of the temple and process all over the city, to bring good luck to one and all. The festival spreads out to a hundred streets and alleys in and out of the city walls, with everyone wanting to show off their talents at the fair, displaying unique skills and remarkable abilities, working as hard as they possibly can to be part of the celebrations. As long as this is going on, the merchants close the markets, and the families empty their houses – they vie with each other to view the spectacle, as the whole city celebrates.

The reason this was called an Imperial Festival is that, on one of his progresses through Jiangnan Emperor Qianlong passed by Tianjin. He was just in time to attend the festival at the Temple of the Queen of Heaven, and he was so delighted by the spectacle that he bestowed a yellow mandarin jacket, a gold necklace, and a double-sided dragon flag on each troupe that took part in the festivities. How can the common people be rewarded by the emperor? As soon as they were so favoured, they began to work even harder. From then on, they changed the name to make it the "Imperial Festival". The parades and performances got grander and more elaborate year on year. For the people who lived in Tianjin, if you didn't go to the Imperial Festival, you might as well be dead.

Blockhead's father was a doctor and was as cautious and careful in his private life as he was in the practice of his profession. In a father's eyes, his son will never grow up – let alone someone like Blockhead who was born stupid and dull. How could you possibly take someone like that to the Imperial Festival? However, this year, an acquaintance had happened to remind him that his son was over eighteen now, and that it was time to let him off the reins a bit, so that was why he was going to be allowed to attend.

But as soon as Blockhead got through the East Gate, he found himself wedged into a vast crowd. By the time he got to the square in front of the Temple of the Queen of Heaven, it was already daylight. The houses and shops around the square had been let out as dressing rooms for the troupes that would be performing, where they could wait their turn. The equipment and weapons that would be used by each troupe were all neatly stacked outside the door. All of them were antiques: flags, umbrellas, all manner of props, and all absolutely beautiful. As Blockhead jostled through the crowd, this was a real eye-opener for him.

Suddenly, a person appeared in front of him. This person was walking on stilts but moved as easily as if stepping on the flat.

Blockhead looked up and saw that it was a woman stilt walker, dressed in a white robe with blue flowers on it, her multi-coloured sash fluttering down, and a crown of pale pink roses on her head, which set off a mischievous little face with delicately flushed cheeks. Her well-defined eyebrows and limpid eyes, not to mention her cherry-red mouth, were all very beautiful. All of a sudden, she seemed to misstep because of something on the ground and stumbled. Her body tilted as if she were about to fall. Blockhead quickly took hold of her arm and steadied her. As she straightened up, she turned to him with a smile. It was a smile of thanks to him, but it seemed to come with some embarrassment. Blockhead was completely unsophisticated, so he just hung his head, blushing fiercely. By the time he looked up again, he could see many others standing high up on stilts all over the place, and he had no idea which one of them was the woman who'd nearly fallen just now.

The sun rose high into the sky, the drums sounded, and the atmosphere was solemn, for the procession was about to set off. The people in the square forged their way over to the Temple of the Queen of Heaven. If Blockhead had been in this main wave, he would have been carried along with them, even if he'd fought against the tide. But since he was far from the temple, he was stuck in the crowds and unable to move. He wasn't particularly tall, nor was he particularly strong, so while he was able to hear shouting up ahead and the sound of the drums, all he could see over the heads of the crowd were some flags, hanging lamps, the top of a palanquin and the spire of the pagoda, as the procession passed in front of him. The strangest thing was that a number of people came past carrying iron woks, huge and black, and spectators were constantly throwing coins at the woks – this was for good luck. The sound of the coins hitting the woks was like tinkling raindrops. Later on, he found out that when the Queen of Heaven set out on her tour of the city, the various troupes would go on ahead and lead the way.

Every year, the procession took a different route. Blockhead didn't know anything about it, so he just followed along with the crowd, with people pushing and shoving him from behind, as he moved forward through the throng. After a while, all this pushing and shoving forced him right to the front. All of a sudden, some men wearing yellow waistcoats and yellow turbans brought him up short against a fat yellow rope. A huge man with a tanned face and yellow clothes shouted at him: "Where do you think you're going? Back up!" The man was holding a triangular yellow flag which he waved at him, and on it were embroidered three words in black: "Yellow Dragon Troupe". Ah, so this was one of the troupes who'd been put in charge of keeping the road clear for the procession. At this time, the Yellow Dragon Troupe were apparently all-powerful, and everyone had to listen to them.

After that, he saw a series of performances that were beyond his wildest imaginings. There were theatrical troupes, acrobats, singers and dancers, and each one of them put forth their very best efforts as they passed by. Every time a new troupe appeared, it was a new experience. Their flags were different, their make-up was different, their performances were different, and the music was different. Where could you see such an amazing scene if not at the Imperial Festival? The performers were wonderful, and the audience was keenly attentive – and pretty soon, with fierce elbow-thrusts and strong-arm manoeuvres, they'd managed to get Blockhead pushed to the back where he could not see a thing.

Today, when the procession departed, it first headed north of the Temple of the Queen of Heaven. Blockhead was squeezed right up against the Flowery Brocade Lantern Shop. He didn't have the strength to fight his way to the front, and just as he was fretting about this, a voice said to him: "Do you want to come up here for a look-see? There's an empty place over there."

Blockhead screwed up his eyes; the speaker was a middle-aged man in a jacket that showed off a fine physique. The man grinned at him, his teeth brilliantly white. Tianjin has bad water, and there aren't too many people there with white teeth. He was pointing with his finger at a low wall, which provided a vantage point for four or five people to watch the procession. There was indeed a little empty space at this end. The wall wasn't very high, but Blockhead simply couldn't climb up it. So the man said: "I'll give you a leg-up."

Blockhead declined, but the man meant what he said. He went down on one leg, crossed his fingers with the palms of his hands facing up, cupping them against his thigh. He told Blockhead to put his foot in his hands. Blockhead just couldn't refuse, and he was lifted up into the air as if soaring into the sky, and with that one hoist he was able to clamber to the top of the wall.

To Blockhead's surprise, he now had a panoramic view of the procession going down the street in front of the Temple of the Queen of Heaven right before his eyes. When he suddenly thought that he ought to thank the man for his help, he'd already disappeared.

Except when viewed from a high vantage point, you could not possibly see the true magnificence of the procession. Stretching northward from the Temple of the Queen of Heaven, down this long, narrow and winding street, the troupes forming the festival procession made their way through the dark crowds in a colourful band, like a huge wriggling dragon. Standing up on high, he could see it all; he could even read the names of the various troupes written out on each set of flags. The cymbals wielded by the Liu family drum-troupe; the Buddhist statues and lampions held by members of the Buddhist benevolent association; the Heluo marching music played by the United Goodness orchestra; the "Song of Immortality" and the "Ode to Longevity" sung by the Eight Immortals of the Western Pool troupe. Blockhead felt that he didn't have enough eyes to see everything. When the Mustard Garden flower-drum troupe came past, they were carrying an elaborate floral arrangement the size of a palanquin, filled with brightly coloured flowers. Blockhead was amazed: how could there possibly be chrysanthemums, azaleas, lilies and peonies in flower now? Were these flowers artificial, or could they be real? He heard someone next to him say: "Don't just look – smell!" The voice was hoarse and thick.

Before he could take a breath, the intense fragrance of the flowers seemed to hit him in the face.

At this moment, he noticed the fat old man next to him for the very first time. He was over seventy, with a small jacket, and wore a cap with ear-flaps on his head. He was not standing but sitting on the wall. How on earth did he get up on the wall when he was so old? The old man remarked: "I come every year just for these people. To have such lovely flowers at this time of year, all in bloom just at the right moment… that's not something just anybody can achieve. Listen carefully, and you can hear that they've even got lots of insects chirruping around them…" Then he turned to Blockhead and said: "OK, I've seen what I came for. It is time to go home. Can you help me down?"

Blockhead was a simple soul: he wasn't thinking about how he would get up again if he jumped down from the wall. He just nodded to the old man and leapt down, and then helped the old gentleman to lower himself. He wasn't expecting that the old man would turn out to be heavier than a water tank, and when he took the weight, it almost knocked him over. Luckily, he was able to use his legs for balance and get the old man safely to the ground. The old man thanked him and then asked: "How many festivals have you been to?"

"This is my first time."

The old gentleman said with a smile: "I love going to festivals." Then he continued in a hoarse voice: "I'll tell you what to do. Here in Tianjin, we have a couple of hundred troupes, and nobody can possibly see everything. You just need to find a troupe that you like and follow on along with them. You go in whichever direction they go." The old man pointed in the direction of the crowd and said: "Here in Tianjin, there are rules about watching the procession. No matter how many people turn up, you aren't allowed to block the roads – there has to be a narrow passage left clear by the wall. You can walk along that. Right! It's time for me to go home and have something to eat – it's almost lunchtime."

How could it be noon already?

Blockhead thanked the old man for his advice and started moving along the wall. Suddenly, a group of people came out of a lane in the opposite direction. Heaven knows who they were or what they thought they were doing! They came rushing forward with great force and pushed him right into the middle of the road, throwing him onto his backside with a *whump*. The fall knocked him silly. When he'd pulled himself together a bit and looked around, all he could see in every direction were hopping stilts. Just as he was panicking, one of the stilt walkers reached down a hand and pulled him to his feet. Looking up, he realised that it was the same woman dressed in white who he had helped when she nearly fell over in front of the Temple of the Queen of Heaven.

What a coincidence! He helped her, and now she had helped him.

Right at that moment, the young woman dressed in white recognised him too. She pouted and then shyly moved away. Blockhead just stood there, his mouth hanging open, surrounded by all manner of characters twisting and turning on their stilts. One of the onlookers shouted at him: "Get away from there! That's Lady White Snake, Xu Xian's intended… you need to keep away from her!" There was a burst of laughter from the crowd. At that, Blockhead came to his senses and ran back, pressing his way through the crowd. Having found his way into a little alley, it was a good long while before he emerged again.

When he returned to the main road, the Imperial Festival was still underway, with one troupe after another performing. The stilt walkers had finished their turn and gone long ago. But for some reason, the only ones he wanted to see were the stilt walkers. He didn't know what the troupe was called, but he knew that they were performing "The Legend of Lady White Snake". He remembered what the old gentleman had said about following the procession, and he made up his mind: that was the troupe he wanted to see. They must be far ahead, but if he ran, he'd be able to catch them up. But when he was almost at the exit of North Street, he found that the road was blocked because a bunch of thugs were there beating each other up. He was hopping up and down with frustration in the crowd, but it was no good. Gradually, the sun started tilting towards the west: he'd left home before dawn, and now nearly a whole day had gone by.

Blockhead realised that his stomach was empty and his legs were feeling shaky. He quickly took out his corn cakes and ate them. Since his bladder was bursting, he found a latrine and afterwards sat down for a bit on a stone step. Gradually, he began to feel better and pulled himself together. Just at that moment, the crowds dispersed enough for him to make his way to one of the main roads. Since there was plenty of space, it was perfect for a troupe to perform. Through the vast crowd, he could see someone jumping about on stilts: it was Lady White Snake's troupe! He ran over but couldn't wriggle his way to the front. Luckily, they were hopping up high enough for him to make out what was going on at least some of the time. Far in the distance, he could see Lady White Snake jumping to the beat of the drums and gongs, like a little swallow darting through the clouds. She seemed to be dancing in the wind, flying through the air, to wave after wave of applause. She was absolutely wonderful!

They moved on past all the guild houses, then onto Youda Alley, through Guodian Street and onto Guyi Street, before heading to Zhenshi Street. These roads were lined with famous shops on both sides. The businessmen here had already been in touch with the masters of some of the most famous troupes, presenting them with certificates and gifts of money. They'd agreed that on the day of the festival, if asked to stop, the troupe would put on a show for them. According to the rules, when someone intercepts the procession, the whole troupe concerned has to stop; and having stopped, then the troupe has to give that person a really good show. That meant Blockhead got to see his fill of Lady White Snake.

From the comments of the onlookers, Blockhead not only learned that this particular troupe came from Gegu, but that their stilt walking was in the "Haixia" style, and he was even instructed in what each of the moves made by the girl playing Lady White Snake was called. Kneeling, squatting, throwing, jumping, turning, pouncing like a tiger; her moves were breathtaking, extraordinary, wonderful and elegant. In particular, he was amazed and impressed by her strong and lithe body as she twisted and turned. Blockhead simply could not get enough of watching her – and he kept walking with them all the way to the corner of Zhenshi Street.

By this time, it was already getting late, but the excitement of the festival was not yet over. The local troupes would follow the Queen of Heaven's procession in and out of the city walls until they went back to the temple; however, the many troupes from other counties would only go so far, and the majority would then leave. Of course, the stilt walkers from Gegu were one of the troupes that was planning to go home at this stage.

Blockhead kept on following on behind the troupe of stilt walkers as they headed off to the west, and the atmosphere gradually calmed down. Not far away, there was a little house built around a courtyard. When the Imperial Festival was underway, there were plenty of troupes from around and about that didn't have a base in Tianjin, so they would hire a house in the city for their props and what have you, as well as renting a few rooms for their people.

Blockhead watched them go into the small courtyard, sit on

high stools and untie their stilts. Then they clambered down from these high stools and sat around on some low seats. After walking on stilts for the whole day, it was obviously impossible for them to move for some time after untying themselves. They just sat there, drinking tea and smoking cigarettes, resting their legs and recovering. There were a few local women looking after them, who wandered in and out of the courtyard: they hung up their sweat-soaked costumes to dry on a line strung across the courtyard. They were spot-cleaning them with alcohol to remove the sweaty smell.

Blockhead did not dare to enter the courtyard, so instead he stayed hidden at the foot of an old willow tree outside, waiting for the woman in white to come out. He just wanted to see how lovely and amazing she looked with no make-up on; considering how gorgeous, charming, brave and fantastic she was when she was all dressed up.

He waited for everyone to come out one by one but didn't see her emerge. He was getting a little anxious.

Now the whole place was quiet and empty. When the old doorkeeper came out to lock up, Blockhead went over to him and asked: "Why I haven't seen the person who was playing Lady White Snake come out?"

The gatekeeper said: "Oh, they've already gone. They were the last out."

Blockhead was very surprised and said: "But the last person out was a tall, thin young man, very strong looking, in a green cloth coat."

"Exactly," the gatekeeper said.

Blockhead was even more surprised and said: "But that was a man! I'm talking about Lady White Snake – a girl!"

The gatekeeper was stunned and then said with a smile: "Our stilt troupe never has female members. The ones who play the female parts are all men dressed as women."

Blockhead was still reluctant to accept this and asked: "So what does he do?"

The gatekeeper said: "He's a sailor. You don't get such good balance except by standing on the deck of a rocking boat day after day."

Having finished his piece, the old man turned and went back through the door and closed it. Blockhead stood for a long time, totally confused, his head filled with the beautiful image of the girl from earlier in the day.

39

PETITIONING THE COUNTY MAGISTRATE

EAST of the Gegu vegetable market, south of the city, there lived a half-disabled man called He Laosan, who really was extraordinarily hideous to look at. He had a huge head with a broad forehead, a nose like an orangutan, the small, squinting eyes of a rodent, and below it all hung a wide, flaccid, toad-like mouth. It was impossible to tell how old he was: maybe forty or fifty? Underneath that enormous noggin was the body of a small child. He had tiny hands and feet, a small body and short little limbs, and when he stood behind the table, nobody could see where he was. This little body could not support the weight of that huge head, which wobbled as he walked. His voice was terrible as well: shrill and high-pitched. Just look at him! How in God's name could anyone look like that?!?

Some people commented that Wu Dalang, in the novel *The Plum in the Golden Vase*, looked not dissimilar. But Wu Dalang was married to the beautiful Pan Jinlian, while He Laosan was over forty and still hadn't managed to find himself a wife. Wu

Dalang supported his family by making sesame buns, but He Laosan could only make ends meet by going out and doing odd jobs. Locals did give him occasional work, not because he was capable, but because they felt sorry for him. He was orphaned at a very young age, and after that he was all by himself. As to why he was called "Laosan"… that ought to mean he had two older brothers, but if so, nobody had ever seen them. When his parents were alive, they looked after him, but once they were gone, there was nobody to care whether he lived or died.

However, He Laosan was a nice guy, and the people in the east of the vegetable market treated him pretty well. He appreciated that. He lived in a one-room shack, and when he was out of work, he would often pick up a boom and go out to sweep the street clean, keeping an eye on the kids playing outdoors and helping his neighbours round up any stray chickens. Although He Laosan was quite hideous, as time went by, everyone just got used to his appearance. And since he was such a sweetheart, people would leave him leftovers to eat or give him their old clothes to wear. Whenever this happened, the donors would just put the things down and leave because they did not want to see his grin of gratitude. He was even uglier when he smiled.

One day, after dinner, several of his neighbours were sitting around and chatting under the old willow tree out on the pavement. He Laosan stood off to one side, listening.

They talked about this and that, and then the conversation turned to a real head-scratcher:

Lots of folk lived in Gegu, and their houses were built higgledy-piggledy one on top of the other, so it was hard to avoid quarrels breaking out. Sometimes, people of quite incompatible tempers had ended up living next door to each other, and as time went on, there would be more and more conflict. And for all that there was conflict, you couldn't say these people hated each other or had any real cause for enmity... it was just that they didn't get along, and there was constant friction. Now what to do about it?

One person said that this wasn't a real crime like robbery or theft, nor did it count as them throwing their weight around and bullying, so it wasn't something you could complain about to the authorities. Then someone else said it would be great if there were an official who could mediate on problems of this kind on everyone else's behalf. But then officials have their own problems to deal with, and who can help them? Someone half-jokingly pointed out that for the festival of the Queen of Heaven every year in the spring, they ought to have a troupe in the procession where there was an "official" so if you had a problem, or if you were arguing with your neighbours, you could report to him and he'd deal with it on your behalf. But how could this pretend official fix anything? Everyone started arguing: they were all full of good ideas. To begin with, it was just a joke, but gradually they became more serious about it. The ideas they came up with would really have worked to fix the day-to-day problems ordinary residents experienced in getting on with their neighbours. But there was just one sticking point – who could possibly act as the pretend official?

When it came to choosing someone suitable for this official role, one suggestion after another was offered, but nobody wanted to do the job. Some simply didn't think they could do it right, others were afraid that everyone else would make fun of them, some didn't dare do such a thing, and some were afraid they'd just get into trouble if they tried. As this went on, the situation became more and more hopeless. Such a wonderful idea, but it was all going to come to nothing. It was just at this moment that He Laosan, who'd been there all along listening to them argue, suddenly spoke up: "I'll do it!"

The group of gossipers looked in the direction of the speaker, and they were first shocked into silence and then burst out laughing: this hideous creature wanted to be an official?

But when old Master Wan from main street spoke up, he made everyone agree that he had a point: "The whole idea right from the beginning was to achieve a good result by unorthodox means. The more unorthodox, the more unexpected, the more out of the ordinary, the likelier it is to be successful! I think He Laosan would be perfect for the job!"

His argument was not only well-reasoned; it spoke to the heart of the matter. Everyone now came together to sort this out properly. On the one hand, they were busy putting the ideas that they'd come up with when they were just chatting into some sort of order and making sure that all their wonderful plans were properly thought out. On the other hand, they were thinking about his clothing: they asked the finest tailor they knew – Master Hong – to make He Laosan a complete costume, a magistrate's uniform. Of course, this wasn't a real magistrate's robe but a theatrical costume; it was all about making a fine show. He Laosan was a pretty stumpy guy, so they would be able to save on the cloth; they could outfit him in about half of what an ordinary-sized person would need. So they put him in a black satin robe, with a multi-coloured mandarin square on his chest, and in among all the gold-thread work, instead of one of the regular symbols of rank, there was a brightly coloured turtle. He had pink-soled boots on his feet and a black gauze cap on his head, and on either side of his head there were two spring-mounted wing-like flaps, each in the shape of a coin, that waggled back and forth with every movement that he made. When He Laosan appeared in this get-up, an absolute roar of laughter went up. Some people laughed so much that they were literally rolling around on the ground, while others peed their pants.

From that day on, the community east of the vegetable market took He Laosan under their wing as they began to arrange and rehearse his performance. At the end of each day, if a couple of people found themselves with nothing to do, they'd call up He Laosan and put him through his paces. Since the time of the Yongle Emperor in the Ming dynasty, many different places in and around Gegu had produced decent troupes to perform at temple festivals, but the area east of the vegetable market was not one of them. Therefore, this community was generally agreed to lack talent. Now, however, they were going to show just what they could do, win themselves some face and bring glory to the whole of Gegu.

The following year, on the twenty-third day of the third lunar month, He Laosan joined the procession at the Temple of the Queen of Heaven. His performance was entitled "Petitioning the County Magistrate", and when he joined the festivities, he was placed between the Great Peace hobby-horse troupe and the Eternal Joy stilt-walkers. The procession consisted of troupe after troupe that would perform as they moved through the streets, but He Laosan only did his Petitioning the County Magistrate performance the one time. As all the other troupes danced and sang the whole way along the route, they arrived at the crossroads leading to Zhong Street. When the Great Peace group moved ahead, riding on their hobby-horses, and the Eternal Joy stilt-walkers paused, there was an empty space left between the two. The gongs then sounded, and the tall, thin and bald-headed master of the troupe stepped forward wearing a blue gown and announced: "We in the East Vegetable Market Festival Troupe will now perform Petitioning the County Magistrate." Then he stretched forward and bellowed: "Let those who have suffered unjust punishment come forward! Let the innocent who have been wrongly convicted step this way! His honour, the county magistrate, has arrived!"

When the crowds heard that, they were amazed. There'd never been a performance like this before: who were these people? What did they mean by Petitioning the County Magistrate? What magistrate? Who could this be?

Right before the eyes of the crowd gathered at the street corner, there appeared a man just half ordinary height but with an astonishingly huge head that wobbled as he walked! He was dwarfish and peculiar looking, hideous and bizarre of appearance. He looked like an official, but at the same time he didn't. His uniform was a costume. Who could this be? One of the sharp-eyed onlookers was the first to recognise He Laosan! And then a great cry went up: "He Laosan!" Immediately, everyone went into gales of laughter. It was not hard to recognise him for all that he was dressed up in this peculiar garb, and he was just wearing the same small patch of white make-up around the eyes that you see on clown characters in Chinese opera. He didn't need anything else to make him funny; he was comic enough to begin with! What on earth was he doing dressed up like this? Was he going to perform the part of a magistrate, and if so, which one?

People were even more surprised to learn that He Laosan, who had always been so peculiar in appearance, could actually act. Who had taught him to do that? Or had he somehow become possessed by the God of Theatre? They watched him take a step forward, his head wobbling and shaking, then he swung his waist and twisted his hip, jumping from his left foot to his right, both hands resting all the while on his belt. As he danced, the coins on either side of his black gauze hat waggled up and down as if to the beat of the drum and the banging of the gongs. As they watched him move his hands and his feet, each gesture was perfectly controlled. The entire crowd just stood there and gawped.

Then He Laosan started to speak in his high-pitched and shrill voice. Every word was carefully enunciated, and each line came out with a theatrical lilt:

"Today, I have come to Gegu to deal with the grievances of the general public and to combat injustice. If anyone is unhappy, if anyone is suffering distress, let them come forward and offer their petition to me, the county magistrate, and I will fix it right away."

As soon as the sound of his voice died away, a man ran up and knelt down in front of He Laosan, saying that his neighbour – the butcher Ma Dadao – had a son who was always throwing his weight around, and just that day he'd forced the man's daughter to kiss him. He went to find Ma Dadao to complain, but instead of punishing his son, Ma Dadao just said: "My son is only twelve years old, and your daughter is nine. What does it matter if he kisses her?" He didn't dare get in a quarrel with Ma Dadao, but he was still furious about this insult more than a year later, and he couldn't put up with it a moment longer.

He Laosan immediately gave orders for Ma Dadao to be brought before him. Having questioned him as to the truth of the matter, He Laosan made his judgment: "Although your son is still small, you must not let him get away with this kind of behaviour. If he carries on like this, he'll be assaulting the local girls when he grows up!" Then he raised his voice and declared: "When a child is badly brought up, it is the parents' fault. Take this man away and lock him up. His punishment is to be kept confined for half a day!"

Ma Dadao still wanted to argue his case, but He Laosan turned his head away and ignored him. Ma Dadao was strong, but the four men who came up to take him away were even stronger, and they were easily able to remove him from the scene.

So he was dragged off, and apparently he really was kept confined in one of the nearby houses. For half the day, nobody saw hide nor hair of Ma Dadao, and he wasn't out there raising a rumpus. Was He Laosan really that competent? Could it possibly be true that he was now the county magistrate?

But who could have imagined that Ma Dadao was enjoying himself enormously as he was locked up – it was so much more comfortable and more fun than wandering around outside. There was a feast laid on for him of fish, shrimp, meat and wine; and the men who brought him in were all part of the Petitioning the County Magistrate troupe. When they got inside, they lit Ma Dadao's cigarette for him and poured him some tea, chatting really politely, playing cards with him and letting him win. They tried everything to keep him from leaving, but he didn't want to go: there was good food and drink here, and he was having a whale of a time. When it was all over, Ma Dadao told anyone who would listen that if he'd been locked up like that for two weeks, he'd have gained ten pounds!

Ma Dadao was happy to pretend that he'd been locked up, and the plaintiff against him was happy to win. From then on, all their grievances disappeared, and they got along together just fine.

Now people realised just how impressive this performance was: it was kind of a joke, all done for fun, just make-believe, but it was nevertheless able to fix problems in everyday life, and that was much more impressive than anything a real government official could do. From then on, the community east of the vegetable market had to be taken seriously: Petitioning the County Magistrate made them famous throughout Gegu. Every year on the twenty-third day of the third lunar month, Petitioning the County Magistrate was an indispensable part of the festival for the Queen of Heaven.

He Laosan was the backbone of their troupe. Although there was only ever one performance of Petitioning the County Magistrate each year, the plaintiff was different, and they would be complaining about all manner of things... but whatever it was, he could fix it. He was never biased or partial but always scrupulously fair and just. In the eyes of the people of Gegu, He Laosan was not only a good official, making decisions to benefit ordinary folk and relieving all the many and various sources of discord among them, but also a natural clown that they all loved deeply. He was ugly, but there was a beauty in his ugliness.

But later, a most unexpected development occurred. There was a county magistrate from some other part of the country who was appointed to serve in Tianjin, and he'd heard all about the wonderful performances put on for the festival of the Queen of

Heaven at Gegu. When he saw the troupe performing Petitioning the County Magistrate, he suddenly looked sombre and said: "I am the county magistrate – what does this mean?"

One of the local officials made haste to explain: "They aren't complaining about you – this performance is all about making petitions, hoping that you will help people!"

This was tantamount to saying that the new county magistrate was only in it for himself. His honour was even more unhappy about that, and he took out his ill humour by complaining about something else: "How can a magistrate possibly look so hideously ugly? And his mandarin square has a turtle on it!"

As he spoke, he hefted himself to his feet and went off to find his palanquin, heading back to the city.

That was all it took to put an end to the performance of Petitioning the County Magistrate at the festival to the Queen of Heaven at Gegu. Nobody ever saw He Laosan there again either.

40
BIG CROTCH

THERE WAS this young guy who lived over in Dashuigou. I don't know his personal name, but his surname was Hou, and he was nicknamed "Monkey". Monkey really did look rather simian with his sharp face and slightly protuberant eyes, shrivelled mouth and sagging cheeks. He was as thin as a rake and always up to tricks. He spent the whole day wandering around at leisure, but the thing he liked best of all was playing nasty practical jokes on people so he could show them up. For a while, he'd been up to his usual fun and games with some sleight-of-hand tricksters over at the Sancha market, and he'd racked his brains for ways to get even with them, pulling all manner of horrible stunts. He'd called in a couple of useless layabouts from other parts to help; they'd order up food and wine, put up a bit of a bluff while goofing around, and then they'd cause a scene, smashing the place up before walking out without paying.

However, there are all kinds of people who live in and around the Sancha estuary; some are real gangsters and some

fine martial artists, but plenty of them are just pretending. The fakes you can find everywhere; those with real skills are hidden away. And there were three individuals there making a living by sleight-of-hand tricks whereby no matter how much Monkey struggled, he just couldn't get a hang of what it was they were up to. People said that Monkey was put on earth to show folk like that up, but when it came to this trio, he was left behind in the dust – it would be hard to say who was showing up whom.

The first of these three men was Mitts Liu. He specialised in the one trick: a kind of shell game. He had two white porcelain bowls and five transparent glass marbles. When he slipped the marbles under the small bowls, it was simply impossible to work out how many were under each bowl. Nobody could guess the right answer, and whatever combination they tried, they guessed wrong; Mitts Liu could put whatever number under whichever bowl he liked. No matter how obvious it might seem that the marbles were under this bowl, with a quiver of Mitts Liu's fat face, they would all shift to the other one.

The sleight-of-hand tricks performed by the inhabitants of the Sancha estuary region were all "open-air". This was not easy at all because they had to perform without props, with onlookers standing around on all four sides, with eyes watching from in front and behind, to left and right – the slightest mistake would be spotted immediately. However fast you move, you cannot outwit the watching crowd. But Mitts Liu had hands that were faster than anyone could see.

But no matter how nimble he was, he wasn't as quick-witted as Monkey.

One day, just as Mitts Liu was performing his act, Monkey

emerged from the crowd and walked straight to the centre of the arena, where he squatted down on the ground. He told Mitts Liu to put the two little bowls about three metres away, one to the left and the other to the right side of his body. Then he told Mitts to put three marbles under the bowl on his left side and two marbles under the bowl on his right. Mitts Liu did exactly as he was told. When that was done, Monkey said to Mitts: "Do you think you can swap the marbles under the two bowls around so that there are two on the left and three on the right?"

As he said that, he giggled because he was expecting that Mitts Liu wouldn't bite; he'd have to admit failure and accept a public humiliation.

The crowd thought that Monkey had made an excellent move here. He was sitting there, right in the middle between the two bowls – no matter how clever Mitts might be, he couldn't possibly move the marbles across.

But nobody was expecting that Mitts Liu would just laugh and say: "Since you've got the marbles in your pocket, how can I possibly be expected to shift them about?"

Nobody understood what he was talking about, Monkey least of all. He put his hand into his pocket and then took it out again – the five marbles had indeed been slipped into his jacket pocket. He was puzzled. The whole time he and Mitts Liu had been three metres or so apart – how could the marbles possibly have made their way into his pocket? He was trying to get at him on purpose!

The crowd started laughing. Monkey had embarrassed himself. He picked up his feet and ran off, never to appear anywhere near Mitts Liu again.

The second was Rope-Trick Li. His was a very simple trick: just a length of fine red rope, about a metre long, but putting it in the hands of Rope-Trick Li was like putting it in the hands of a god. It appeared and disappeared in the blink of an eye, twisting and turning, transforming itself this way and that. He'd throw the rope straight up into the air, but it wouldn't come down again. Where could it possibly have gone? He'd say it had been taken away by the seven fairy maidens. But then as he was walking around his performance area, complaining about how the seven fairy maidens had been stealing his stuff, all of a sudden he'd lower his head and spot the rope on the ground. He'd bend over, pick up one end of the rope and then raise the whole length – this was indeed his red rope. Then he'd say: "The seven fairy maidens must have told Earth Traveller Sun to bring my stuff back."

You had to admire him for it; he was performing right there in broad daylight, with everyone watching him.

One day Monkey turned up with a shiny pair of scissors in his hand. Reaching out, he grabbed the rope out of Rope-Trick Li's hands. Then with a couple of snips, he cut it into bits and then put them into his mouth and swallowed them down in a few gulps. Right, what was Rope-Trick Li going to do about that? Rope-Trick Li just stood off to one side, not saying a word. Then suddenly, he pinched his fingers together behind Monkey's left ear and started to pull – bit by bit, he pulled the whole red rope out, completely undamaged. That put Monkey in his place! Ever afterwards, he gave Rope-Trick Li a very wide berth.

As for the third man, his name was not very nice – Big Crotch.

Nobody seemed to know his real name; everyone called him by this nickname. He was a tall man with a long face, who went about dressed in a fine cotton robe in summer, and a long padded coat in winter, buttoned up to his neck and reaching right down to the ground, with long sleeves that fell over the wrists. He spoke with a Shandong accent; the moment you heard him speak, it was obvious he'd come to Tianjin from elsewhere. Big Crotch lived in Beidaguan without any family or friends – he was all on his own. People said that the reason he didn't have any family was that all his earnings came from sleight-of-hand; he could make enough to feed himself, but not a wife or kids. The reason he didn't have any friends is that sleight-of-hand is all about the know-how, and he didn't want anyone else to see what he was up to. When he set off to perform, he didn't bring any props with him, just his long robe. But you should not underestimate it – that robe had all kinds of things tucked away inside it. If he was hungry, he could magic up a stuffed bun or piece of fruit, or a big bowl of spicy noodles out of thin air, while if he was thirsty, he would conjure up a pot of hot tea. If it started raining, he'd produce an oiled-paper umbrella and head off home, keeping dry underneath.

How could he possibly be pulling all of these things out from his robe? Where on earth could be hiding these things – in his crotch? That was how Big Crotch got his name.

One day, Big Crotch was performing, when all of a sudden, one of the local traders started loudly hawking their fish. That produced a response from him: "Fish is good for you... Let us have one too, and a live one at that!" As he said that, he bent over and felt under his robe, and then with both hands he pulled out a big, round, shining goldfish-bowl, filled with clear water, and inside there was indeed a big goldfish swimming back and forth! That gave everyone around the Sancha estuary pause. From that day on, whenever he was performing, there was always a vast crowd packed many deep around him. And every day when it was time for him to pack up, the crowds would only disperse after he'd magicked up a bowl of water with a live goldfish swimming in it out from under his robe.

All this meant Monkey went on the warpath. After thinking for seven days and nights, Monkey finally came up with a peculiar – and peculiarly nasty – trick. He caught a one-eyed stray cat and starved it for three days in his house, until it was so hungry its eye was shining with a blue light. Then he took it over to the Sancha marketplace. Spotting Big Crotch in full flow, he sneaked up behind him, and while he wasn't paying attention, he slipped the starving one-eyed stray down the back of his robe. What followed next was that Big Crotch's padded coat bounced hither and yon, as if he had half a dozen rabbits hopping about underneath it. Heaven only knows what was going on under there... but Monkey was cackling away to himself: with the cat being so hungry, wouldn't it be making a nice meal for itself of the live fish?

But just at this moment, Big Crotch looked down at his trousers and said: "I think my audience would like a nice hot brazier to keep warm by... what are you making all of this fuss for?" As he said this, he reached under his coat and pulled the cat out from inside. Its fur was completely coated in ash, and it scampered away, whimpering.

Big Crotch laughed heartily and then bent down to grab something else out from under the cotton-padded robe. But this time, it was no live fish; it was a big charcoal brazier scattering sparks! Big Crotch said: "This weather is so cold, so I'd like to invite you all to move closer to the warmth. I wouldn't like anyone to freeze while they're standing around…"

The charcoal brazier was burning well, with flames a foot long shooting out. How could something like this be possibly carried under his robe? Big Crotch laughed and looked back to see if he could spot Monkey, wanting to say something in his moment of triumph, but Monkey was already long gone.

This performance resulted in a scholar from the old city commemorating the occasion in verse:

> *Braziers and fish bowls are easy for him to hide.*
> *Even gods and spirits seem to halt by his side.*
> *His tricks and teases will ne'er be forgot.*
> *What a remarkable man is our Big Crotch!*

Big Crotch was originally his nickname, but now it became a famous stage name.

But this time, Monkey did not accept defeat. In the case of Mitts Liu or Rope-Trick Li, these were men of great ability who worked with simple things, but Big Crotch was just working the space under his robe, wasn't he? It was obvious to one and all that the things he pulled out were concealed about his person. He would have loved to just rip Big Crotch's coat off him in public and reveal to everyone what was under there – that would show him! He thought about it for a long time, and suddenly he came up with a great idea. He would climb up onto the roof of his house and take off some of the tiles so he had a peephole from which he could see everything: then he'd know. So while Big Crotch was off performing by the Sancha market, Monkey rushed round to Beidaguan and climbed secretly onto the roof of Big Crotch's house, right up onto the ridge. Then he removed a couple of the tiles to make a hole. When it started to get dark, as normal, Big Crotch made his way home dressed in his heavy coat. He sat down for a rest, but his rest seemed to go on and on and on. By this time, Monkey had already been sitting up on the ridge of the roof for two hours in the greatest discomfort, given that the tiles were so bumpy and his arse was so bony. He was just about to give up when suddenly Big Crotch stood up and started taking off his clothes.

Monkey was thrilled; he thought that he was about to see through the mystery, but who could have imagined that having undone the buttons on his coat, Big Crotch would just toss it aside like a rag, without the slightest concern. Underneath, he was just wearing a regular coarse cotton shirt and trousers – there was absolutely nothing else under there! Monkey thought he must be seeing things: that was the only possible explanation for why Big Crotch wasn't hung about with a million different items for his show!

The shock almost had Monkey rolling down off the roof. He didn't care any more about whether he would make a noise with his feet – he scrambled down and made off to the sound of the breaking of tiles, scared that Big Crotch would chase after him and catch him.

Many years later, long after the events described above, Big Crotch retired and moved back to his old home in Shandong Province. Monkey was chatting with an old buffer who lived up in the north part of town and knew what was what, and happened to mention this story because it still bothered him. He simply couldn't understand it.

The old buffer grinned and explained just exactly what had been going on there. As he said: "Actually, Big Crotch was putting on a performance for you that day – he knew that you were up on the roof peeping in. He gave you a really fine show, all to yourself, and you ought to be grateful to him for that."

41
LI'ER

LI'ER WAS Stammerer Liu's daughter.

Stammerer Liu's real name was Liu Ba. People called him Liu Ba to his face and Stammerer Liu behind his back.

Stammerer Liu's wife was long gone, and so he lived with his daughter, Li'er. He had a little snack place near the Sancha junction between the river and the Grand Canal, where he made just the one dish: *guobacai* – thick green bean flour pancakes served with a rich, spicy sauce. People secretly called his *guobacai* "Stammerer pancakes".

Liu Ba's stammer was so bad that all the greeting of customers and hospitality was done by Li'er.

Ever since she was a little girl, as soon as she was big enough to see over the top of the tables, Li'er had helped her father wash up and clean their shop, moving the tables and chairs, and serving the customers. This had kept her busy right up to the age of nineteen, and she was still working hard. Nowadays, though, she was working towards a goal – saving up for her dowry.

Mr Guo the schoolmaster, who lived next door, had seen what a splendid girl Li'er was: hardworking, careful and honest – and he'd fixed her up with his son. Mr Guo knew that Liu Ba wasn't at all well-off, and so he wasn't expecting him to spend any money on the wedding, but what girl goes to her marriage without something in her bottom drawer? So she was doing her best and making every effort to earn a bit of money for herself.

Liu Ba's little snack shop stood at the intersection of two small streets by the river. It was the sort of place where people came and went, so it was just right for his business. He just had the one room, and then outside there was a shed in which he kept his pots and pans, and then there were a few tables and benches: a perfectly normal little eatery. In the summer, you could eat outside; in the winter, he'd hang up heavy awnings to keep the cold wind out, and then it was a fine little snack shop.

When you make *guobacai*, you take your pancakes and chop them into chunks, serving them with various toppings. However, Tianjin people care about their snacks – they may not be expensive, but they've got to be good. Liu Ba's little eatery didn't even have a name, but with customers coming and going the whole day, he got almost no free time. There was a constant stream of boatmen and porters coming in from the river; they'd be hungry and want to have a bowl of *guobacai*, piping hot, ready to eat, rich and spicy. And having eaten their fill, they'd be on their way again.

One day, two men wearing long robes turned up. It was very rare for customers dressed like that to eat at little snack shops such as this. They were very smartly dressed, they looked delicate and refined, and their every gesture was elegant. This kind of refinement isn't something you can learn; and the tall, thin one was particularly outstanding, with his handsome face and gentle smile, as he constantly looked around him, as if everything was fascinatingly new. Maybe they were some kind of businessmen? No, they didn't look right for that – businessmen in this part of town were big, hearty types. How about educated gents? That was more like it: that tall thin one had a silk fan in his hand, with sticks made of sandalwood, which he kept opening and closing – there was a poem written out on one side, and a painting on the other... all very elegant.

When these two men came in, they chose one of the tables outside the shop. Li'er immediately dashed over like a little bird and asked them what they wanted to eat. The man holding the fan looked up at Li'er, and his eyes lit up. She was the kind of girl people liked at first sight. She might not have been from a grand family, and she certainly wasn't the delicate kind brought up in the lap of luxury. Nor did she rely on powder and paint, and she wasn't fabulously good-looking or striking in appearance, but she was really sweet-looking and cute, like a flower or a slender sapling, like a baby bird or bunny rabbit. Working hard every day the way that she did, she was neither thin nor feeble; exposed to the sun and the wind, her cheeks had a ruddy glow. Growing up under her father's wing, she was a good and obedient girl, and when she dealt with customers, she was friendly and good-natured. Looking at her, she was a real Tianjin girl. But with her slightly slanted eyes, tip-tilted nose and pointed chin, she had something of the look of a Jiangnan beauty. People said that her mother originally came from Yangzhou.

Li'er was wearing a rough-weave dress tied with a belt, her waist cinched by a faded red cloth band. Her coal-black hair was braided and wound round her head, pinned in place by a "hairpin" that was actually a branch of flowering peach. However, this possessed a pure, natural beauty that all the gold and silver hairpins in the world could not rival.

As soon as the two customers had ordered, Li'er immediately brought out their *guobacai*. The man holding the fan asked her: "Miss, I can see you get a lot of customers here, and everyone wants different things. How on earth do you remember all of their orders without getting confused?"

"Dad says that if you pay attention, you don't get confused," Li'er told him.

The man with the fan nodded and said: "He's quite right." Then he ate a mouthful and continued: "Your *guobacai* is very good – much better than what I got to eat last time in the city."

"That's because Dad is really careful," Li'er said. "You have to get the batter just right, and then the pancakes must be cooked until they are crisp but not burned. Dad is also really particular about choosing the spring onions, greens and chilli peppers that he puts in… if anything's not perfect, I'll go and tell him."

"That's a lot of work for your father. He puts in a great deal of effort just to make this one dish!"

"Dad says that it may not be expensive, but you've still got to get the flavour just right. If you skimp, then you're cheating your customers." Having said that, Li'er turned away with a smile.

This conversation deeply impressed the man holding the fan. Clearly, there were some really good people out there.

After a while, when they had finished eating, the man holding the fan asked his companion for twenty coppers, which he put down on the table. Li'er came past to clear their bowls and collect the money, but when she saw how much was there... it was ten times what two bowls of *guobacai* cost! She hastily waved her red, work-roughened hands at them, telling them that they'd paid far too much. The man with the fan insisted that she take it, and he turned around, ready to walk away. Li'er felt that she had no choice but to call for her dad.

Who would have guessed that when Liu Ba arrived on the scene, he too would wave the money away? He stammered, and the more stressed he became, the more he wanted to say, and the more difficult it was for him to get a word out. The man with the fan suddenly asked Liu Ba: "I heard you call your daughter Li'er, but obviously that's just a nickname. What's her real name?"

Liu Ba could only shake his head.

Whenever it happened that Liu Ba couldn't speak, it was Li'er who spoke on his behalf. She now said: "I don't have a proper name. I'm just called Li'er."

"Well, it is a very unique name – a grain of rice. Why are you called that?"

Li'er frowned; it seemed that the question troubled her. However, since he was asking nicely, she felt she had to answer. It transpired that her birth had been difficult. Her mother hadn't had enough to eat, and so she didn't have any energy – it seemed as though the infant would suffocate inside her mother's womb. Fortunately, her father had saved some rice scraped from the bottom of the pan, and he'd stuffed that into her mother's mouth; that was how she was able to give birth. However, her mother died immediately afterwards. Her father was so grateful to the rice that had saved her life that he named her that: Li'er.

When she got to that part of the story, her voice became choked, and she started to cry.

The man holding the fan was moved, and he said to Liu Ba: "What a lovely girl your daughter is! I'd like to make her my god-daughter. I know that you don't want to take the money I've offered today, so I'll take it away. But if in the future you ever get into difficulties, come and find me. I live in the capital."

"But the capital is huge," Li'er said. "How can we find you?"

The man with the fan thought for a moment and then said with a smile: "Go and find the building on top of the tallest flight of steps in the city, because that is where you will find me. If the people at the gate won't let you in, then you must show them this fan, and they will be sure to let you in." He handed his beautiful fancy fan to Li'er as he said this.

With that, the two men said goodbye and left.

It sounded like a joke, but the fan she held in her hand was very much real. A close look at the sticks revealed that they were exquisitely carved, inlaid with ivory and jade – an extraordinary piece. Who were these two people? They seemed to be very rich, but why would someone like that come to a little snack stall and eat *guobacai*? And why on earth would such a person be willing to make a poor girl like Li'er his god-daughter? There was nobody they could ask for help. Neither of them could read, so they couldn't understand what was written on the fan. They didn't dare tell anyone else about these peculiar events, not even the father of Li'er's intended – Mr Guo the schoolmaster. All they could do was put the fan somewhere safe and decide what to do about it later on.

A year passed, and Li'er still wasn't married and still hadn't managed to get her dowry together. After some discussion, the two of them decided to go to the capital to look for Li'er's nameless godfather. They were quite clear about their goal: to find the building on top of the highest flight of steps. But when they got to the capital, they wandered around for three days, getting themselves completely lost and confused. How were they to find the house on the tallest steps? Li'er was a clever girl, and she said: "Dad, we've got to count the steps. If we don't count them, how are we to know which building is up at the top of the tallest flight?"

So the two of them counted steps all over the capital for the next seven days, and then they finally found themselves outside a huge mansion with a magnificent stairway leading up to it. A bunch of soldiers were standing on guard by the gate, armed with guns and swords. Liu Ba looked at the building and said with a sigh: "Woah! This looks like the sort of… sort of… place that an emperor lives."

Li'er wasn't afraid; she was there looking for her godfather, so she felt she had nothing to worry about. She walked over to one of the guards and said that she wanted to see her godfather. When she explained, it seemed that she might have a point; on the other hand, she could easily just be some loon. The guard didn't know what she was talking about, so she took out the fan – that was evidence that her story was true. The soldiers by the gate took the fan, asked her where she was staying in the city, and told her to go back there and wait.

The two of them waited until the afternoon of the third day at the little inn they were staying in, but there was no news. When they came back from eating lunch, the innkeeper came up and asked them what they had got up to in the capital. It turned out that four officials had just been there looking for them; they didn't say anything, but they looked pretty aggressive.

Li'er and her father had never been in trouble with the law, so when they heard this, they started shaking and went cold all over. Neither of them had liked much how the man had decided to become her godfather the year before, and they worried that something bad might have happened. They decided to leave straight away and go back to Tianjin.

The capital is more than two hundred *li* from Tianjin. Not daring to hire a carriage, they walked back. They didn't travel on the main roads either, but down little side tracks. That meant that they did not get home for three days. When they arrived, their neighbours told them that people had come out from the county yamen looking for them the day before. They'd said that if anyone saw them, they should report it immediately. Liu Ba wondered if there was a warrant out for their arrest. Their neighbours asked what it was that they'd done, and they couldn't answer. It wasn't just that Liu Ba was stammering so badly that he couldn't get a word out, Li'er couldn't explain either. Anyway, when you get into trouble with the law, there will never be an end to it. The situation was very scary, and in the circumstances the best they could do was to run away.

Liu Ba pointed out that it is easy enough for one person to hide, but hiding two together is difficult. Li'er had a cousin who was a Buddhist nun in a nunnery over on the west side of the city – the place was surrounded by water on all four sides and very quiet. He thought that Li'er should go there to hide for a bit while he went to stay with a distant relative over in Lutai Village.

That was not the end of it all. Apparently, one day, all of a sudden, a group of officials turned up at the little nunnery over on the west side of the city, with a banging of drums and a sounding of gongs. Right by the gate, they put up a ladder and hoisted up a wooden plaque, with gold letters on a dark ground, reading: "Abode of the Imperial Lady." The calligraphy was very formal and impressive. And what does "Imperial Lady" mean? That's a title used by the sister of the reigning emperor. They'd brought a palanquin with them, and one of the officials shouted that his majesty had sent them to collect Li'er and bring her to the capital.

No one understood a word of this.

As soon as the temple door had creaked open, a shaven-headed nun of about forty came out, dressed in a plain Buddhist robe. It was not Li'er. She explained that she was all on her own in this nunnery. The girl called Li'er had stayed with her for a few days, but then her father had come to collect her. Heaven alone knew where he'd taken her.

Ever afterwards, the little nunnery was known as the "Abode of the Imperial Lady". A plaque given by the emperor could hardly be taken away again. But gradually, everyone forgot about who this "Imperial Lady" might be.

42
CUI FAMILY FIRECRACKERS

WHEN IT COMES to fireworks and firecrackers, you could get good ones from Shangli, Pingxiang, Liuyang and Liling. As a port city, Tianjin gets goods coming and going, and you could certainly find fireworks from all these different places there. However, Tianjin people don't buy fireworks from other parts of the country – they only use their own. Tianjin's own fireworks can really put the stars in your eyes; Tianjin's own firecrackers went off with a report like a foreign gun. Making firecrackers is a dangerous business and was banned from the old city and anywhere with lots of residents – you had to make them out in the villages in the middle of nowhere. As to the best village for fireworks, absolutely everyone knew that it was the Cui Family Village in Yanerzhuang Township, Jinghai County.

 Everyone who lived in Cui Family Village had the surname Cui. It was an old village, but very few people lived there. Half of them had been killed through being blown up making fireworks. The survivors were tough as anything; they risked

their lives every day, after all – a real bunch of heroes. This situation came about because firecrackers are so dangerous. Those who make firecrackers are up for anything, and that is how they can cope.

Black Cui was the best firework maker in Cui Family Village. His ancestors had worked out long ago that the dazzlingly white saltpetre that crystallised on the ground out in the wilds could be scraped up and used to make gunpowder with the addition of some charcoal and sulphur. The explosives his family made could be used for mining or blasting rocks, and everyone called these things Cui Family Firecrackers.

Black Cui had three sons. When his second son was sixteen years old, he was lying on a pile of big rockets out in the courtyard having a siesta, when all of a sudden the whole lot of them exploded for no reason at all. His second son was killed on the spot, ripped to pieces by the blast.

That left Black Cui with two sons: the eldest and the youngest. At this time, his eldest was thirty and still single; nobody would marry him for fear of being blown up and killed. The whole house was coated in gunpowder, and the air was filled with saltpetre. How could you not be scared? Black Cui was so dark-skinned because of all the explosions he'd been in. His third son was only thirteen and disabled. When he was little, Black Cui had been repairing the roof. In a moment of carelessness, he'd dropped his axe, and when it hit a stone on the ground, it gave off a spark. That spark had set off a half-bag of gunpowder at the foot of the wall, destroying half the house and injuring his third son's right ear and his leg. Black Cui's third son was left with two different disabilities: he was deaf in one ear and walked with a limp.

Firecracker makers only do two things: they produce firecrackers and they sell them. Selling their firecrackers is the more important. That is because they are the only people who can really understand how to bring out the best in their own firecrackers, so they can get a good price for them. Black Cui was getting on a bit, so he kept an eye on the manufacturing process, while selling them was entirely left up to his two sons. Every year in the run-up to New Year's, his youngest son would go to the market to sell his wares, while his oldest son headed off to Fushen Street, near the Temple of the Queen of Heaven in Tianjin.

To know how powerful the Cui family's firecrackers were, and how amazing these men were, all you had to do was look at how the two brothers sold their products. From the outside, you would never have guessed that the two of them shared a mother: the oldest brother looked like a tiger, his younger sibling like a cat. But when it came to selling their firecrackers, it is hard to say who was the better.

In the last month of the year, there would be a fair every three days in Jinghai County. On fair days, the residents of Cui Family Village would carry the finished firecrackers out of their homes and pile them onto a cart, which would be covered with a red cotton quilt to ward off evil spirits. They would move these carts to the bank of the Qinglong River, outside the village, and halt on the high embankment, lined up under a row of old willow trees. The Qinglong River flows into the Ziya River, and in the autumn the waters there dry up. This riverbed, frozen hard, was the site of the firecracker market. Each family would take their own firecrackers, run down the side of the embankment, and then set them off on the riverbed, competing with one another so that each made a bigger bang than the last. The people who'd come out to buy would stand on the top of the embankment, watching and making their selection. There were merchants trading in fireworks and firecrackers from all over the place in among the crowd. It was like watching a play.

Yanerzhuang Township was the most famous of all the makers of firecrackers in Jinghai County. There were at least twenty or thirty firework-making villages within its purlieus, and at this time every year they all brought out their works to the banks of the Qinglong River to compare and sell. When it came to making comparisons of firecracker quality, you had to admire them. There would be some young guys with individual rockets tucked separately under their belts, and a long pole in their hand, from the top of which a long string of bright red mini-firecrackers hung down. The pole would be a couple of metres long, and when the fuse was lit, they'd run down the side of the embankment shouting at the tops of their voices, waving the pole about so that the long string of firecrackers danced through the air like a St Catherine's wheel: exploding with endless reports, spitting out smoke and flying scraps of paper. When they'd run to the middle of the river, they would continue waving the pole about and shouting up into the sky, each one braver than the last. Their performance, waving the pole about as the firecrackers exploded, was not just about showing off; they were demonstrating that the gunpowder used in their family's firecrackers was sound. It was only if each and every mini-firecracker went off properly that the whole string would go in one.

At this time, as soon as the third son of the Cui family appeared, everyone would quiet down and wait for him to show his unique skills. They'd also – quite unconsciously – make sure to plug the cotton in their ears a bit tighter. The Cui family's firecrackers were guaranteed to make your ears ache. The crowd that came to Qinglong River firecracker market, even the animals who pulled the carts, all had large lumps of cotton wool stuffed in their ears.

The third son of the Cui family did not look in the least like a hero. He was under five feet tall and very thin. He wore a long cotton-padded robe, very thick and soft. He looked like a cat, and a pretty sick moggy at that, with his little grey peaky face and dull, small eyes. He had a felt hat on his head, supplemented by ear-muffs, and the fur lining of the muffs poked out in long thick strands. Unlike the other participants of the fair, he did not scream or shout but just walked slowly out to the middle of the riverbed and set off a string of firecrackers or perhaps one or two fireworks. That done, he would walk away. However, the couple of cartloads of firecrackers he'd brought with him from home would be gone in an instant, the crowds fighting to buy every last one. Once the Cui family's firecrackers had been displayed, everyone else's sounded no louder than a fart from an old ox.

Last year, when the third son of the Cui family was walking down the embankment, he was carrying a string of tiny little firecrackers – quite honestly, they looked about the same size as bean sprouts. What was up with these itty-bitty firecrackers? Well, when he lit the fuse, they went up with a report like a foreign gun, the most amazing bang. It seemed to cut right through your ears! These really were proper "super-crackers"!

But just then, a stout, fat boy, bare-headed and wearing a Tibetan blue short jacket, took up position opposite him, holding a long thick elm-wood pole, from which was suspended a string of firecrackers. No one had ever seen such huge firecrackers before – they were the size of cucumbers! The fat kid didn't say a word; he just lit the fuse. When the firecrackers had finished exploding and the smoke cleared, the third son of the Cui family was nowhere to be seen. Some folk said he'd just gone back home; others said he'd been blown to smithereens.

Afterwards, the story of the fat boy became more and more widespread, and more and more mysterious. One person claimed that he came from over Dacheng way in Hebei Province and that his surname was Cai – people called him Fatty Cai. His family had made fireworks for many generations, and they were sold all over Manchuria… even your Russians would set off Cai family firecrackers for New Year's. (Of course, Russians did nothing of the kind.) Then there was this other person who said that his family had military connections, and their gunpowder was the same as that used for artillery shells – in fact, their firecrackers had a metal casing on them like a shell. As the rumours swirled, the Cui family's firecrackers were soon forgotten.

At this year's Qinglong River firecracker market, the third son of the Cui family was nowhere to be seen. Fatty Cai turned up looking pretty pleased with himself and immediately set off a string of firecrackers, even larger and louder than before. Just as he was showing off, the third son of the Cui family walked slowly down from the top of the embankment. He seemed relaxed and at ease, as if he were going for a leisurely stroll. He was deaf in his right ear anyway, so he had nothing to fear there, as he held a string of firecrackers in his right hand. This string was something quite out of the ordinary: it was just two feet long or thereabouts, with eleven crackers in all. None of them were very big… maybe about the size of a carrot. Aha! A string of carrots! He was obviously up to something: there must be something very special about this string of carrots.

When he got down off the embankment and set foot on the riverbed, the third son of the Cui family lit the string of firecrackers in his hand. The first one went off with the sound of a bomb exploding – it was like the most enormous clap of thunder. It panicked the beasts of burden up on top of the embankment, and some of them started dragging their carts down as they stampeded. The third son of the Cui family was small, and the string he was holding was not far off the ground, so earth was kicked up by each of these huge explosions. They went off slowly: he would take a step, and then one of the firecrackers would go off, there would be the most enormous bang and a fountain of earth. It was like he was walking through a minefield, step by step. He took eleven paces, and the last one took him right in front of Fatty Cai, which meant that the last explosion was right in front of him too. That gave him a turn! When everyone had calmed down enough to be able to see straight, the third son of the Cui family had a line of eleven craters behind him, each one of which was big enough for a man to squat down in! That was a shock for one and all.

Suddenly, Fatty Cai clapped his two hands over his ears and started to bawl. He had lost his hearing.

After that, Fatty Cai wasn't to be seen again around the Qinglong River. The Cui family's firecrackers, on the other hand, were now famous, under the name "Eleven Bangs". When they celebrated New Year's at the Tianjin naval base and the Dagu Forts, they would be sure to buy this kind.

The firecracker market in the old city of Tianjin was on Gongqian Street outside the city walls.

Every New Year's, the shops and pavement stalls along here were filled with candles, silk flowers, clothing, ornaments, statues, offerings, rice cakes, dried fruit and nuts, bonsai arrangements, pots of narcissus flowers, cakes, snacks, wine, New Year's auspicious prints, lanterns, celebratory calligraphy couplets written on red paper, toys, posters with the character for "Good Luck" in every size, and so on and so forth... everything that the citizens needed for the occasion. Firecrackers, on the other hand, were sold on Fushen Street – a crossroads lying beside the Yang family mansion north of the Temple of the Queen of Heaven. One reason for this was that there are lots of merchants and businessmen in Tianjin, and they like to use firecrackers to ward off bad luck and summon good fortune, so they bought in really huge quantities necessitating a separate specialist market. The other reason was for fear of something going off... it would be easy enough for an accident to happen, so it was best to put everyone together in the same place.

Fushen Street was really too narrow for all this, so the market was arranged in a very unusual way. There were stalls for firecrackers down one side of the street, while pedestrians used the other. Actually, they didn't have stalls for firecrackers – they just piled them up. They had bundles of big firecrackers, rockets and boxes of fireworks, and if you added them all together, they'd make a small mountain. Next to the mountain of firecrackers would be any number of fireworks in every colour under the sun. Traders in firecrackers from Jiangxi and Hunan Provinces would be there as well; the firecracker market was like a test site for the whole industry. The majority were done up in bright red paper, so that the whole street was crimson. However, the very best space – the most eye-catching and exciting – had been held by Black Cui's family since the time of the Qianlong Emperor. According to the rules governing the Gongqian Street market, in the last month of the year, the Cui family would put up a piece of red paper on the wall in the prime spot, right at the end of the road, and on it was written the four words: "Every Year As Normal." Below, he signed his name: "Cui of Yanerzhuang". Nobody would have dared to try and muscle him out.

The Cui family only sold two kinds of fireworks: strings of firecrackers and "Double Shots". On both sides of the stall, there was a bamboo pole, the size of a thick arm, with a string of firecrackers hanging down from the top. This was a couple of metres long and sufficiently heavy to bend the bamboo pole over like a bow. At the bottom, the string reached to the ground, and in the middle there hung a red wooden plaque, on which was written in black lettering: "Ten Thousand Crackers". Everyone in Tianjin knew that this was the best that the Cui family of Jinghai County produced. It had nice round casings and plenty of powder in each firecracker, which would go off in order, with a loud, crisp bang – they never misfired or turned out mute.

Back in the day when Black Cui set up a stall here to sell firecrackers, it was forbidden to set them off in the market. Even if just one spark got out, the results would have been appalling: half the city could have fallen down and no end of people killed. During the reign of the Daoguang Emperor, a rich man came to the market and insisted on setting off a "Yellow Smoke Rocket" on the spot. He was rich and didn't believe in consequences, but the result of this was that he set off a heap of firecrackers, and more than a dozen firemen had to risk their lives in the ensuing inferno, in which half the street was burned to the ground. When this came to court, the rich guy was ordered to hand out pretty much everything he owned in compensation, so he ended up in poverty. After that, nobody dared to set off a firecracker in Fushen Street. But if you don't set them off, how do you know which one is good and which is not worth the money?

When Black Cui started to feel his age, his oldest son took over his father's business. Standing by the junction to Fushen Street, he decided he had to set off his firecrackers. He had the guts to do this, and he knew he could do it safely. He gave a public performance of his amazing skill in releasing a hand-held "Double Shot"...

Double Shots consist of a paper tube in which there are two charges, which result in two separate explosions. The fuse leads into the lower charge of shot. When most people set off one of these rockets, they hold it by the top part. After they have lit the fuse, the bottom charge will explode first, and that's the first shot. The top half then flies off to explode in mid-air: that's the second shot. Setting off a Double Shot requires you to hold it in your hand, and for that you need steady nerves. Nobody would dare set off a rocket anywhere near Fushen Street because after the top half flies out of your hands, it could go anywhere! If it went and landed in a pile of firecrackers, wouldn't you blow the whole place up?

Black Cui's oldest son's trick was to keep both shots in his hand.

He first held the upper part with his left hand, lit the fuse, and allowed the lower half to explode under his left hand. Then he grabbed the exploded part of the rocket with his right hand and held on tight as the upper half went off. Inside each Double Shot were two coils of fuse – top and bottom – and when he swapped hands, the fuse had just burned through to the top part, which meant that it exploded above his right hand. In this way, using both right and left hands, one hand for each shot, he could make sure that it went off in a controlled way and did not go flying off anywhere.

Who had ever seen a Double Shot being set off in this way? With this one move, the oldest son of the Cui family made sure that everyone in the city who wanted the real thing would buy the Cui Family Firecrackers: you had to admire the quality.

But when you've got a skill, that just makes other people jealous; if one person shouts acclaim, someone else will be tearing them down. When preparing for his show, the oldest son of the Cui family had the habit of putting the Double Shot down on the little table behind him. He wasn't expecting anyone to quietly pierce the casing with a needle so that the two charges were combined into one – the Double Shot would now go off with a single massive bang. He had absolutely no idea when he picked it up from the table at the back, holding tight to the top half with his hand and lighting the fuse with a match… the two charges exploded as one. The Cui family's firecrackers were fierce, and a Double Shot going off together was doubly fierce. His hand was very badly burned, and his thumb was torn off and hurled up towards the rooftops.

Not long afterwards, everyone on Fushen Street was saying the same thing: "You shouldn't buy Yanerzhuang 'Double Shots'. If the two charges go off together, you'll just kill someone!"

If your backbone can be broken just like that, it's no backbone.

The next winter, on the wall at the corner of Fushen Street, the same poster was put up for the Cui family of Yanerzhuang: "Every Year As Normal." On the fifteenth day of the twelfth lunar month, the eldest son of the Cui family took his place at the firecracker stall, grinning from ear to ear. On either side of the stall were two great bamboo poles, each bearing a string of Ten Thousand Crackers. His mouth was smiling, his bald pate was shining, and his face was as ruddy as ever – in fact, he might have put on a little weight. However, without the thumb on his left hand, how could he possibly set off his Double Shots? He'd come up with a trick nobody could possibly have imagined!

What he used to do with both left and right hands was now done with one. It was his left hand that was missing a thumb, so he now used it to light the fuse. He gripped the upper part of the Double Shot with his right hand, and once the first charge had gone off, he loosened his grip and spun the rocket around so that the other half could explode. Then he'd be holding onto the spent half while the second charge went off over the same hand.

His demonstration had changed, and his show had become even more dangerous, even more amazing and even more impossible to match. He was as impassive as ever, and each time he made no mistake. You had to admire the people who made Cui Family Firecrackers.

But just think how brave you would have to be to run such a risk… to come up with a trick like that?

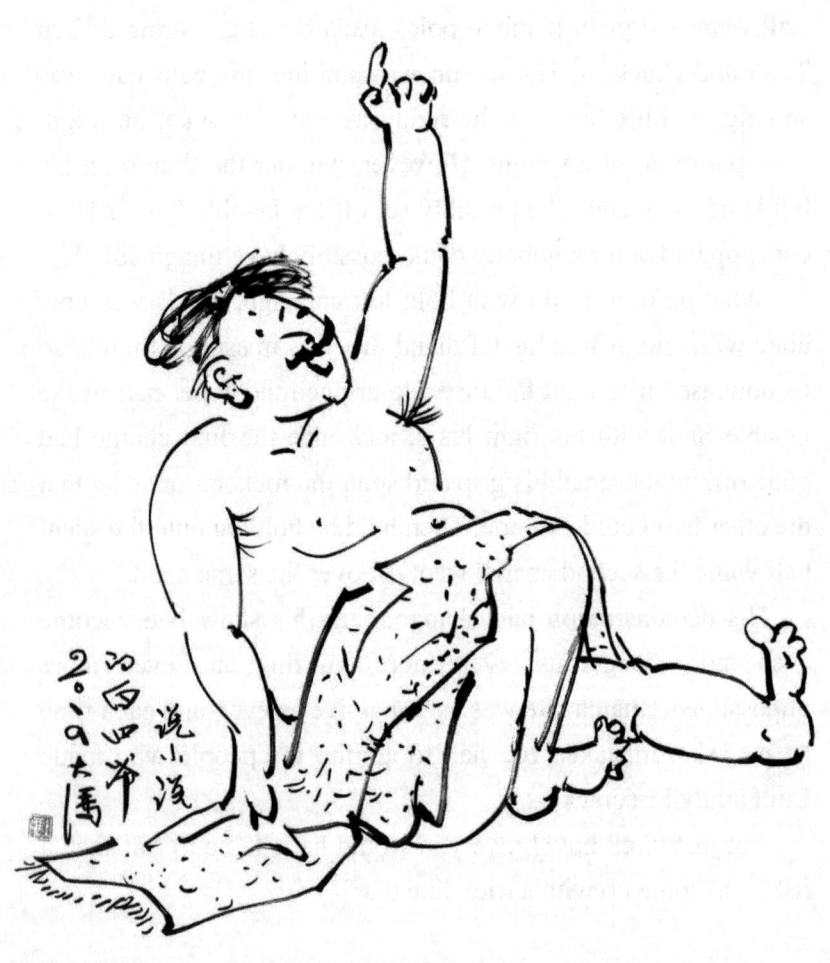

43
FOURTH MASTER BAI TELLS A STORY

ROMANCE NOVELS WERE popular in Shanghai, while martial arts books were widely read in Tianjin, so most of the famous writers of martial arts novels ended up living in Tianjin. The top three were the Master of the Returning Pearl Belvedere, Zheng Zhengyin and Gong Baiyu. There was also one other, who was much more famous when he was alive, but he took a different path to fame. Whereas the other three wrote martial arts fiction, this man dictated it.

His name was Bai Yunfei. His family were salt merchants and made a lot of money at it, which even now serves to keep them out of the gutter. He was the fourth son of his family, and so he was called Fourth Master Bai. Fourth Master Bai was odd-looking and certainly struck even the most casual observer as unusual. He was big-bodied but with stumpy arms and legs, a round stomach, low-slung buttocks and a face the size of a cartwheel. But his head was even more amazing than his face: he had a photographic memory, and his mind worked like greased lightning – he was one really smart guy. He wasn't what you would call well-read, and the time came when he'd written more books than he'd read. To begin with, he did author books, but his pen just couldn't keep up with his imagination, so he stopped writing and started dictating.

At that time, there were lots of newspapers and magazines being published in Tianjin; every kind of periodical was sold there. They wanted to attract a readership, so they'd ask famous authors to write martial arts fiction serials for them. For the magazines, it was a new instalment every issue; for the papers, it was a new instalment every day. Famous writers sold their work like hot cakes. Every day, they'd be chained to their desks by their editors, scribbling away from morning till night, and then the next day they'd get up and start all over again. But Bai Yunfei got off lightly: he didn't have to write a word since he dictated his own works, and running his mouth wasn't exactly hard labour. In saying that he got off lightly, it is no more than the truth...

Fourth Master Bai liked to spend time in the bathhouse. To hear him tell it, he'd feel filthy if he went a day without a good scrub; and as for two days, he'd turn into a werewolf or something! He rented a single cabin for himself at the Huaqing Springs, the big bathhouse right next to the Quanye Bazaar. He had Cabin No. 4 in Row A. He wanted No. 4 because that matched his name: Fourth Master. He thought it was auspicious, and it was easy to remember. Through all four seasons of the year, except for New Year's Eve and the Mid-Autumn Festival, he was there every single day and spent the entire afternoon in the place.

He first had a good soak in the hot water pool, and a foot spa, then retreated to his cabin to lie down on the small bed, naked except for the big white towel wrapped around his waist, and then he would raise the curtain separating off No. 4 in Row A. The individual cabins in this bathhouse all had two small beds in them, left and right, with a square table in between. He'd relax into one bed, and the other served as a seat for the people who came to visit him. Once he was in position, a staff member came round and got busy, first giving him a brisk rub-down and then massaging his feet. Once this had been done, he looked as if he'd been polished, like a snake that has just shed its skin. He would be shining from head to foot, and his arse cheeks looked like large white enamel bowls.

Afterwards, one of the staff would bring round a few small dishes, each bearing a different snack: melon seeds in a soy sauce dressing, salty dried plums, sugar-glazed peanuts, candied orange-peel from Zhao's on Dafeng Lane and luscious slices of daikon radish, as well as a pot of strong and hot jasmine tea. Eating and drinking like this, enjoying these snacks whether they were hot or cold, sweet or salty, crisp, sticky, hard or soft... well, that's really good living, the best that it gets in this vale of tears.

It was just at this moment, as soon as the curtain was lifted, that a man walked in. He was dressed in a long robe, wearing glasses, and in his hand he held a small briefcase – a single glance would tell you that he was an editor from some rag. He sat down on the little bed opposite Fourth Master Bai and took out a pen and some paper. Then he said: "We didn't have an instalment from you yesterday, so we'd better have one today – in fact, two instalments of the story would be best." Then he smirked at Fourth Master Bai.

"Which paper are you from?"

"I'm from *Commonalities*. I come every day... how can you not remember me?"

"I've got eight different papers coming every day to pester me, wanting another instalment of this story or that... How can I possibly remember everyone? If I don't give you the next instalment of someone else's story, I reckon I'm not doing too badly."

"What a head you've got on your shoulders, Fourth Master, to have eight different stories on the go at the same time! I'm sure there's not your like in all of Tianjin... in all of the world!"

Fourth Master Bai was pleased by this flattery, and he calmed down. Then he said: "Where have I got to with your paper's story? Hmm... you'd better read the last paragraph out to me, and then I can continue."

The bespectacled newspaper editor smiled and said: "For us, you're writing *The Heroes of Wudang*. I've brought today's paper with me, hot off the press, so let me read it to you... the last paragraph goes..." He took a newspaper out of his briefcase and opened it out to read:

> Xie Hu whispered to Liao Hanying to get out a handkerchief, soak it in water, and wrap it around his face, protecting his nose. After blowing out the lamp on the table, he lay down fully dressed and pretended to sleep, his sword by his side. After a while, the shadow of a human figure appeared against the paper-covered window, as the moon shone brightly outside. The shadow outside the window suddenly became bigger. Whoever it was had come right up to the window frame; extending their tongue, they licked the paper until they'd silently worked a hole in it. Then a fine bamboo pipe was

inserted. The man put his mouth to his end of the bamboo pipe, and a plume of grey smoke was puffed out into the room, turning blue where it was touched by the moonlight. Undetectable... invisible... this was that notorious life-threatening drug – Dawn Awakening Incense!

The editor, with his glasses perched on his nose, stopped at this point and said: "Your last instalment ended there."

"Great! I know just where we are now... Let me begin, and you take notes..." Fourth Master Bai took a long pull at his cigarette and collected his thoughts. Up until now, he'd been lying down, but now he sat up, his pale-skinned torso bare, his eyes glittering, and from the moment he opened his mouth, the story just came tumbling out:

> Having introduced his drug into the room, the man outside the window waited for a good long while, but he did not detect any movement from inside. He bent his ear, but all he could hear was the sound of snoring. Having unsheathed his sword, he quickly and easily slipped open the window, and launched himself inside.

Having got to this juncture in his narrative, Fourth Master Bai cast his eye about the room in a hesitant way, as if he were searching for the right word. He looked at the two beds in his cabin, and then up at the ceiling, before carrying on his tale:

> The man was extraordinarily agile. As soon as he'd righted himself, swords appeared in both his right and left hands, and he started to hack away at the two beds on either side. When he

heard the sound made by the fall of his swords, he suddenly realised that something had gone terribly wrong... looking around, there was no one on either bed. Where could they have gone? He knew he was in trouble, but before he'd had time to look about him, two shadows suddenly dropped from the ceiling... Xie Hu and Liao Hanying had been lying in ambush up on one of the exposed beams. They did not allow their attacker a moment's reflection – they flew down upon him, their hands gripping at him like the claws of an eagle seizing a rabbit. Once their attacker was in their power, they had him tied up with ropes in a trice. Lighting the lamp to have a look at him, they were deeply shocked. At one and the same moment, they exclaimed: "It's you!"

Fourth Master paused. The bespectacled editor said: "I'm on the edge of my seat. You've got to keep going!"

"Well, that's your five hundred words for today, and it ends on a cliff-hanger. Didn't we agree that I'd provide you with five hundred words per day?" Fourth Master Bai said with a smile. "If you want to know what happened next, read on! As you can see, poor old Mr Qin from *369 Illustrated News* has been standing out there, waiting for ages..."

The editor from *Commonalities* looked about him and realised that Mr Qin from *369 Illustrated News* was indeed standing by the door. They both often came to get copy from Fourth Master Bai, so they'd bump into each other from time to time and thus become acquainted. Since neither of them liked to interfere with the other, he just picked up his papers and made haste to leave. Mr Qin then entered the cabin and took his seat on the bed, while Fourth Master Bai took a couple of gulps of tea.

Not waiting for Mr Qin to start speaking, he said with a grin: "If I remember correctly, I'm writing a serial for you lot entitled *The Beautiful Swordswoman*. As I recall, we'd just got to the bit where the swordswoman had gone into a tavern out in the mountains and demanded a plate of stewed leopard meat... is that right?"

"What a memory you have, Fourth Master!" said Mr Qin. "It is always so impressive the way that you can organise your eight different sets of characters and never get them confused! Your last sentence was: 'She picked up a big lump of leopard meat in her chopsticks, but just as she raised it to her lips, there was a sudden blinding flash of light, like a silver star, that came spinning in from the doorway with a draught of cold air. It was aimed right at her head. She could neither duck nor dodge...'"

As he spoke, Fourth Master Bai was listening carefully and gathering his thoughts while lifting a bright green slice of daikon to his mouth, held between thumb and index finger. He looked at the piece of daikon radish in his hand and then began on today's instalment of the story: "Suddenly, her hand twitched and there was a loud clang. Now what was caught between her two chopsticks was no longer a lump of leopard meat, but a six-inch-long, shining bright throwing-dagger!"

"Wow!" Mr Qin exclaimed. "That's a fantastic opening! What a great start! You always seem to be able to pick up right where you left off, and you've got such wonderful tricks up your sleeve!"

Mr Qin was an old hand in the newspaper industry; he knew how to inspire the authors he worked with and keep them up to the mark. His praise made Fourth Master Bai put out further efforts: immediately, his imagination ran riot, and a whole new story came out at considerable length... Before he realised it, there were two men sitting down with Mr Qin, one tall and one short. Both of them were editors here to collect copy. All these men were dressed in long robes and coats, but one wore glasses, the other one did not, and the third had sunglasses on. Some wrote with pencils, some of them used modern fountain pens, and the more old-fashioned came with brushes and inkpots, the tips of their brushes covered in bronze caps. Although all of these editors were good at keeping minutes, it was not an easy task to take dictation of Fourth Master Bai's novels. The most difficult aspect was that when Fourth Master Bai was declaiming, he would put in so much expression and characterisation that his auditors would get caught up in the story and stop writing.

It seemed utterly incomprehensible: where did all of his stories come from? Unlike other authors, nobody ever saw him lost in thought and struggling for an idea, chewing the end of his pen, frowning and grimacing. He never locked himself away in his study. He would have a good soak in the hot tub, get himself rubbed down, drink some tea, nibble a few snacks, and then he'd start pulling all the tangled threads of his tale together. Without so much as a wave of his pen, it would all come pouring out... and he could write half a dozen or more different serials all at the same time. He had the gift of the gab, that's for sure, and when he gave dictation, the story came out fully formed – it never needed any polishing or revision from the editors. It did not matter what order the people from the papers turned up in, whether this one came ahead of that one or the other way around; he would have the next instalment of the tale ready to go. The stories fermenting in his brain seemed like Tianjin's very own tramlines – each of the seven lines were marked in red, yellow, blue, green, white, spotted and purple – all going their separate ways, never crossing. It was impossible for anyone to board the wrong tram by mistake.

Did all of his characters and stories, and their marvellous settings, all leap into his mind – into that pumpkin-like head – impromptu? Who knew? According to the man who came to give him his daily foot massage, the wife and four concubines of Master You in his classic *The Heavenly Guardians* were the five toes on his left foot. Apparently, one day as he was massaging Fourth Master Bai's feet, the man suddenly pointed to his little toe and said sadly: "Look how miserable my little concubine is, so tiny and thin... she spends all day every day picked on and crushed by the others, without daring to stand up for herself." Then he said: "Right, I'd better give her some knowledge of kung fu!" A few days after he said this, his toes had been transformed into the women of the You family in *The Heavenly Guardians*. His little toe became the remarkable Fifth Lady with her amazing martial arts techniques, who finished the novel taking over the family business of transporting goods through bandit-infested country.

And then there was another thing. A big screen stood right by the entrance to the bathhouse, and in the centre there was depicted a red dragon fountaining water. Behind the screen, there was a big silvered mirror so that customers could arrange their clothing before heading out of the door. Every day, Fourth Master Bai would begin by soaking in the hot pool, then he would declaim his novels, and then he'd get dressed again and leave. But before he did so, he'd always stand in front of the big mirror to fix his collar. There was a nail knocked into the frame of the mirror with a string hanging from it, tied to a greasy comb. Every day when he checked his appearance in the mirror, Fourth Master Bai would grab the comb and sweep it through his hair a couple of times. Somehow or other, this became the fearsome blade known as "Copper Comb" wielded by the Lakeside Assassin in his novel *The Three Heroes of Eagle Gulf*.

People said that everything in his books was steamed out of him in the bathhouse. In actual fact, there was one time when a couple of distant relatives came to Tianjin from his old hometown back in Hubei Province, wanting to borrow money, and there was a nasty quarrel on the back of it… that ended up in one of his novels the very next day. When he put true events into his stories, it wasn't at all how it had really happened. On some occasions, he'd make it all so much grander and more magnificent; on others, so much more vulgar and base. It was completely transformed in his mind. A joke would be metamorphosised into a murder; a petty crook and a whore could end up becoming towering figures of romance in one of his novels. Who knows how events might not be recast in Fourth Master Bai's ever-fertile imagination?

People in the same line of work understand their co-professionals. However, nobody in artistic circles was prepared to acknowledge Fourth Master Bai's natural abilities – they cursed him as a clown because he didn't write his own books but got rich and famous from others taking dictation. It was a well-known author of the day who made such complaints. Other people, irritated at this, then cursed the complainant in his turn: how about you lie down in the bathhouse and dictate a couple of instalments and see how well you get on? Fourth Master Bai didn't just have a marvellous imagination; his stories hung together, and he didn't need his editors to change so much as a single word. If someone started writing down everything that you said, wouldn't it be a mess?

Fourth Master Bai was a renowned novelist for some thirty years. All of his serials were reprinted as books by reputable publishing houses, and they were huge bestsellers – in demand from Heilongjiang in the north to Hong Kong in the south. But then in 1947, a block fell from the roof over the hot tub in the Huaqing Springs bathhouse, loosened by year upon year of steam, and broke Fourth Master Bai's neck. He survived, but the accident left him subject to fainting fits, so he had to give up writing serials for the newspapers, and the following year he retired to his hometown in Hubei Province to recover.

As a consequence, a new version of the old story came to be told: Fourth Master Bai stopped writing once he was no longer spending his afternoons in the bathhouse – all his inspiration came from lying around in the nude. But it doesn't matter what people said about him; as soon as you open one of his books and start reading, well, you just have to admire the man.

44
CROSSPATCH

On Guodian Street, not far from the Ruifuxiang Silk Store, there lived a man, balding and single, some forty years of age, who was called "Crosspatch". Of course, Crosspatch wasn't his real name, it was just an epithet. But calling him Crosspatch was just perfect: it described his character and also his appearance. He was the kind of person who went around all day with a frown on his face for no reason that anyone else could see, always looking irritable, and whatever happened, he was simply never pleased. No matter how delicious something was to eat, or how good it was to look at, or how much fun it gave everyone else, or how amazing it was… he wasn't interested in the slightest. On the other hand, when horrible things happened, when things got nasty or dangerous, he didn't care either. It seemed as though he was fully occupied with his own troubles, a burden that he could never set down and was never relieved… What could that be? Nobody had a clue.

What no one knows, everyone wants to know.

Let's take a good look at him…

He went around with his forehead knitted in a frown all day long, as creased as the pinched folds in a wonton. His face was otherwise stiff and hatchet-like, his eyes as dull as a dead fish, and he never seemed to really look at anything. These mannerisms were natural since you couldn't possibly learn them.

Why he was such a crosspatch nobody could work out. It was like an intractable knot which had everyone worrying at it, but which proved impossible to undo.

Some observers said it was all because he was an orphan and unmarried – he was really unhappy. Some said he was so miserable because he didn't have a wife. Actually, both these explanations were wrong. His father was a dealer in ceramics out of Jiangxi Province, specialising in top quality blue-and-white porcelain. He'd take the very best, the very finest items from Jingdezhen and transport them to Tianjin by cart or boat, where he sold them in the Foreign Concession at Zizhulin. In addition, he had a fancy shop over on Guodian Street. His family had got rich out of the ceramics trade. Not one of them would be seen dead wearing cotton – it was all silk and fine brocades for them. However, once his parents died, the family lost their mainstay; there was nobody to carry on the business, and he had to shut the shop. In spite of this, he was still living in a grand two-courtyard house. If he'd wanted a wife, was there any family with unmarried daughters that wouldn't have been happy to see her move in? Why was he such a crosspatch? Some people said he'd had a foul temper from birth, and there was nothing that could please him. Certainly he'd been called Crosspatch ever since he was a kid. If you are born contrary, there is nothing much that anyone can do about it.

However, the people of Tianjin come one sharper than the last, and there is nothing they can't fix if they put their minds to it.

Maybe if he'd never met Chen Liu, he might have spent his whole life as a misery guts; he'd have been a crosspatch until the end of his days. However, he did meet Chen Liu, and that changed him. Chen Liu was an amazing man, and he got things done – make no mistake about that.

Chen Liu wasn't originally from Guodian Street. He sold sugar-glazed roast chestnuts over in the west part of the city. His chestnuts were roasted until they were deliciously sweet and fragrant, glossy, plump, easy to peel and just ready to eat. The thing is that the inhabitants of the west side of the city were poor, and they just had coppers in their pockets; those over on Guodian Street were rich, and they were weighed down with silver. You've got to go where the money is, so Chen Liu headed over to Guodian Street to set up his stall and earn a crust. He didn't know that over on Guodian Street, each stand was worth its weight in gold. The whole place was carved up by the local hoodlums, so not everyone was able to set up shop there. However, in the case of Chen Liu, from the very first day he showed his face around Guodian Street, nobody tried to cause trouble for him. He didn't look especially fearsome, so why did nobody try to move him on? The reason will be found in the story given below.

One day, a few of the local thugs were gossiping with him, and they happened to mention Crosspatch. Sooner or later, whenever anyone was chatting about him, they'd bring up the same subject: why was he so miserable?

Chen Liu just said: "If his house burned down, he'd cheer up."

So one of the thugs laughed and said: "Then he wouldn't be Crosspatch any more. Maybe he'd even take a header into the Grand Canal…"

They joked about this and that, but about a month later, there was a fire on Guodian Street, filling the sky with thick black smoke and shooting flames into the heavens. Then the fire brigade came rushing forward with a loud pounding of gongs. Everyone had their eyes peeled: it was Crosspatch's house that was on fire. They watched as Crosspatch himself – his torso naked but wearing pyjama trousers – was carried out of his home, his body blackened with smoke, looking for all the world like a stray cat that had fallen down a chimney. He was struggling and screaming all the while. It was very rare for Crosspatch to open his mouth, so nobody had previously heard his hoarse voice. Now they were listening to it, and some people claimed he sounded like cloth being torn, while others said it was like the hooting of an owl.

This was a real conflagration that burned his house down to the ground, leaving only an empty shell. Everything inside was reduced to cinders – the only things to survive were a few ceramic jars which were pulled out of the smoking ruins. Porcelain can withstand the heat quite well. Having been through the kiln, they have nothing to fear from further fires.

Apparently, when the fire first started, a gang of hoods turned up and dashed straight into the flames. They screamed that they were trying to save the contents of the house, but actually they were there to rob the place. All sorts of fine antiques and fancy ornaments were just carried off by them. From start to finish,

Crosspatch – looking like a black monkey – was standing by the gate, jumping up and down, screaming and shouting. But the following day, there was peace and quiet. A thin blue haze of smoke hung over the charred ruins of the house, but Crosspatch was nowhere to be seen. He was all alone in the world, with no family and no friends – where could he possibly have gone? Someone said that the fire had driven Crosspatch over the edge: he'd thrown himself into the river.

Someone else happened to mention this to Chen Liu as he was selling his glazed roasted chestnuts. Chen Liu just remarked: "Well, it's true that it's not the depths of winter, so the river ain't frozen solid. Anyone who wants to jump in the river can go right ahead. But there's no need to assume he's dead. You never know, this fire may be the making of him."

Chen Liu's remarks didn't seem to make any sense at all, and nobody took them seriously. However, one young thug did call one thing to mind... this fire seemed far from accidental. Just a few days before, they'd all been chatting, and Chen Liu happened to mention his house burning down... and now lo and behold, it had been burned to the ground! Who could have set the fire? And why? Was it all about burning him out so that they could rob his place?

Six months past, and someone happened to mention seeing Crosspatch working as a porter over at the wharf by the Foreign Concession. Nobody believed a word of this, since in the old days when he'd bought a watermelon or two, he'd always hired someone to carry them home for him. How could he possibly be working as a porter himself?

After this lie was put to rest, there was no more news of Crosspatch.

Four years later, the pharmacy opposite the Ruifuxiang Silk Store, which was supposed to sell medicines better than anything the foreigners had, closed its doors. After it ceased operations, a sign went up seeking new tenants. A few days later, a neat looking middle-aged man took over the store. He opened a ceramics shop specialising in blue-and-white porcelain from Jingdezhen. When they first went into business, the shop looked wonderful: blue-and-white porcelain, blue-and-white vases, blue-and-white jugs, blue-and-white basins, blue-and-white dishes, and blue-and-white bowls, stacked up all the way from the inner shelves till they spilled out onto the street. A pair of blue-and-white vases, the height of a man, painted with a design of cavalry officers waving their swords, stood to the left and right of the entrance, like door gods. There were only three people working there: the boss and his two assistants. The boss was called Yang Guangzheng, and he was supposed to come from Jiangxi, though he spoke with something of a Tianjin accent. He was short and slight, looking more like a senior assistant than a boss. He was a hard worker too, in and out of the shop along with his assistants, and he pretty soon got the business on its feet so the place was hopping. Even the foreigners living over in Zizhulin came to buy from him. It reminded the old hands of the days when Crosspatch's father had his porcelain store.

Suddenly, one of the brighter sparks said: "Crosspatch's father had the surname Yang, and here is another one. And wasn't his father from Jiangxi originally? Can this man possibly be Crosspatch, who was burned out of house and home a couple of years back?"

This man was called Yang Guangzheng. But round here,

everyone had called the other Crosspatch, and nobody could remember what his real name was.

It was all just a guess; this man didn't look the least like Crosspatch. With his bright eyes and smooth forehead, there was nothing to call to mind Crosspatch's knitted brow. Look at how chirpy this man was, smiling day in and day out, and then think of Crosspatch's ugly mug – he was as miserable as if every man he came across owed him money.

No matter what angle you looked at it from, he wasn't a bit like Crosspatch. But thinking about it, he did have something about him that called Crosspatch to mind…

Anyway, the little hoods in those parts came up with various nasty tricks, trying to find out if he was the person they thought. Chen Liu found out about this and immediately moved his chestnut roaster over to opposite this Mr Yang's porcelain shop, and he put out the word: "Anyone who tries bullying him will have me to deal with."

Nothing much happened after that.

One day, when a young thug was having a chat with Chen Liu, he said: "I don't care if he is Crosspatch or not – what I want to know is how a right misery-guts turns out OK?"

Chen Liu understood what he was trying to ask and said with a smile: "You wouldn't understand. People like Crosspatch aren't hurting for money, they are hurting for something to do – the misery comes from boredom. When you're poor, you're kept busy. It's the rich guy who turns into a crosspatch."

45

THE THIRTEEN PROBLEMS

AMONG THE LITERATI, there was a man who was both inside and outside the group: his name was Wang Wuqi. He was a refined-looking man, not at all vulgar, and in the ordinary way of things, he liked to wear a long sky-blue gown, with clean socks inside his well-polished shoes – so he looked somewhat scholarly, but at the same time, not quite.

He was accounted a member of the literati because they all knew that here was a man who could make brushes, and his brushes were very good quality – in addition to which he knew how to paint and do calligraphy. Supposedly, he was pretty good. But on the other hand, he could also be considered an outsider because he did not have too many dealings with the literati, and it was pretty rare for anyone to be allowed to see any of his artworks. To put it bluntly, he was just someone who was occasionally mentioned in passing in literary circles.

His father was a brushmaker from Huizhou in Anhui Province. Huizhou produces some good brushes, and in those days, Tianjin's brush shops all brought in their stock from the south. He was impressed by Tianjin's position as a port city connecting various different trade routes, so he uprooted his family and moved them there, making his brushes in situ and opening a shop where he could sell them. The name of his shop was very well-chosen: he called it "A Brush With Spring", and it was located on Zhenshi Street. He had a nice five-room house overlooking the road with a garden out back, so he could have the shop in front and the workshop behind. That meant he could essentially work from home, and he made a good life for himself. Wang Wuqi studied brushmaking with his father from childhood, and when he grew up he joined him in the family business. He seemed to have a natural talent for painting and calligraphy, and was highly intelligent – he learned how to do these things without ever having a teacher. However, given that he wasn't involved in literary circles, nobody knew whether he was any good or not. Besides which, he didn't care what anyone else said about his works. It was his nature to be happy, having followed his dad in making and selling brushes – he was not looking to become famous for his paintings and calligraphy. After his father passed away, he carried on the same as ever, and his art was just for his own personal amusement. He enjoyed his day job, since it was not onerous and left him free to be himself.

Wang Wuqi made Huizhou brushes with tips of sheep hair, wolf hair or a mixture of the two. However, when he was painting or doing calligraphy, he would use a chicken-feather brush that he had made for himself. The feathers were plucked from the rumps of the cockerels he had running about at home. He painted something in the style of the early Qing dynasty artists Shitao and Bada Shanren, while his calligraphy was modelled upon the clerical script of the well-travelled Chan Buddhist monk, Andaoyi, who lived during the Northern and Southern dynasties. These untrammelled styles suited him, since they left him free to paint as the fancy took him.

However, he did not anticipate that although few people outside had seen his calligraphy and painting, there would be many to praise them, and gradually the story developed that here was an artist of genius. If he happened to hear anyone speak of this, he would just laugh, since he thought that it was just other people making fun of him.

But he could not understand it… why did these people talk about him? He was just a brushmaker, after all, and it did not matter a jot whether he could paint or not. He did not like the feeling that other people were making it their business. He painted and did calligraphy purely for his own amusement, and if he was happy with the result, that was the only thing that mattered.

One day, Yu San from Guodian Street came to find him. Yu San was an aficionado of calligraphy and painting, and he had a fondness for the equipment he bought from A Brush With Spring. This man was everywhere in artistic circles, and he knew absolutely everyone. Today, right from the moment he arrived, he was bellowing about how the famous local artist Sheng Dengyun wanted to meet Wang Wuqi. He followed this up by saying: "His paintings sell for gold bars – you won't be buying one of them if you can only pay in silver! If you want to get hold of one of his artworks, for all that you'll have to pay up front, you won't get your hands on it until the year after next. For some reason, he's determined to see you and asked me to bring you over."

Wang Wuqi was curious and asked: "I only sell brushes. I never sell my paintings. Why would I want to see him?"

"It's not you that wants to see him – it's him that wants to meet you. That's why he told me to come and find you. You might as well meet him… maybe he wants to buy some of your brushes."

Wang Wuqi had never met anyone famous and was quite nervous at the prospect. But when he heard that the man might possibly admire A Brush With Spring's products, he went off with Yu San. On arriving at Sheng Dengyun's door, he was struck dumb. He was overcome by the sight of the house, the vast gateway, the huge living room, the pomp and circumstance with which the man was surrounded, and the relentless vigour of Sheng Dengyun himself. He just wanted to run away. It seemed to him that Sheng Dengyun had white eyeballs – how could it be that his eyes did not have pupils? He looked like the White Guard statue at the Temple of the City God. Later on, Sheng Dengyun managed to glance at him, and it was at this point that he discovered he did have pupils – it was just that he kept his eyes rolled up towards the ceiling so that he didn't have to look at him directly. However, if he despised him so much, why did he want to invite him round?

Moreover, Sheng Dengyun did not ask him to sit down but plumped himself down on his own chair, carrying on as if there were nobody else present. He was in full flow praising himself. Wang Wuqi had never met anyone quite so self-satisfied. Sheng Dengyun declared that in Qin Zuyong's *Discussions on Painting in the Shade of a Paulownia Tree*, the critic had divided all artworks into four categories: relaxed, spiritual, remarkable and technically competent, but that he himself had trampled the word "relaxed" underfoot some ten years previously.

Yu San was curious and asked him: "So how do you categorise your own works?"

"Naturally, mine are works of genius!" Having said this, Sheng Dengyun threw his head back and laughed, allowing his guests to see right down to his tonsils.

Wang Wuqi stopped listening at this point and began to squint at the paintings hung up on the wall behind him. It would have been one thing if he had never seen them, but once he got a good look at Sheng Dengyun's artworks, he nearly burst out laughing. He thought to himself: Can you be famous for painting rubbish like that? He felt he couldn't stand it a moment longer and made his farewells.

As they departed the Sheng mansion, Wang Wuqi asked Yu San: "So what position does that man Sheng hold among Tianjin artists?"

"Oh, he's the best, of course… or at least one of the best," Yu San replied. "I wouldn't drag you off to meet someone second-class, now would I? If there's someone else you'd like to meet, just say the word – I can introduce you. Ma Jiatong? Zhang He'an? Zhao Zhixian? Whichever one you like… I know all of them. But when you see one of them, you mustn't mention Mr Sheng – they all hate each other, and say the most horrible things."

"Whatever, it doesn't matter," Wang Wuqi said. "I don't want to meet any of them. I just paint for fun. I really can't be bothered dealing with any of that lot."

Wang Wuqi thought that all he had to do was close the door and he would be isolated from the world. In fact, this was not true at all; he had to sell his brushes, and therefore he was dependent on painters and calligraphers to buy them. Besides which, he had a few friends who were interested in art – none of them were in the least bit famous, and nobody wanted to buy their pictures, but they stuck around. These people admired him greatly and said that he was a very talented artist. They thought that he ought to be better known and went about praising him. As a result, he became more and more renowned in artistic circles. However, they were just making this stuff up... none of them had ever seen one of his paintings. It was just as well, though, because that way there was nothing to criticise; they could only talk about how wonderful they were.

However, that was OK too.

But one day, an old man came to visit him carried in a sedan chair. This man was well dressed and was clearly somebody of position. He was followed by two servants clad in green. The moment he entered, he wanted to see Wang Wuqi's paintings and calligraphy. Wang Wuqi realised that he must be some kind of official, and he was scared of officials – he didn't want anything to do with him. He claimed that he was just a brushmaker, that he'd never really had an education, and that he couldn't paint. As he said this, a new idea flashed into his mind, and he suggested: "I think you've found the wrong person. I've heard that there's someone else with the same name living in Tianjin – he's a painter and calligrapher, and he's been here to buy his brushes. I think he's called Huang Wuqi... or it might be Wang Wuqi, the same as me... I don't really know. He's a famous man, so he wouldn't want to waste his time talking to me."

When the old man heard this, he looked sombre and turned away.

As soon as Yu San heard about this, he started to complain: "Why didn't you just show him some of your paintings? There are lots of painters here in Tianjin, so why would he come and find you if not for the fact that he's heard about your genius? If one of the eight great families of Tianjin were to sponsor you, you'd be in clover!"

Who could have imagined that when he heard this, Wang Wuqi would just smile and ignore him!

Afterwards, there were rumours about this in circulation, especially among the literati. These events were made to sound most shocking: apparently, the man who came to visit Wang Wuqi that day was none other than the magistrate, Liu Mengyang! Liu Mengyang was a scholarly man noted for his painting and calligraphy collection, and he wrote a pretty good hand himself. However, Wang Wuqi had simply refused to show him any of his paintings – his honour the magistrate had been sent off with a flea in his ear!

The people who spread this gossip had their own opinions on the matter. Some of them said that he was a genius, so he was allowed to be a bit peculiar; even if the magistrate turned up to visit him in plain clothes, he did not feel a need to make an exception. Some said that he was just a jumped-up nobody who didn't know his arse from his elbow, and if he insisted on annoying his honour like that, sooner or later he would find himself in serious trouble. There were some individuals who speculated on whether he was ignorant, or mad or just plain stupid, or off his head in some way, or whether he just did not care about the money and did not want anything to do with officialdom. However, they never came to any conclusion about this.

After this, literati circles began to take him very seriously indeed.

There was this minor artist type named Meng Jieyuan, who liked Huizhou-style brushes and hence often called in at A Brush With Spring. One evening about six months later, Meng Jieyuan arrived with another middle-aged man. Wang Wuqi disliked dealing with strangers, but he could not say no because of being friends with Meng Jieyuan, so he let the man come in. This middle-aged visitor spoke with a Beijing accent and seemed very friendly and refined – there certainly was not anything obvious to object to. Meng Jieyuan introduced him as a visitor from the capital, a painter, with a particular interest in landscape monochrome ink painting. He had been painting all afternoon over at Meng Jieyuan's house, and then suddenly he had had the idea of bringing him over so that he could do a painting for Wang Wuqi. He thought that Wang Wuqi might be interested in seeing the kind of artworks in favour in the capital. Meng Jieyuan explained: "He's from Beijing after all, and I'm the only person he knows in Tianjin – he doesn't have any other friends here. He's going back home first thing tomorrow morning."

It was this sentence that made Wang Wuqi relax his usual vigilance. He led them to his study out by the back courtyard, where he spread out his paper and ground his ink. The visitor from the capital rolled up his sleeves and grabbed a large sheep's hair brush, with which he swept up a dollop of ink. With a twirl of his brush, the landscape began to appear... a vista of endless mountains and deep waters wreathed in clouds and mist, and all conveyed through thick brushstrokes and thin washes. Although the painting could not be accounted anything other than pedestrian, it served to arouse Wang Wuqi's interest. When painters feel an urge to paint, there is nothing that can stop them.

He waited until his visitor had finished painting, then he removed his artwork and spread out a piece of fine white Xuan paper for himself. He used one of his own chicken-feather brushes to paint with. Chicken feathers have their own unique characteristics: there are thick and thin filaments, some soft and some hard. And there is oil in them, which means that when dipped into ink, the feathers will react in an unpredictable and interesting way; each brushstroke will be individualised, scattering the colour in wonderful ways.

The visitor from the capital exclaimed in amazement: "What a wonderful painting of water lilies. You are every bit as fine an artist as Shitao or Bada Shanren! This is the first time I have ever seen anyone paint with a chicken-feather brush – but it might as well be made from phoenix feathers!"

Nobody had ever seen Wang Wuqi painting before. Even Meng Jieyuan was seeing this sight for the first time. He was surprised and excited, cheering on the artist as if he were watching a play. Wang Wuqi was still feeling inspired to paint, but he was hot, and his forehead was beaded with sweat. He took off his long coat, and now, dressed only in his trousers and a shirt, he produced another painting of wind-tossed bamboo.

The visitor from the capital then happened to remark: "How about doing some calligraphy with your chicken-feather brush? I guess that would be much more difficult than painting with it…" When he heard that, without saying another word, Wang Wuqi spread out a piece of paper and swapped his original brush for a really fat, two-foot-long chicken-feather brush that he now dipped in the ink, before writing the words: "The wind blows, whipping up the waves, exciting our true feelings."

The visitor from the capital said: "Just those few characters – particularly the word 'true' – really, nobody today could write that better!"

Wang Wuqi was thrilled to hear these words. He felt as though he had finally met someone who could really understand him. He was not expecting that, all of a sudden, the man would reach into his coat and pull out a very heavy package, which he handed to Wang Wuqi. Wang Wuqi did not understand what he meant by this, so the visitor from Beijing explained: "That's three gold bars right there. I'm buying these two paintings and the one piece of calligraphy. Just put your seal on them to authenticate them for me!"

Wang Wuqi was now feeling even more baffled and irritated: You didn't ask me if I was prepared to sell them or not, and now you're ordering me to put my seal on them? But he merely replied: "I sell brushes – I've never sold one of my paintings or pieces of calligraphy before. Besides which, why are you giving me so much money?"

The visitor from Beijing replied: "Tomorrow, your calligraphy and painting will be worth an awful lot more! Let me tell you... I have a gallery at Liulichang in Beijing, and I've heard an awful lot about you. That's why I came here today specially to meet you. Now I've seen you paint, and your work is a whole lot better even than what they told me. I'm going to help you sell your paintings! If you trust me, we can sell your works on commission, split sixty-forty: you get sixty per cent, and we'll take forty. But I am telling you right now that after we've set up the deal, you will have to guarantee that you will only sell your paintings and calligraphy through us – you won't be able to market them through anyone else. Even if you are going to give one of your works away to someone as a present, you'll have to get my agreement first. I know you don't have any dealings with people here in Tianjin... well, neither do we. But once your paintings start selling for big money in the capital, I can guarantee you that you'll be doing OK here in Tianjin too!" When the visitor from Beijing said this, his face split in a huge grin – there was not the slightest trace of the refined and elegant air he had displayed earlier.

"When you are famous," Meng Jieyuan chipped in, "I'll come and grind your ink for you."

Neither of them could have imagined that when Wang Wuqi heard this, he seemed to turn into a different person on the spot. Not only did he refuse to take the gold bars, he acted as if they had insulted him in some way – he looked absolutely furious. He turned round and grabbed the paintings and calligraphy he had just produced and ripped them into shreds. Then he thrust his visitor's landscape painting into Meng Jieyuan's arms before walking them to the door without a word. Once the two men had left, they walked for a long time, but they still looked surprised and puzzled.

From then on, Wang Wuqi refused to have dealings with anyone in the literati. Yu San came round twice, only to be thrown out on both occasions. Meng Jieyuan did not dare to show his face round there again. Everyone was baffled: Tianjin is all about making money – here was the money, so why didn't he want it? He made his living by making brushes, but that was just small change... The God of Wealth was right there wanting to make him rich, but he'd ignored him. It was almost as if he wanted to be a beggar for the rest of his days!

Meng Jieyuan told this story to everyone, and nobody could understand it. Some suggested that Wang Wuqi was nothing but a fool, while others said that it was his destiny to be poor, and that sooner or later he would die in misery.

Whatever people said about Wang Wuqi, he just carried on as usual: he was busy making his brushes and selling them, and then he relaxed afterwards by painting and doing calligraphy. This was his hobby, and he did not care what anyone else thought about it. One day, Wang Wuqi's wife was off playing cards at a neighbour's house, and he went to collect her. Someone asked him if he knew how to play, and he replied: "When I was younger, I did, but I only ever played one game: The Thirteen Problems. You lay it out with the one, four and seven; the two, five and eight; or the three, six, and nine; and you put your cards out north, south, east and west, together with the centre, and you play and play until you're blue in the face. But this card still can't be put together with that... I only know this one game, and it's the one I like. The rest of them I don't know how to play." Then he added: "It's very difficult because it's a kind of Patience – you play against yourself, and that's the best thing!" Having said this, his eyes brightened, as if he had suddenly come to some kind of resolution. When he got home, he wrote the words "The Thirteen Problems" with his chicken-feather brush on a horizontal board, which he hung up on the wall of his studio over the entrance. This became his studio name.

On one occasion, someone asked him what exactly it was that he considered to be the Thirteen Problems? He pointed to the left-hand side of his horizontal board, where there was a line of little characters about the size of your fingernail, which read:

> For me, the Thirteen Problems are powerful men, celebrities, rich snobs, criminals, family connections, so-called friends, women, narcissists and users, confidence tricksters, people who want to give me calligraphy or paintings, people who want to buy my calligraphy or paintings, and the sort of people who don't care what they do.

In Wang Wuqi's mind, the last three kinds were the most important. He did not like people who gave away their artworks because they were using something they loved for the benefits they could get out of it; he did not like people who sold their calligraphy and paintings because they were prepared to betray their art for money; and he did not like the sort of people who do not care what they do because you have to have moderation in everything, to find pleasures where you can.

Wang Wuqi died sometime in 1922. About a week before his death, it seemed as though he realised his time was nearly up. He burned all the calligraphy and paintings in his study and the chicken-feather brush he had used all his life.

✥ 46 ✥
SLINGSHOT YANG

YANG KUANGHAN WAS A MIDDLE-AGED MAN, six feet tall, with long arms and legs, and a waist as thick as a tree trunk. Everyone called him Big Yang. He was super strong, probably thanks to his love of steak tartare, with a physique practically corrugated with musculature. And he ran to a pretty high metabolism, which meant that he'd still be going round bare-armed when it got towards winter, never feeling the need for a coat – at the most, he would just put on a waistcoat. Outside the North Gate, beyond the Houjiahou red-light district, there was a kind of no-man's land, where local hoodlums liked to mess around lifting weights and practising their swordsmanship, and he would go there to mess around himself. However, he never used a sword or a spear: he was only interested in his slingshot. In the normal way of things, he had it tucked into his belt behind him, but when the time came for him to perform, he would pull it out and give everyone a show of what real skill looks like.

Big Yang originally came from Cangzhou in Hebei Province.

Everyone in Cangzhou is good at martial arts, but on arrival in Tianjin, they would find that was a different story. This is just like how clever people from provinces across the country would make their way to Beijing to serve as government officials, only to discover that the world of officialdom is a shark-tank – if you can hold your own, it is a sign that you have got something to you. Tianjin is quite different from the capital, but it has its own sharks. For example, out in No-Man's Land, it might look fun on the surface with all these people practising their martial arts skills, not to mention the musical and theatrical performances held out there along with booths for fortune-tellers, snake-oil salesmen, barbers and hairdressers. However, there were all sorts of remarkable folk with strange and special skills lurking in amongst them. But this was far from being a happy place; they called it No-Man's Land for a reason. This was a place where bodies were dumped or hastily buried, and the authorities did nothing to investigate; where people were tricked or swindled out of their money, and nobody cared; where fighting broke out, and people could beat one another up without anyone attempting to intervene. There were professional criminals here, mixed in with the crowds, each one more evil than the last. If you were trying to scrape a living out here, they would not care where you came from, and they would not care if you were part of a gang – they would just jump you and fling you into the Bai River.

When Big Yang first arrived at the wharves in Tianjin, he realised that this place was very colourful. The ordinary men and women were very kind-hearted, while the criminals were extraordinarily cruel – you had lambs and tigers living side by side. However, these tigers had no interest in the lambs: they only went after other tigers. Big Yang was a huge guy, overtopping everyone else by a head. In those days, he rented a hut over by the Grand Canal, and one day as he returned home in the evening, he suddenly felt something catch against his ankles. Those who practise martial arts are very sensitive in every part of their body, so he immediately realised that somebody must have set a tripwire for him. He bent over and grabbed hold of the cord, giving it such a fierce tug that he dragged out the two little thugs lurking in ambush on either side of the road and pulled them over to where he stood. He then clouted their heads together with such a bang that they ended up all bruised and bleeding.

Big Yang thought no one would dare to provoke him again. Three days later, he went back home and lay down, only to find himself itching horribly all over. When he lit the lamp, he realised that there were bedbugs everywhere. Where could they have come from? It turned out that those nasty little thugs had emptied a big canister of live bedbugs over his bed while he was off out of the house.

This really annoyed the big guy from Cangzhou. The very next day, he was out in No-Man's Land showing off his martial arts skills, his torso completely bare, but with a yellow cloth bag slung over his shoulder. The bag was half-full of slingshot pellets the size of grapes. These pellets were made of black clay, and who knows what was inside them, but they were as black and hard as iron. His slingshot was also most unusual: a fork of willow-wood one and a half foot long, with a thick two-foot-long buffalo sinew sling hanging between the two upper ends. If you shot these iron-hard pellets out of a slingshot like that, wouldn't it be like firing one of those foreign guns? When Big Yang put one of his pellets into the leather pouch hanging in the middle of the buffalo sinew, it was like putting a bullet into the breech of a gun. The bystanders watching the fun started to worry that he might go off of his own accord. If that pellet headed your way, it would break your head open like a watermelon!

Big Yang, solid and unmoving as a pine tree, stood in the middle of the open ground bolt upright, bellowing in his deep, booming voice: "Don't worry, everybody! I'm just going to shoot up into the sky!" As he said this, he raised his slingshot and pointed it straight upwards, pulling back on the sling, and then shot the pellet up into the air. Who knows where it ended up... somewhere in the clouds maybe?

As they watched, Big Yang stretched out his arm and held out his hand, and then with a sudden thud, the pellet he'd shot into the sky fell straight back to earth and landed right in the middle of his palm. How accurate is that? What amazing kung fu! What a fantastic thing to be able to do with your bare hands!

Without waiting for the crowds to cheer him, Big Yang took out another two pellets from his bag. His first shot was a backward one, straight up into the air, in the position "Buffalo Facing the Moon". Having shot off his first pellet, quick as a flash, he turned round and fired off the second, his head tilted right back – this was the pose "Turning to Face the Moon". It was quite obvious to one and all that his second shot went off with a great deal more force behind it, and the pellet flew out that much faster. A moment later, there was a crisp report somewhere high, high up in the sky, as the second pellet caught up with the first one and smashed it to smithereens. The crowd shouted their acclaim. This was the first time in their lives that any of these Tianjin people had seen such skills – and in Tianjin, if there was one thing that got people's admiration, it was real skill.

Just at this moment, someone stepped out from the crowd – a man wearing a black jacket and black trousers, with black shoes and a dark-skinned face, and an expression filled with malice. He walked forward aggressively, and every single person out in No-Man's Land recognised him straight away, for this was the famous gangster, Blackleg.

Without saying a word, Blackleg had the old man running the nearby tea stall bring over one of his tables, and in the middle he placed a blue-and-white porcelain teapot. Then he took a glass marble out of his pocket and balanced it neatly in the spout. Afterwards, he turned his head and said to Big Yang: "You see this? This here teapot is Qianlong-era blue-and-white, and it's worth a gold bar. If you've got the guts, I want to see you knock the marble out of the spout of this teapot but without damaging the spout. If you break my nice Qianlong-era teapot, you're going to have to pay me for it! If you reckon you can't do it, then I want you to get down on all fours and crawl across the ground for me, banging your head three times in submission, and then piss off out of here and never show your face again!" His tone was like a flick of the whip against raw skin.

This teapot was just one of the regular ones from the stall and was not worth more than a few coppers – yet here he was claiming it was Qianlong blue-and-white. But in No-Man's Land, if Blackleg said something, then that's what it was.

Big Yang heard him out with the abstracted air of someone listening to a cicada chirping; he was not remotely bothered by all these threats. He just took a pellet out of his bag and then said to the people standing behind the table: "Can everybody move back a bit for me?" They all immediately shifted out of the way. Big Yang spread his arms out wide, with his front hand holding the slingshot and the back hand pulling on the leather pouch where the pellet was nesting, the buffalo sinew humming with the tension as it was jerked back. Then, with a twist of his body and a bend at the waist, he got himself into the position called "The Hegemon King Draws His Bow" and suddenly released the leather pouch pinched between his two fingers. The sinew flew through the air, and there was a giant bang from the teapot. Everyone thought that the teapot must have been smashed to bits, but when they looked more closely, it was sitting there just fine, with the spout not even chipped. The glass marble lodged in the spout, however, had essentially exploded, and there were glittering shards glinting all over the ground.

Everyone was stunned. Blackleg seemed to deflate before their very eyes.

Now Big Yang spoke out: "I've only got five pellets. I've already used up three, and the last two I have a specific use for – they are set aside for two little thugs. Anyone who thinks they're going to get away with bullying me... or anyone else that I see... well, one of these days they're going to be paying with an eye. I'll be having their left eye off them!" Having said that, he put a single pellet into the leather pouch on his slingshot. By now, everyone had seen enough to be terrified.

From then on, Big Yang had his space over in No-Man's Land, and as long as he was there, everything was nice and quiet. He could use a slingshot with the same deadly accuracy as one of those foreign guns, and he was even faster – who could say that he might not beat someone with a gun to the draw? If he set to, you might easily lose an eye; of course people were scared of him! After this, Big Yang had a very impressive nickname: he was Slingshot Yang.

Seven years later, during the Boxer Rebellion, the foreign armies destroyed the northern part of the city of Tianjin, setting fires and murdering people, robbing every shop they came across. The residents of Tianjin were hardly going to stand for this, and they fought back hard. Apparently, one foreign army officer who died was not cut to pieces with weapons but taken out by a single shot. Many saw him fall, his left eye reduced to a black hole with blood pouring from it; it was a terrible way to die. At that time, all of the soldiers in Tianjin's Wuwei Corps were armed with foreign guns, so they thought it must have been a Wuwei Corps bullet that did for him. Then locals started to say that it wasn't a bullet that killed him at all but one of Big Yang's pellets, and this was because he lost his left eye. They said that this foreign officer had been a horrible man, who'd killed all sorts of innocent people, and so Big Yang had made him pay.

As to whether any of this was true or not, who knows? Big Yang was never seen alive again after the Boxer Rebellion, and No-Man's Land was reduced to a wasteland. It was only twenty years later that something of the same sort was reconstituted in the Southern Market area outside the South Gate.

47
JIAO QI

As we all know, in Tianjin, the worst thing that can possibly happen to you is to have trouble with the local gangsters. Sometimes, gangsters are also called hoodlums, but the fact is that gangsters are something quite different – each one is worse than the last. You have cruel ones, you have evil ones, you have tough guys and you have tricky ones. However, the most horrible of all are the hidden ones – those who are hidden away are much, much worse than the ones that you know about. How bad can they possibly be, you may ask? Well, right here, there are certain people who did certain things, and when you hear the story, you will understand just how nasty they can get.

This particular gangster was called Jiao Qi, and to look at him, you would think he was half-disabled. He had a bald head and a clean-shaven face, with long arms and stumpy little legs, blackened lips and dull eyes. If he walked for any length of time, he would start panting, so he clearly did not have much strength. Nor was he possessed of any particular skill, so he never held down a job. But for all of that, he had a pretty comfortable life, with wine and meat at every meal, and he lived in a huge fancy house over in Liangjiazui, with a whole host of young thugs looking out for him and carrying out his orders. You would never see him getting into a fight or killing people, nor was he about to throw his weight around whenever he went out, yet he was the most famous gangster in all of Tianjin. Traditionally, gangsters have divided themselves into the quiet and the loud, and he was the quiet kind. He had not got to where he was by brute force and fighting all comers; he had his own nasty little tricks. With good people, you can see their skills, but with the wicked, outsiders do not get to see a goddam thing. If you want to understand what he could do, you had to catch him at it.

Jiao Qi's favourite food was sausages. Everything else in life he entrusted to others, but he made his sausages himself. He would only eat his own home-made sausages: he would buy the meat, mince it up, toss in his seasoning, fill the casings – he had his own recipe. As to how much white wine to put in and how much pepper, whether to add soy sauce, oil, spring onion, ginger, or sugar, how much fat meat should go with how much lean... he did not trust anyone else to get it right. He would eat them all himself too, since he was not going to share them with anyone else: even his wife very rarely got so much as a taste. It is a fact that cruel people like to keep things to themselves.

When he had just moved into his house at Liangjiazui, he discovered a huge old elm tree out in the courtyard, with lots of branches and good leaf cover, letting the breeze through but not the sun, which meant that it was just perfect for drying sausages. He would loop his strings of fresh sausages round the branches of the tree, because by drying them out a little, he would get the texture just right – they would be really good to eat. But having done this a few times, he suddenly realised he was not taking down as many sausages as he put up. That was odd! Were the crows taking them? Or was it a cat? The next time he made sausages, he came up with a plan. He counted exactly how many strings he had, and having hung them up in the branches of the tree, he settled down to keep an eye on them. One day, he suddenly saw a bamboo pole appear over the wall to the neighbour's house, and on the end of this pole someone had lashed a hook. With a twist and a tug, a whole string of sausages sailed over to the other side of the wall. Bugger! They were being stolen!

"How dare you touch my sausages!" Jiao Qi was in a rage. However, he was not the kind of person to show his feelings; he just swallowed his anger and set himself to thinking exactly how he would take his revenge. He thought of this and that, before he came up with the most perfect, most sinister plan: something that would send the greedy pig next door to hell as he deserved for his sausage-stealing antics.

The next day, he went out to buy a lump of meat, a bag of sausage casings, some spring onions and ginger. Then he made a detour, which took him past a pharmacist, where he bought a small package of arsenic. When he got home, he minced the meat and mixed up his seasonings out in the middle of the courtyard, adding in a sprinkling of arsenic before stuffing the casings with this mixture. Having made fifteen strings of poisoned sausages, he strung them up in the tree. Afterwards, he spent the next couple of days on a chair out in the courtyard, smoking cigarettes and drinking tea, keeping his eyes fixed on the poisoned sausages hanging from the branches of the tree, just like a fisherman squatting on the riverbank waiting to catch his fish. A couple of days passed, and finally he got to see the pole with the hook lashed to the end come over the top of the wall and pull away two strings of poisoned sausages. He smiled to himself, and the rage he had been feeling all this time simply vanished.

Afterwards, he took the remainder of the poisoned sausages down from the tree and put them into a bag. Once it got dark, he nipped out of the house and threw them all into the river.

That night, he suddenly heard the sound of screaming and shouting coming from next door – first there were calls for help, and then there was wailing about people having died. There was the sound of weeping and dogs barking, and what with one thing and another, the racket went on all night. The next morning, one of the thugs came by to say that Mr Hu next door, who was something or other big in the lumber business, had been poisoned to death. The authorities had sent a couple of officers out to investigate. Jiao Qi carried on as if this had nothing at all to do with him; as insouciant as if he had been hearing about a truck running over a stray dog.

That afternoon, there was a thunderous knocking on the door. When Jiao Qi went to open up, he saw several officers standing in the entranceway, dressed in black. They did not wait for him to say anything, but one of them gestured to three sausages lying on a piece of paper and asked: "Are these yours?"

The officer must have imagined that he would deny it. But the pale face in front of him simply smiled coldly. Then it was Jiao Qi who asked the officer: "How on earth have you laid hands on some of my sausages?"

The officer started and replied: "Look, I'm asking the

questions here. Why have you been putting arsenic in your sausages?" That was getting to the crux of the matter.

Jiao Qi replied straight away: "These sausages were never meant to be eaten – I wanted to kill off those bloody weasels. Of course I put arsenic in them! What else would I use?"

The officer was nonplussed by Jiao Qi's answer and had no idea how to proceed. His next question was much milder: "You know that your sausages killed Mr Hu senior next door?"

Jiao Qi pretended not to have the slightest idea what the man was talking about. "That's impossible!" he said. "My weasel-poisoning sausages were all hung up safe and sound in the tree in my courtyard – how can he possibly have eaten one? Did he steal it?" Then he suddenly burst out laughing and said: "That's nothing to do with me. Suppose he climbed over the wall into my house and cut his throat with one of my kitchen knives – are you going to say that was my fault too?"

The officers were left with nothing to say, and they stood there in silence.

Everything that Jiao Qi said was perfectly logical. He did not deny that these were his sausages, or that he had put arsenic in them, but he had done so in order to poison the weasels that plagued him, and that is not a crime. Mr Hu senior had stolen the poisoned sausages and eaten them, but that was hardly Jiao Qi's fault. No matter how you cut it, this had nothing to do with him. In the end, even the Hu family had to admit that if anyone was to blame here, it was Mr Hu senior himself; if he hadn't stolen those sausages, he wouldn't have died. In the end, the authorities closed the case – Mr Hu senior's greed had brought about his death, and it was nothing to do with Jiao Qi.

However, these events demand that we think deeper about

the whole situation. What kind of person makes poisoned sausages to kill weasels? The Jiao family did not keep chickens, and nobody had said anything before about the place being infested with weasels, so why did he want to poison these wretched animals? Why would anyone go to so much trouble for no good reason? On the other hand, Mr Hu senior had stolen Jiao Qi's sausages once before and annoyed him very much – wasn't that why he came up with this horrible plan and killed him in this terrible way?

Gradually, everyone came to understand exactly what had happened here, but there was nothing anyone could do to bring him to justice. The authorities could not do anything about it, and nothing much ever happened to Jiao Qi. He certainly was not the kind of person you want to needle.

The person who came off worst in all of this was Mr Hu senior, who lived well for so many years, only to ultimately fall victim to his own greed. Even his family felt shamed by it, and in the end they quietly moved away from Liangjiazui.

48
MR MAO AND MR JIA

THIS IS A TRUE STORY, but nobody is quite sure when exactly it took place.

There was a latrine over on Dan Street, which ran alongside the bank of the Grand Canal. During the day, there was light to see by, but at night, nobody put up any lanterns, so no one dared to use it after dark. If you had to feel your way through the pitch darkness, it was all too easy to stumble into the latrine pit.

On the night in question, someone did make his way in – a man so thin that he was just skin and bones, carrying an empty basket. He walked right to the middle of the latrine, whereupon he turned the basket over so its bottom was facing upwards. He stepped up on top, and as he did so, he loosened his belt because he was going to sling that over the beam – he intended to kill himself.

But when he looked up, he saw that there was already a noose hanging from the beam. Who on earth had put that there? He reached out a hand and tugged at it: the noose had been very

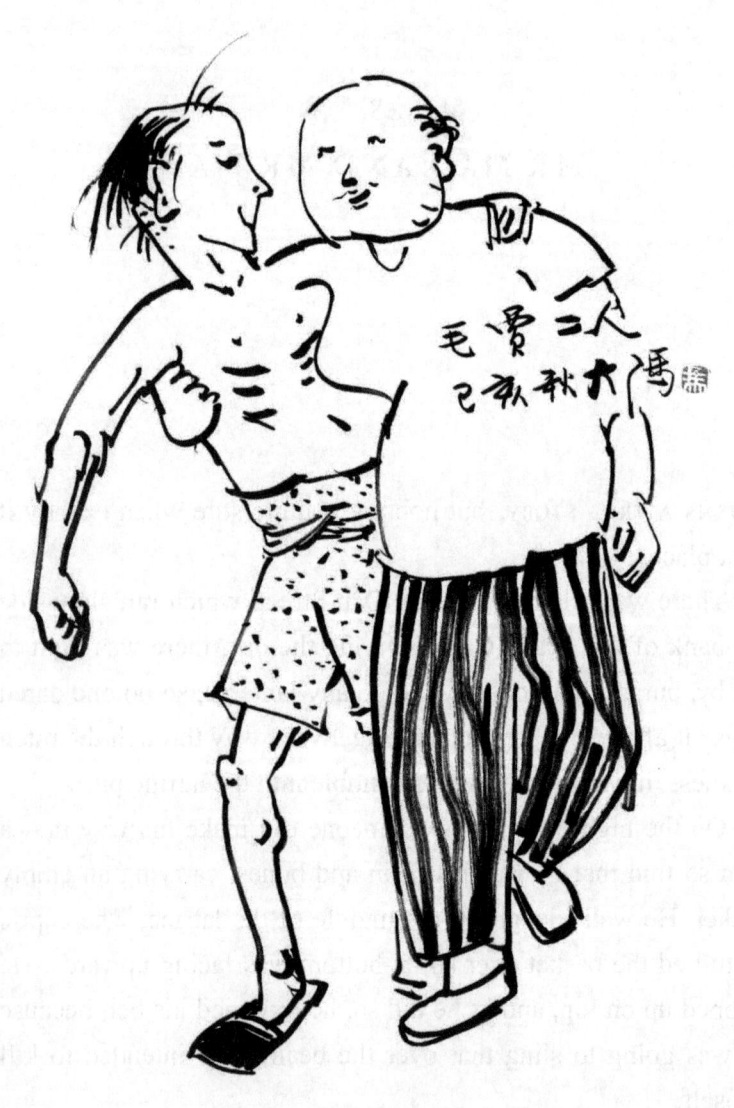

neatly tied. He made up his mind to use that instead and was just about to thrust his head in, when a voice came from the blackness beneath him: "You're not to use that! It's mine!"

The thin man was startled. He thought he must have encountered a ghost. He was in a panic and jumped down from the basket. Then he spotted a figure sitting on a stool.

"Who are you?" the thin man asked.

"It doesn't matter who I am. Anyway, we both want to die, so we can each kill ourselves separately. What's the point of asking all these questions?"

"Given that we've met and we're both about to die, what's wrong with chatting a bit first?"

"Oh, sure, I get you. Well, you first… Why do you want to die?" the man sitting on the stool asked.

At this time, the scene within the dark room gradually became a little clearer. Although he could not really see what the man sitting on the stool looked like, he could make out the broad outlines of his figure – he was a fat guy. The thin man said to the fat guy: "OK. I have a little business selling groceries, and I've got into serious financial difficulties. I've had to borrow, and I can't pay back. The longer things go on, the worse they get. I've racked my brains for any idea about how to fix this, and nothing will do me any good – I've decided to die. What about you?"

The fat guy didn't answer but just enquired: "How much money do you owe?"

"Forty taels. How can I ever pay that back? I'll have to kill myself."

Unexpectedly, the fat man said: "You're prepared to die for such a small sum of money… if you're not careful, your whole family may end up topping themselves." The fat man then said sombrely: "I've got a silver ingot here, fifty taels all told. I'll give it to you so you can pay off your debts. There's no need for you to die!"

When the thin man heard that, he said: "You're suicidal yourself, and yet you want to make fun of me! If you've got so much money, why should you want to kill yourself? Haven't you got money troubles too?"

"Oh, sure. I used to run a local bank – but I got swindled by a gang out of Linfen. I've lost the house, and my wife ran off. I can't face anyone any more. That's why I decided to kill myself." The fat guy didn't say any more about this because there was nothing to say. He just told the thin guy: "Just take the money. There's enough there for you to pay off your debts. It can save you, but it can't save me."

The thin man did not like to take it and said: "You're about to die, and here I am taking money off you. What does that look like?"

"It's not like I can take it with me on my way to hell," the fat man pointed out. "Just take it and go. I'm going to sit here in peace and quiet for a bit. Once I've hanged myself, that will be an end to it all."

The thin man could never have imagined that as he was on his way to die, someone would extend a helping hand. Yama, King of Hell, apparently did not want him... a whole silver ingot seemed to have dropped from the sky! He got down on hands and knees before his saviour and kowtowed three times. Then he picked up the silver ingot and ran off home.

When the thin man got home, he found his wife and told her everything that had happened. His wife burst into tears, furiously upset that he had been so selfish as to think of killing himself, leaving her and the kids behind. But when she saw the silver ingot, she cheered up – they would now be able to pay off all their debts. They could start again with a clean slate. Then, all of a sudden, she said: "That man saved your life, and you left him there to die…"

"What else could I do? He's lost absolutely everything – he's ruined. What could I do to help him?"

"At the very least, you could have brought him round here to eat a plate of dumplings. That would have been only polite. He can kill himself *after* he's had his dumplings. Right, I'm going to mix the dough and chop the veg. It's the middle of the night, so you won't be able to find anyone to sell you some meat, but if you go next door to the Zhang family, they'll let you borrow a couple of eggs." That was what the thin man's wife said.

The thin man rushed off to borrow some eggs. Meanwhile, his wife was busy chopping vegetables, making dough, and rolling out the wrappers for the dumplings. As she rushed around, it so happened that she dropped her rolling pin on the ground. The floor was uneven, and the rolling pin rolled off into a corner of the room. The odd thing was that as the rolling pin went rolling off, when it hit the wall, it somehow or other rolled so that it pitched into a mouse-hole with a thump, end on. She reached into the hole to pull it out, and as she did so, her fingers touched something – what could it be that was so hard and so heavy? Pulling whatever it was out to have a look at it… this was no rolling pin but a huge and shining bar of gold! What on earth was happening? Had the God of Wealth decided to take up abode in their humble home? First a silver ingot, and now a whole bar of gold! She felt as if she were dreaming, but clearly she was wide awake.

A short time later, the thin man came back clutching his eggs, and he was quite overwhelmed by the sight. The two of them quickly moved everything out of that corner of the room and set to with a hoe and shovel. Pretty soon, they'd dug out two jars filled with gold bars, and when they counted them, there were one hundred and ten.

The thin man was quite overcome, but his wife kept her head. She told him to run back to the latrine as quickly as possible and tell the fat man that on no account whatsoever was he to kill himself: the money was there.

That brought the thin man to his senses, and he said: "You're quite right. He gave us that silver ingot to save us, and now it's our turn to do the same by him."

"You'd better be quick," his wife said. "For all you know, he's already hanging from that beam."

The thin man ran to the latrine so fast it seemed he was flying. The moment he looked around him, he knew all was well – the fat guy was still sitting there crying. He went in and dragged the fat guy out of the latrine, hauling him all the way home. When the fat guy saw the two jars filled to the brim with gold bars, he was puzzled as to what this could all be about.

"With all of this gold," the thin man said with a laugh, "there's no need for you to go and kill yourself."

The fat guy waved his hand vigorously; he had no intention of taking their money.

"What are you talking about?" the thin man demanded. "You gave us that silver ingot, and that saved my family – what do you mean by saying I can't save you?"

Now the thin man's wife said: "If you hadn't given us that silver ingot, we'd never have found the two jars of gold bars. It must be that God on High felt sorry for the pair of you, and that's why all of this happened with one thing after another. It would make a great play, this would."

The two men divided up the gold bars, each taking half, so it was one jar per person. Later on, the pair went into business, each of them opening a store.

The thin man had a big grocery store over by the North Gate; he sold produce coming up from the south on the Grand Canal, such as salted duck, bacon, spice-cured chicken, salami and other household items. The fat guy opened a shop for foreign products on Xiaoyanghuo Street near the Temple of the Queen of Heaven, and everything in the place was newfangled fashionable stuff brought in from overseas via the Foreign Concession at Zizhulin. In both cases, business was good – good enough for the two of them to make a name for themselves, and they earned a decent amount of money at it. But no matter how rich they got, they never forgot their friendship – the two men continued to be in regular contact. One day, they were discussing what had happened and sighing over it. They decided they would build a house together over on Dan Street north of the city, and then they would both move in so that their kids and grandkids could all grow up together. They had been through some bad times, and now things were good for them – that was where things had been at their worst, but they had brought each other through it safe and sound, so for the two of them, it was hallowed ground. They found a suitable empty spot on the right-hand side of Dan Street, and they bought it together. Then they brought in a construction company to build them two long houses, eight rooms on each side, with their front doors facing each other. An alley ran down the middle between them, which both families shared, so that the two households would constantly be meeting one another as they came in and out, as friendly as if they were all one family.

This alleyway needed a name. The thin man was called Mao, and the fat guy was called Jia, so this was the Mao-Jia Joint Alley. However, I don't know whether they chose this name for themselves, or whether it was given to them by other people.

If they chose it themselves, then it was to commemorate their friendship, in the hope that it would continue forever. If it was given to them by other people, then it was in appreciation of the kindness and good feeling shown by Mr Mao and Mr Jia, who went through the worst of times together and shared their later happiness with one another.

49
THE MALLET-SHAPED SNUFF BOTTLE

FACES COME in six different colours: there are yellowish faces, blackish faces, ruddy faces, pale faces, greyish faces and bluish faces. But Third Young Master Ni from Houjiahou did not have any of those kinds; he had a fleshy face. What do I mean by fleshy face? Surely everyone has some flesh on their faces? How could his face be completely colourless?

Of course, it had some colour, but it was not a pure colour. When he was hungry, his face showed a yellowish tinge; if he stayed hungry, his face went pale; if he was hungry for a very long time, it went greyish; if he was so starved that he got sick, his face went bluish; when he was basically starving to death, his face turned black; and when he finally got something to eat, then his face took on a pink tinge, and if he got a bit of wine, it went quite ruddy.

But wasn't he the Third Young Master of the Ni family? How could someone like that possibly go hungry? As a young man, it is true that he did not have to worry about making a

living because his father was rich. But later on, his father died, the family went bankrupt, he did not have any means to make a living, and pretty soon he ran out of cash. When you have picked all the jujubes off the tree in the back yard, how can you not end up going hungry? But Third Young Master Ni wasn't one to let the side down, no matter how poor he got. Even when he had sold everything in the house right down to the portraits of his ancestors, there were still some things he kept back, which he decided never to sell in his own lifetime. These were the things he needed to make a good impression every time he went out, and they would include his clothes, shoes and hat, which gave him the air of a rich young man, as well as the knick-knacks that a fashionable gentleman would have about his person – glasses, brush and comb, ear scoop, folding fan, snuff bottle, rosary and so on and so forth. All of these items, when not laid away in lavender, were neatly kept in their hard or soft cases, each covered in silk satin and embroidered with auspicious designs, all with beautifully matching colours. Each one of these cases had a really pretty silk cord attached so that they could be suspended from their owner's waist, hanging all around his body. When he walked along, they would sway below his stomach, attracting everyone's attention. These things were how the rich gentlemen of Tianjin showed off their position.

It did not matter that Third Young Master Ni had sold or pawned everything in the house, to the point where the only thing left at the bottom of the empty chests were some mouse droppings – the things he wore about his person were never going to be got rid of. When he walked down the street dressed like that, everyone had to give him the time of day. Who was to know that he was going hungry with it? There was one occasion when he went over to the Foreign Concession dressed like that, and a foreigner proceeded to stop him very politely and then immortalised him in a photograph right then and there. Apparently, even the Dowager Empress Cixi had been snapped the same way. As to what it was all about, he did not care. When the foreigner photographed him, he was asked to put on his little round dark glasses, while in one hand he held a folding fan, and in the other he gripped his ear scoop and gestured as if he were clearing his ears of wax.

One day, he got up early in the morning and dressed, only to realise that he was feeling a little hungry and there was nothing whatsoever to eat in the house. Having eaten the left-over tea leaves out of his cup and thus pulled himself together a bit, he went out into the streets. After crossing the Old Bridge, he walked from north of the Temple of the Queen of Heaven to the south, pausing every time he met an acquaintance to chat a little bit about this and that. This also gave the passers-by an opportunity to admire his fine appearance. When he walked out of the East Gate to the old city, he was feeling almost faint with hunger, and his face was quite pale, his palms and forehead beaded with sweat. Just by the side of the road, there was a small restaurant called "The Many Blessings". He'd been there many times before, so he just lifted the curtain in front of the door and went straight in. The waiter knew him well, and did not bother asking him what he wanted to eat; he just slapped down on the table in front of him a vegetarian aubergine dish and two buns, together with a bowl of salty soup, and he didn't even bother to chop up some coriander for the soup. This meal would cost two or three coppers, and it was what the poor ate in those days to fill themselves up.

Third Young Master Ni chewed slowly, since he did not want anyone to know he was going hungry. By the time he got to his soup, he was prepared to take his time over it, and he swallowed it with every sign of enjoyment, for all the world as if he were drinking a bowl of sea-cucumber soup. Every so often, he would put it down so that he could take his comb out and run it through his hair; or else he would undo his snuff bottle case from his belt so that he could pull out the bottle itself and put it on the table. He was not going to actually take any snuff; this was all about showing off.

In the good old days, Third Young Master Ni's family had owned any number of fine snuff bottles, but after his father died and his mother got sick, they'd had to sell them all. This one bottle was left because it didn't have a lid. It was quite an ordinary bottle, very simple in shape, without anything in particular to recommend it. It was the kind commonly known as a "mallet" bottle, made from white porcelain, thickly glazed and with plenty of pinholes in the top part. It was painted with a picture of a Pekingese with golden yellow fur. The painting wasn't great either, and there was just the dog – no background at all – so it was far from being a work of art. On various occasions, he had tried to sell it to antique shops, but nobody wanted it, so in the end he had just kept it for himself. He had a very fine cover which had lost its bottle, so he put his "mallet" in there. However, his snuff bottle had lost its lid, and he did not have any money to get a new one. Having turned over all of his boxes and bags, he could not find anything suitable to act as a topper, so what to do? One day when he was walking along Shang Street with his head down, he happened to notice a little knucklebone in the gutter, and the idea came to him. He picked it up and took it home, and then popped it onto the mouth of the bottle: it fitted perfectly! The little knucklebone was just the right shape, nice and round, and it made the perfect lid. Once it had been polished up a bit, it looked like it had been made for it.

Just as he was about to pick up his bottle to take a pinch of snuff, he suddenly spotted an old man sitting opposite him. The old man was dark-skinned and thin, with a sharply pointed nose, a moustache, a narrow face and brightly twinkling eyes. He was dressed in a blue robe, and from his appearance, it was not at all obvious who he might be. The old man was not looking at Third Young Master Ni; his eyes were riveted on the mallet-shaped snuff bottle. He could not understand why he was staring so hard at his rubbishy little bottle.

Before her could ask, the man spoke first: "Would you be interested in selling your snuff bottle?"

This sudden remark came from out of the blue.

The thing is that when people are poor, they become very cautious. Third Young Master Ni had been forced to learn how to bargain, and although he did not quite understand what the old man was up to, he knew how to reply to such an overture. He opened negotiations: "How much silver are you prepared to pay for something that has been an heirloom in my family for hundreds of years?" He was using this gambit to try and see what the other man wanted, since he did not believe for an instant that anyone would pay good money for his wretched bottle.

Apparently, however, the old man was not trying to tease him. He raised his hands and spread all five fingers to indicate the price: five taels of silver.

That gave Third Young Master Ni pause for thought. Five taels of silver? That would be enough to live off the fat of the land for three whole months! However, the poorer you get, the trickier you become. Third Young Master Ni now suddenly started to wonder: might this snuff bottle that he had inherited from his father have something special about it? Maybe no one who had looked at it previously had seen it properly, but this man was actually a real connoisseur? When he reached this point in his thinking, he laughed and said: "Do you really think I'm going to sell you this heirloom for that little money?"

The old man stood up and said: "In that case, I hope you look after it." Then he turned and walked away. The whole thing seemed very odd. If he really wanted to buy it, then why didn't he haggle a bit with Third Young Master Ni?

Third Young Master Ni watched the old man walk away, his jaw sagging. Could he stop him? Of course he could not. He didn't know whether there was anything special about this particular mallet-shaped bottle. If he went and stopped the old man, was he really going to sell it? And if so, how much for? It might be that his father had left him a real treasure here.

This idea made him feel a lot better than he had for a long time. However, his snuff bottle did not have a lid, and he was just using a bit of bone as a stopper. If it were really worth money, it ought to have a nice lid, so he decided to sell the last remaining hardwood octagonal table he had at home and used the money to get a jeweller to make a proper red agate stopper for his snuff bottle. The lid was set in bronze, gilded in pure gold, and the workmanship was very fine indeed.

Mr Ma, the owner of the jewellery store, said: "To tell you the truth, your snuff bottle is really poor quality. The way you've had it done is like wearing a second-hand cotton-padded jacket and putting a mink hat on your head."

Third Young Master Ni smiled mysteriously and said: "If you've got such a good eye, you should be in the antiques business."

Having put such a good lid on it, he did not dare have his snuff bottle hanging from his waist any more because he was worried that in a moment of inattention, someone might steal it off him. Instead, he had to tuck it inside his jacket. Then whenever he wanted to show off, he would ostentatiously pull it out so that other people could admire it – at that moment, he would be feeling pretty grand.

As time went by and the novelty passed off, a problem arose. He could not keep his treasure always about his person if that meant his stomach was empty. You can do without all kinds of things, but you cannot do without food. You need three meals a day, and missing out on any one of them means that you won't be able to carry on. He quietly took his treasure off to the Studio of Gathered Beauties to ask them how much they would give him for it, only to be told that the red agate lid was worth some money, but the rubbishy ceramic bottle underneath he might as well just throw away.

Third Young Master Ni was so angry he was left speechless. He turned around and walked straight out. But when he had taken his snuff bottle to seven or eight different antique shops between Majiakou and Guyi Street, they all took one look at it and turned up their noses. He had no idea what was going on. Then he remembered how he had met the narrow-faced thin old man with the darkly tanned skin and the little moustache over at the "Many Blessings" restaurant by the East Gate, so he had his aubergine and buns there day after day, but the man never turned up. He asked the waiter about him, but he just said: "He wasn't a regular. I have no idea who he might be..." But he seemed to be the only person to recognise what a treasure he had in his possession! Third Young Master Ni now started to dream about the dark-skinned old man, regretting that he had ever allowed him to just walk away.

After the dog days of summer, the autumn turned cool. One day, walking through Beidaguan, he felt a little hungry and bought two freshly baked sesame cakes, hot and steaming from the oven. Then he went over to a teahouse by the side of the road and asked for a bowl of hot tea so he could drink it with his snack. Turning around, he saw that the old man was just sitting there drinking his tea at the table by the window. He felt like a lost child who had suddenly spotted his mother in the crowd – he ran over and, without saying a word, pulled out the snuff bottle that had taken so much criticism from others and put it down in front of the old man. His gesture seemed to be saying: Look at this! Look at this bottle... and this lid! How's about it?

The old man, quite unexpectedly, appeared neither amazed nor pleased. Just like the owners of the various antique shops, he just closed his eyes and refused to look at it; it was as if it was an entirely different object from last time. Third Young Master Ni was sure that the man still wanted his treasure, and he controlled his excitement. He told the old man: "I've added an agate lid to the bottle... it's something really special now! I'm sure you'll appreciate it all the more!"

The old man just said lightly: "You'd better keep it for yourself."

"You don't want it?" Third Young Master Ni said with a smile. "Last time, didn't you want to buy it for five taels of silver?"

The old man looked sombre. "This snuff bottle isn't the same as the one I saw – you've ruined it." He seemed quite upset.

Third Young Master Ni was stunned and said: "Ruined it! You're having me on. I've just added a top… a red agate lid."

The old man shook his head but did not say a word. Third Young Master Ni was starting to feel a little bit anxious. This old man was probably the only person in the world who would pay real money for his mallet-shaped bottle – if he did not want it, nobody else would have it. Third Young Master Ni now said: "If you don't want it, see if I care. But you've got to tell me exactly how I ruined it…"

The old man looked at Third Young Master Ni's anxious face and was silent for a moment. Then he spoke: "There's a dog painted on your snuff bottle, right?"

"Absolutely," Third Young Master Ni said. "To be precise, it's a Pekingese."

"And what do dogs eat?" the old man then asked.

"Meat and bones," Third Young Master Ni declared. "Dogs aren't exactly vegetarian."

Then the old man continued: "And what was your lid last time? Was it perhaps a knucklebone?"

"Oh, yes," Third Young Master Ni said. "It didn't have a proper lid, so I made one for it myself."

"There you have it!" the old man said. "Let me tell you – your knucklebone lid matched the dog on your snuff bottle perfectly – dogs need a good bone the same way as people need their rice. But now you've swapped it out for this one, so your poor dog doesn't have anything to eat. Sooner or later it's going to starve to death. That's why I said you've ruined it!"

Third Young Master Ni was now panicking, and his voice

grew louder and louder. He almost seemed to scream as he said: "You're having me on! That Pekingese is painted on there – how can it need bones to eat? If you want a bone on there, I'll go right out onto the street and find you one!"

The old man looked at him, half-smiling, with an expression that nobody could read. "Quite obviously, you don't understand what I've been talking about," he said to Third Young Master Ni. "You've got to this state... how can it be that you still haven't grasped the situation? I don't have any more time to waste on all this." Having said these words, he walked away and never looked back. No matter how much Third Young Master Ni shouted at him, he simply did not stop.

Third Young Master Ni stood there, staring blankly. He simply could not understand what the old man was talking about – none of it seemed to make any sense.

Afterwards, someone said to Third Young Master Ni: "You shouldn't pay any attention to his bluff. He loves your snuff bottle and was just trying it on. All I can say is that for the next six months, if anyone comes to find you wanting to buy that bottle, you'd better not sell it to them. You can be quite sure that anyone wanting to buy your snuff bottle is going to be acting for that old man."

Third Young Master Ni believed him. But nobody ever came to find him wanting to buy that snuff bottle – not in the next six months, nor in the following year. Instead, he tried to sell it, but that proved impossible. In the end, he stopped caring about whether it was worth any money or not, but he still never quite got his head around what the old man had told him. When the story got out, all sorts of people tried to explain what the old man meant, but their explanations were all different. Some said the old man never had the slightest intention of buying the snuff bottle and that he was just teasing Third Young Master Ni; some said the old man had the money the first time round, but the second, he couldn't afford it; and others claimed the whole thing was made up by Third Young Master Ni, trying to drum up some interest in his rubbishy old bottle.

There was an educated gentleman who lived over in the northwest corner of the city who had a quite different explanation. He said that the old man was someone of remarkable intelligence, and when he was talking about the dog on the snuff bottle, what he actually meant was Third Young Master Ni – he matched well with the bone found in the street, and not all this gold and silver and agate. However, this explanation was the most baffling of all.

50

BIG NOSE MENG

BIG NOSE MENG was the nickname of the Second Young Master of the Meng family. You can tell how he got this nickname easily enough – he had an extra-large nose.

Big Nose Meng was not a tall man, and when he stood in a crowd, he was hardly going to stand out, with his thin neck, sloping shoulders and just the suspicion of a hunchback. However, there was one thing about him that was terribly noticeable – his out-sized nose, bulbous and glossy, like a newly peeled chestnut. Since it is located right in the middle of your face, the nose is a very conspicuous feature, so the moment you caught sight of him, the very first thing you'd notice was his absolutely enormous nose.

He hated the fact that every day, wherever he went, he was preceded by his nose, which made everyone burst out laughing as soon as they saw it.

However, for all that this was a cross to bear, there is a silver lining to every cloud. Second Young Master Meng's nose was far

from being a superfluous feature or an excrescence. It was in its own way a gift to him and possessed remarkable powers.

Do not be fooled by the bulbous appearance of this nose, boring and mediocre, with its cavernous nostrils from which you might see some hairs protruding, like weeds emerging from the mouth of a dry well. These nostrils were possessed of remarkable qualities, which was something ordinary people could never understand.

Everything in the world has not only its own appearance but also its own smell. Some things you can smell, and others you cannot. However, Big Nose Meng could smell absolutely everything.

In this world, all kinds of scents are mixed together. You cannot tell one from the other, but Big Nose Meng could. There was the smell of wood; the smell of iron; the smell of vegetables; the smell of an old cotton-padded jacket; the smell of feet... his enormous snout could distinguish each one at first sniff, like the gigantic eyes of an owl focusing on a tuft of new autumn growth. There was not one of the myriad scents that he could not identify.

People said that if a mosquito bit him, he would have no problem in finding the mosquito. Then he would take off his shoe and kill it with a single blow from the sole. Could he even smell where the mosquito was sitting?

Surely that is impossible? But do not imagine it to have been just baseless rumour, because there is another story about him...

One day, it so happened that he had a drop too much to drink at the Heavenly Perfumes restaurant over on Guyi Street, and the waiters helped him over to a chaise longue where he could sleep it off. A little hoodlum saw that he was so inebriated, and he felt inside his jacket for money, stealing three silver taels off him. A couple of weeks later, he happened to bump into the hoodlum over by the entrance to the Shanxi Guildhall. He went straight up to him and said: "If you hand over the three taels you stole the other day, that'll be an end to the matter. However, if you deny it, I'll report you to the yamen."

The little hoodlum thought he could get away with it and asked: "What do you mean by accusing me? Did you see me do it?"

Big Nose Meng answered: "I don't need to have seen you do it. You take your body odour with you everywhere you go, so whatever you do I can smell it."

The little hoodlum listened to this peculiar explanation and then looked at the huge nose on his face. Suddenly, he remembered all kinds of rumours about Big Nose Meng. He did not dare to deny it; he just took out the silver and gave it back to him.

On another occasion, Big Nose Meng invited a group of friends to dinner at the Spreading Spring restaurant in Beidaguan. The waiter serving them presented a dish of "Leaping" carp and said: "This is the speciality of the house – our chef's finest dish. The fish is freshly caught, cut up and cooked while still alive. You should eat it straight away."

"When Tianjin people eat fish, they want to eat them live – once they're dead, they're no good to eat," Second Young Master Meng said. Then he sniffed at the dish of fish and immediately stopped smiling. He said sternly to the waiter: "I'd like to speak to the manager."

The waiter had no idea what the problem was, but he brought the manager over, a man named Qiao. Before Mr Qiao had so much as opened his mouth, Big Nose Meng said: "This carp died yesterday."

When Mr Qiao heard that, he was dumbstruck. However, Tianjin is a port city, and businessmen in a port city need to be quick on the uptake. You have to be able to respond quickly, not to take things to heart, and you need to be able to talk your way out of any trouble. Mr Qiao immediately pasted a smile onto his face and said: "Oh, I do apologise. How terrible! Let me take this dish away now. I'll go and pick out a live carp for you, and I'll stand over the chef while he makes it for you. Please wait a moment."

That put an end to the matter, but the manager could not understand how Second Young Master Meng could possibly have known whether the fish was alive or dead before it was put into the pot. Could it really have been all down to his enormous nose?

There were other people present on both occasions to witness these events. From then on, nobody dared to bother Big Nose Meng. Or rather, it wasn't that they were scared of him, but of his nose. They could not quite be sure just how special that strange snout on his face really was.

Every cabbage leaf has its caterpillar – this is an important principle.

Big Nose Meng was a friendly man who liked a good crowd, and he came from a rich family and was happy to throw his money about, so naturally he soon picked up a bunch of good-for-nothing cronies who were happy to go along with whatever he wanted to do. He spent all of his time wandering here and there, eating and drinking, and getting up to trouble. He lived in a spacious mansion over on Liangdian Street, and he did not have any children – just a pretty and lively wife kept idle at home.

If you are bored and idle for long enough, trouble will come looking for you. Neighbours started to talk about how his wife was having an affair. This rumour began as a whisper, but as time went by, everyone was gossiping about it, and it was openly discussed. Gossip spreads as if on wings, because everyone enjoys a good story, and we all want to be in the know. These humiliating rumours about Big Nose Meng's home life were spread throughout the neighbourhood and in and out of his house, and then even his cronies were talking about it. The odd thing was that Big Nose Meng himself seemed oblivious and showed no sign of having heard what everyone else was saying – he just carried on as normal. There was also one other odd thing: nobody knew who it was that Big Nose Meng's wife was supposed to be having an affair with. There are always all sorts of experts in human affairs at the marketplace, and no matter how private the matter, they will keep on digging until they have got every last salacious detail squeezed out. But as to the identity of the man who had put the horns on Big Nose Meng – well, from start to finish, nobody ever saw hide nor hair of him.

People started to question the powers of Big Nose Meng's snout. Even if he was out and about all day every day, at night he would go back home and sleep with his wife, so how come he could not smell the stranger? If he could smell out a pickpocket who had swiped his cash and a mosquito that had bitten him, how was it possible that he could not smell the supposed lover of his wife ? What kind of nose was that? But if he had smelled out the man, he would not be talking and laughing every day as he usually did, as if nothing whatsoever were the matter.

Over the course of the next year, things gradually became clear. The name of the man who was cuckolding Big Nose Meng eventually floated to the surface: a military officer serving in the central administration of Zhili Province named Liao Zhengcao, who was a very smart guy and pretty damn tough with it. Even the thugs over round Houjiahou did not dare lay a finger on him. When his name was mentioned, everyone understood that Big Nose Meng must have smelled him out long ago, but he had to pretend not to have noticed. It must have been horrible for him to have to make as if he didn't know what was going on, so it was obvious that Big Nose Meng must have suffered greatly over the course of the last year. Some people claimed that the officer had such terrible body odour that Big Nose Meng had to stuff cotton wool in his nostrils every time he went home.

Once all was revealed, Big Nose Meng started to keep out of the way, and his wife never showed her face in public again. He changed his way of life: he was no longer hail-fellow-well-met, throwing his money around at parties, and so naturally people didn't want anything to do with him any more. His good-for-nothing cronies vanished pretty quickly, not one of them staying behind. He would appear every so often to do some business or buy something or other, and he had changed a lot; he seemed much smaller, as if almost literally crushed. The really odd thing was the huge nose he'd had in the middle of his face now seemed to have suddenly grown smaller, as if it had deflated and become less bulbous. The mysterious sense of self-confidence he had always had before had vanished.

Once his nose stopped working, Tianjin stopped speaking about Big Nose Meng.

51
FLYING BEAR

IN 1934, which was the twenty-third year of the Republic of China, there was a strange man known as Flying Bear in the city of Tianjin. This name might suggest that the man was a bear who could fly. Which he sort of was…

This man was not a bear, but his surname was Xiong, which does indeed mean "bear", and he certainly looked like one. He had a heavy, fleshy face and a huge burly body. His back and chest, not to mention his arms and legs, were all covered with a thick pelt, right down to the backs of his hands; and a pair of black eyes glittered from beneath heavy eyelids. Nobody could look more like a bear than he did.

Long, thick hair covered his entire body. Supposedly, mosquitos never bit him because they could not find a way through this fur. If he stood right next to you and opened his mouth in a smile, it looked quite terrifying. But he had his own problems. Thanks to being so very heavy and slow, he could not walk very fast, and if he tried to run, he would end up panting.

If anyone annoyed him, all they had to do was run away; he could not possibly chase after them.

However, once he added the word "Flying" to his surname of "Bear", that was something else again. He did not add the word "Flying" himself; this was what other people called him. And there was a very good reason for that…

Originally, Flying Bear was working as a coolie on the Grand Canal, and he got into a fight with a gang of thugs working the red-light district in Houjiahou, and those people bore grudges forever. The thugs knew that he was pretty strong, but they were still determined to find a way to beat him up – they wanted to thump him into next week so he would never dare run up against them again.

Eventually, these thugs thought of a way to get at him. He liked his drink and was often to be found boozing in one of the bars or houses round there; if he was roaring drunk, he would be easier to beat up. One day, he was knocking back the booze upstairs at the "Three Cups or More" over by the East Gate until he was half-drunk, and that was where the thugs caught up with him. Each one of these bastards was armed with a white stick, and every single one of them was prepared for a fight to the death. The man was pretty drunk, but even if he had been much drunker, he would not have tried to fight this one out – there were far too many of them, and they obviously meant business. If he tried to go for them, he would simply end up dead.

Although the restaurant was spacious, the stairway had been blocked by the thugs. There was only one way to escape: the big window facing south. The window was open, and outside there was a big tree. But the big tree was at least eight feet away from the window. Even the great Huo Yuanjia couldn't make the jump to that tree. If he could not jump, then he would fall to his death; but if he did not try, he would be beaten to hell and back. However, the man was clumsy and heavy – weighing over two hundred pounds – so that was dead weight. How could he possibly jump?

There was no time to think about it! They saw him leap up, turn around and run straight to the window. The thugs were pretty quick on their pins, and the first thumps from the sticks had already landed on his back. Those blows seem to beat his head clear of the fumes of alcohol and make him furiously angry and desperate! He looked like a wild animal leaping through the flames of a forest fire. He threw himself towards the window, and without the slightest hesitation, he launched himself out of it. The thugs ran to the window where an amazing sight awaited them – he was right over there in the tree, his arms wrapped around its trunk, staring straight back at them. He looked just like a big bear climbing up a tree. How could such a huge and heavy man have jumped so high and so far? Had he flown over there?

No one saw how he got down from that tree. The thugs were all scared into running off.

Many diners in the restaurant saw this scene, and seeing is believing. From then on, he was accorded the fine nickname "Flying Bear", and no one dared to provoke him again. He became a real celebrity in the city of Tianjin.

Flying Bear was very proud of his nickname. He didn't care about the prestige it garnered, but he did like the name. He found it very useful; wherever he went, people showed their respect for him – they would chat to him and say nice things, maybe even invite him to eat and drink with them. The guards at City Hall invited him to come and teach them martial arts, but he refused. He said that he could teach martial arts that he had learned himself, but natural skills could not be taught. Natural skills are a kind of genius; you cannot set yourself to learning them. That made people admire him even more.

There was a certain Master Tang from the Japanese Concession, who came from a family with plenty of money, and he had nothing whatsoever to do. He spent all his time eating and drinking and having fun. One day, Master Tang invited a couple of friends to join him for a meal, and they were gossiping away, when someone happened to mention Flying Bear. Master Tang said: "I don't believe someone that heavy could fly."

His friends said that many people had seen it, and they could name some of them – it had to be true.

Master Tang now had an idea and said: "How about we invite him to drink at the 'Three Cups or More'? We can have him fly again, and this time we'll be there to watch!"

Everybody declared that this was an excellent idea. But one of their number said: "He's famous now. Why would he do what we tell him to?"

Master Tang said with a smile: "We'll get him drunk. Once he's drunk, we'll challenge him. That way, he's sure to fly."

His guests proclaimed that all this was much better than watching any drama starring Yu Shuyan and Cheng Yanqiu.

A few days later, Master Tang's friends invited Flying Bear to the "Three Cups or More". They had a table set up just where Flying Bear had been drinking before, the top completely covered with food and wine. Having eaten his fill and drunk cup after cup, his companions started talking about his feat, as if he had "crossed five passes killing six generals." Flying Bear loved hearing people discuss his exploit, and he was getting more and more excited. But then Master Tang asked him coldly: "Can you really fly over to that tree outside the window? Are you really so much better than the Swallow, Li San?"

"Everyone in Tianjin knows what I can do," Flying Bear said. "Of course it's true!"

Still in the same cold tone of voice, Master Tang said: "There are plenty of lies printed in the papers in black and white, let alone gossip passed from mouth to mouth... How can it possibly be true?"

Flying Bear was now breathing heavily. He'd had far too much to drink, and now the wine went to his head, his face flushed bright red. He hauled himself upright and asked Master Tang: "So... who would you believe?"

Master Tang smiled and said: "I believe what I see with my own eyes."

At the same time, some of Master Tang's friends were pleading with him; some of them coaxing him; some challenging him – demanding that Flying Bear fly for them, to show them just what he could do.

Flying Bear really did pull himself together. Just as when he came under attack by the thugs, he turned around and launched himself straight at the window, leaping up onto the sill. But this time when he was standing on the windowsill, everything suddenly changed. The tree seemed to be miles away from him, and the ground below was like an abyss – he was terror-struck! How could he possibly have jumped over to that tree? He could not explain it himself. Needless to say, Mr Tang did not believe he could do it – in fact, he did not have any faith himself.

How could he know that sometimes, in extremities, people

have a special reserve of strength they can draw upon – but only once, for it will never come back again.

He stood on the windowsill for a long time. None of those present dared to make a sound, for fear that they would frighten him into falling.

Seeing his legs shaking, they rushed forward to help him down from the windowsill. When he got down, his legs buckled under him, and his body twisted. Half-fainting, he collapsed to the ground with two people under him, one of whom ended up with his arm broken.

These events ensured that Flying Bear would henceforth be known by a hitherto unheard-of nickname: "Scaredy-Bear".

52
PEDALLING

In old-time Tianjin, cycling was not called cycling, but pedalling. Riding a bike was all about appearance; it did not matter how you pedalled, providing you put your back into it. As a result, people would raise their knees and bend at the hips, open their mouths and gulp for air, as they pedalled as hard as they could. At that time, little was known about traffic regulations and few would care to follow them anyway. Wherever they wanted to go, they'd pedal there, and so it ended up that they found themselves in opposition to another kind of people – traffic police.

Tianjin folk are fond of banter, so no matter how aggressive they may seem, they are not really going to attack their opponents – it is just a kind of game to them. They like to run their mouths, to compete verbally, and when it is all over they have enjoyed themselves.

The group that really put the traffic police in their place were the Master Pedallers. The Masters were rich men, and very

honest and good people, but they all had a temper and were tough as old boots. They could give you a pretty good tongue-lashing too, because each one of them was quick to get his words out and always kept the upper hand. They were also pretty nippy on their pins, and could do tricks on their bikes like the clowns at the circus – even the police gave them a wide berth. But every so often, there would be a new policeman on the job who did not know what end was up, and they would try to deal with the Master Pedallers; but it always ended up with them biting the dust.

That one year, Tianjin's traffic calming measures got an upgrade, and the police moved from standing in the middle of the street to direct the traffic to a glass hut by the side of the road; in addition to which, traffic lights were installed at the crossroads, with red and green lights. The traffic police would sit in their round guard box, looking out in all directions through the glass, manipulating the red and green lights with the flick of a switch, out of the sun and the rain, with no risk of getting sunburned – that was the life! A new traffic policeman, Young Chen, arrived at the police box with a four-sided clock mounted on top, bright eyes glittering in his pale, clean face, dressed in a brand-new uniform and helmet, looking very spick and span. That day, far in the distance, Young Chen spotted a Master Pedaller coming from the east. It was cold that day, but this particular Master was highly skilled. From time to time, he would let go of the handlebars and rub his frozen fingers up and down against his face. Young Chen knew that the man was just showing off and wanted everyone to see his skill... to make them admire his abilities. Young Chen pretended not to have noticed a thing, but when the bike got to the crossroads, he suddenly flicked the switch, so that the green light changed to a red: do not cross. At that time, traffic lights were all still manual. If they wanted you to move, they would give you a green light; if they wanted you to stop, it would be red.

As soon as the Master saw the light change, he hit the brakes, and his bike stopped. When the brakes are slammed so hard, the bike will fall to one side, and the rider will have to get off. But this Master was hot stuff: his bike came to a halt, and he did not so much as move – his bottom was still right there in the saddle, and both feet were clamped against the pedals. Nevertheless, his bike was standing upright on the spot, neither leaning nor tilting, not moving by so much as a fraction – this technique was what was known as "fixing your bike". When Young Chen saw that he had fixed his bike, he thought to himself: OK, stay right there. How long can you keep your bike fixed for? If I do not change the lights, what are you going to do about it? Do you really think you can stay there forever? As time goes on, your bike will tip over and you'll have to come off – that'll be embarrassing!

The Master was an old hand at this sort of thing. He understood just what the little policeman was thinking. He did not just keep his bike fixed there in place, he proceeded to reach into one of his pockets and pull out a cigarette, which he lit with a match. Afterwards, he crossed his arms in front of his chest and slowly smoked his cigarette, waiting for the lights to change, for all the world as relaxed and at ease as if he were sitting on a chair at home. The longer the light went unchanged, the more relaxed he was just sitting there. And all the while, his bike sat in the middle of the road as if it had been nailed down.

As a result, the two of them were challenging each other, and some of the passers-by along the road stopped to watch the fun.

Look at them – one was like the little Lord Guan that guarded the temple over by Huarong Road, and the other was an old fox who had scrapped his way through the markets and lanes. Who would be the one to blink first?

If the red light does not change, no one can move. But as time goes on, things will change. It was not just the Master Pedaller that was being held up in the middle of the road any longer – more and more cars had joined the stationary queue. Some of them were hammering on their horns, while others were shouting: "Are the police here asleep or what?" However, the Master stayed calm and fixed in place, as if none of this were anything to do with him.

In the face of this situation, in the end, it was Young Chen who could not hold out a moment longer. He had to pull the switch and give him the green light. When the Master looked up and saw the light turn green, he tossed aside the butt of his cigarette and put his two hands back on the handlebars, pedalling away on his bike. As he passed the post, he turned round to glance at the over-confident and under-experienced little policeman. Young Chen kept his eyes fixed in front of him, not daring to look at the man. Nevertheless, he could feel his triumphant and mocking gaze sweep over him, so that his face burned with shame for a very long time.

Another example of a policeman defeated by a Master was the traffic policeman stationed at the crossroads leading to the area round Daotai Huang Yinfen's private villa. Again, it was a new policeman that was involved, but this time he had the surname You. Young You was a much tougher proposition than the previously-mentioned Young Chen. This Young You came from Qiande Village over on the west side of the river, and he'd grown up in and around the alleyways and markets over there – he had the gift of the gab and was not about to take anything from anyone. Furthermore, in the space of just a couple of months after taking up his new profession, he ran into one nasty situation after another and dealt with them all beautifully, which gave him more and more confidence.

One afternoon in the depths of winter, a Master some way down the road to one side of his guard post was trying to get onto his bicycle. There was a bundle of wood strapped to the rack at the back, which was pretty wide. The Master himself had short little legs, and he was dressed in thickly padded cotton trousers, so he simply could not straddle his bike. Having tried a number of times, it was impossible for him to get on top. It was getting towards rush hour, so the streets were full of people with their bikes. Young You was worried that the Master might get into trouble that way, so he wanted to tell the man to go somewhere else with fewer people and get on his bike there. Even though Young You had good intentions, Tianjin citizens like to be passive-aggressive in their approach, and they often speak with a sting. Of course, this can be a lot of fun, and people enjoy it. So he opened up the window to his police box and said to the Master with a giggle: "Hey, sir, if you want to practise riding your bike, how about you find somewhere a bit quieter?"

Everyone heard what Young You said, and they really enjoyed the backhanded joke.

The Master Pedallers of Tianjin were hardly about to be bested in this way. If someone can make a joke at their expense, it's a real humiliation. So the man turned his head round and said to Young You: "Don't worry about me. That's nothing to do with you. Your job is to stay right there in that canister!"

He said the word "canister" because the round police boxes of those days did look like one. There was a vulgar saying in Tianjin: "Every canister has its bastard; they sit in there and play with themselves." Everyone knew this saying.

This was even more fun, and everyone burst out laughing. Of course, they were also laughing at the young policeman for not knowing his place – how could someone like that stand up against such an old fox? Young You was left stunned and speechless.

The Master finally succeeded in hauling himself atop his bike, and once he was in place, he pedalled off with vigour, never once turning his head.

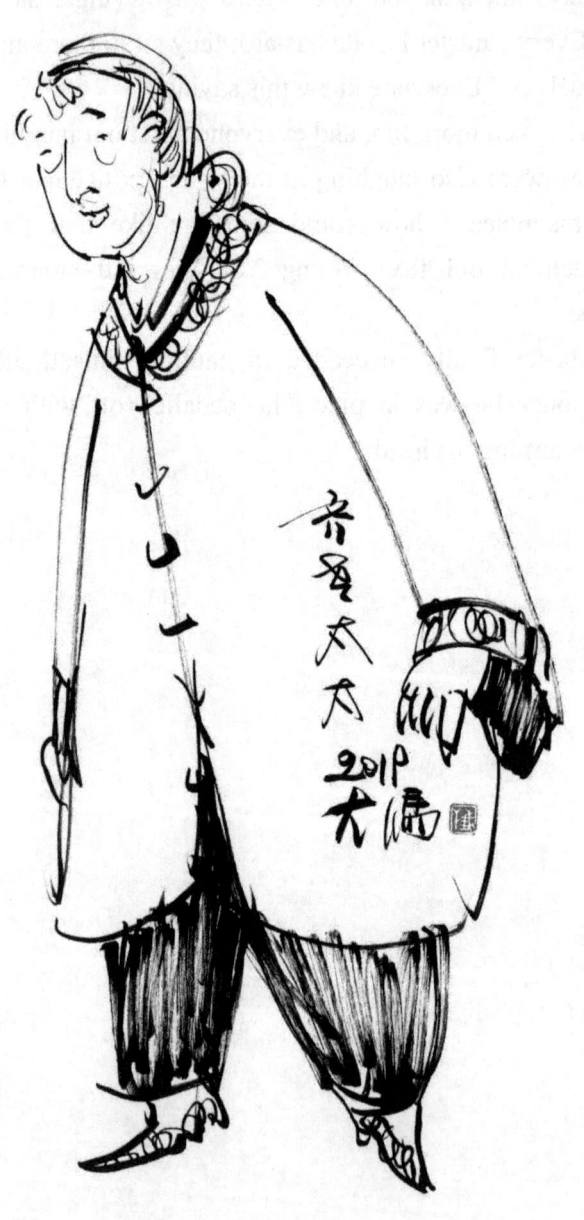

53
OLD LADY QI

OLD LADY QI lived a comfortable life in a small courtyard house in the western part of the city. After her husband died, she had just one idea – she wanted the family to stay together.

She had three children – two sons and a daughter. Her daughter was her youngest child and unmarried; her two sons had wives but were still living at home, looking after their elderly mother. The two sons lived in the eastern and western wings of the house. The main building had three big chambers: the one on the right was where the daughter lived; the one on the left was kept by the old lady for herself; and the middle room was empty, because this was set aside for the whole family to use.

The old lady had a very specific picture in her mind: in the spring, the whole family would get together to plant the courtyard with flowers; in the summer, they would sit around chatting while trying to keep cool; in the autumn, they would pick up their poles with which to knock ripe jujubes to the ground; and in winter, they would sweep the snow up to make snowmen. In the ordinary way of things, the whole family spent their lives around the square table in the main room. That was where they ate three meals a day, and even though the food was far from fancy, there was enough meat and vegetables for everyone. They ate together, and they enjoyed life together. When she had some spare time, the old lady would call on her daughter and daughters-in-law to play cards with her. The grandkids could play out in the courtyard. The various members of the Qi family were all peaceful folk; they never quarrelled and argued with each other, nor did anyone ever get into a rage. The old lady felt herself to be in paradise. But when one day she was genuinely called to the celestial realm, would she not miss her family? However would she manage? Whenever she thought of this, she would start to cry.

Playing cards was the old lady's one vice. But once she got past the age of seventy, after playing for a while, she'd want a little rest. A couple of the kids had arranged a nice soft sofa for her in one corner of the main room, so when she felt tired she could lie down on the sofa and stretch out her arms and legs. When she felt recuperated, she would ask her daughter and daughters-in-law to continue the game. Anyway, the whole family obeyed the old lady's call without the slightest murmur, and every day they would make it so that she would win their final game.

Old Lady Qi's two daughters-in-law were both very nice. Every day, when their husbands went out to work, they would take care of the chores at home, coaxing their children to play nicely together, taking turns to cook meals for the whole family, while looking after their mother-in-law and playing cards with her. Playing cards was fun for everyone; they would chat together, eating snacks and drinking tea. It would be boring to play cards without putting down a stake, but the family did not have much money, so they would play for a few coppers at a time, while regularly losing to the old lady. When playing cards, the old lady liked to keep her back-scratcher to hand. Whenever she won, her back would start itching; but by contrast, her daughter had a little round mirror by her side so that she could keep an eye on her appearance whenever she felt like it. The eldest daughter-in-law had her cigarette case; that way, when she felt the need for a nicotine fix, she could take a few puffs. The second daughter-in-law had a more unusual trait, since she would take off the gold ring she wore on one hand and wrap it in her handkerchief – she was worried that when she shuffled the cards, the soft gold would get scratched. She came from a poor family, and when she got married, that gold ring was the most expensive gift her family gave her. Although it was just a plain band without any special workmanship, it was quite solid and had a very good colour.

She played cards every day, and all that time the ring was sitting by her right hand. But then one day, she took some time filling up the thermos flask, and when she came back, suddenly – "Aiyo!" – the ring was gone. She looked for it, the others helped her to look for it, and they searched on the table and around the floor. They looked everywhere, but they could not find it.

The old lady said: "There's nothing to worry about! How can anyone possibly lose something at home? We just need to look carefully…"

Her second daughter-in-law was angry and panicking about

having lost her treasure, so she could not stop herself from saying something cutting: "I just popped out for a moment to pour some water into the thermos. How can it have vanished in broad daylight? Unless we've got poltergeists in!"

As soon as things start going missing, people get very upset and on edge. The eldest daughter-in-law found she could not keep her mouth closed: "Hey, I was sitting right next to you. I do hope that when you talk about 'poltergeists' that you don't mean to say I took it."

The second daughter-in-law said: "Why do you have to make everything all about you? I didn't say it had anything to do with you. I was just blaming myself for leaving something so valuable on the table." Obviously, she was upset, but now with each one of them chipping in, it was just adding fuel to the fire.

If they kept going on like this, there'd be an open quarrel.

Nothing of this kind had ever happened in the Qi family before, and the old lady was very concerned. She went as pale as a sheet and suddenly gripped the table and gave it a push. At her age, it was only possible for her to push it a few inches. Then she spoke up in ringing tones: "Nobody is to leave the room. I want this place searched from top to bottom – and we're going to do this properly, so everyone is also going to have to have a body search! I refuse to believe that we won't find the ring. I refuse to believe that we in the Qi family can have things go missing like this!"

The old lady was furious for the very first time in her life!

Everyone calmed down and did as she said. They searched all the nooks and crannies in the room, high and low: every single inch of ground was gone over carefully. Even the sofa where the old lady took her rest was pulled out and gone over. The sisters-in-law searched each other from top to toe. At that moment, Old Lady Qi closed her eyes as if she were dying. She felt quite sure in her mind that this was the end, that the family was ruined. No matter who the ring was found on, once it appeared, it would be a stab to the heart for everyone. But the strange thing was that the ring remained missing. Once even the vases on the mantelpiece had been upended, where could it possibly have gone? Perhaps the second daughter-in-law had it right: there were poltergeists in the house!

As to whether or not there might be such a thing as ghosts, she did not know, but a dark cloud now seemed to hang over the Qi family. Everything was different. The family members seemed preoccupied, and they were no longer talking to each other. If they did speak, they were obviously just trying to make conversation. If they smiled or laughed, it was forced. Who knew what the rest of them were thinking? Even though they still ate every meal at the same table, it felt like a group of strangers had happened to sit down together. The old lady carried on playing cards, but she just did not feel like it any more. One day, she suddenly threw all of her cards down on the table with a crash, and then said sadly: "I just can't do this any more, I don't feel like it." After that, there were no more games. When the card games stopped, the Qi family became even more miserable.

The images in the old lady's mind of how her family ought to be were torn down one by one.

No one knew how to break through this impasse. Anyway, as long as the gold ring remained missing, it was impossible to put the whole thing behind them.

One day, Miss Qi asked her elder brother: "Do you think the cat might have got that gold ring?"

"You really do like to consider every possibility!" her brother said. "I've never heard of a cat going after anything gold – after all, it couldn't eat it. Besides which, even supposing it did, you don't know where it has gone, nor could you bring the ring back…"

That put an end to all speculation. It seemed an impenetrable mystery.

But one night after dinner, before anyone had time to get up from the table, the old lady suddenly said to everyone: "I want to tell you something. Listen up! There's no need to go on guessing about that ring – I took it! I needed the money… but don't ask me what for. I'll do my best to make it up to you."

The old lady's words were like a bolt from the blue – everyone just looked at each other, not daring to believe it. But the old lady had never told a lie in her entire life; she would not say something if it were not true. Whatever she said, they all believed it. And there might be something to it. On the day when the ring vanished, they'd all searched each other, but nobody touched Old Lady Qi. None of them would have done a thing like that! If she hadn't taken it, then where had the gold ring got to? But if she took it… how? What good could it possibly have done her?

If the old lady did not choose to explain, no one would dare to ask her, or even discuss it among themselves. But from that moment onwards, everyone unconsciously changed their attitude towards her. How could she steal from her own daughter-in-law? They hated to think of it. Their former respect for the old lady naturally dwindled. She might not say anything about it, but she felt it nevertheless. Although she had explained the truth of the matter so that their mutual suspicion and embarrassment could be set aside, from then on she clearly thought badly of herself, speaking less and less to her family, and her body grew ever more hunched over. In a flash, Old Lady Qi had aged enormously – she emerged but rarely from her room, and now she called upon her daughter to bring meals in to her, since she did not like to be seen by the others. Maybe she felt too ashamed to be seen?

Somewhat over a year later, the old lady passed away.

The whole family participated in the funeral and tidied the main room. When the sofa in the corner of the main room was removed to clean the floor, her daughter suddenly spotted something shining in the crack between the floor tiles. This was a little strange. She squatted down, pulled out one of her hairpins and used it to wiggle the item out to have a look. Then she yelled for her brother and sister-in-law. Everyone came and clustered around to see what she'd found, and they were all amazed! It was the lost gold ring. It had been here all the time!

On the day the ring was lost, this place had been searched too, but because it was late at night and there was no light in the room, of course no one had spotted it. Now it was afternoon, and a ray of sunlight slanting into the room had illuminated the crack in which it lay – and so the gold ring had returned to the Qi family thanks to its glitter and shine.

The mystery was solved.

Miss Qi was weeping as she said to the ring: "Why did you hide down there? You killed my mother!"

The whole family thought about this benevolent old lady who took all the blame on herself in order to ensure that everyone else could live in peace together. To keep them united, she had endured humiliation and a great mental burden, so much so that she wished to die. Without really being aware of it, they all started to cry.

54
THE FLAGPOLE

IN THE PAST, tall people in Tianjin were called tall 'uns, and the tallest of them all were called flagpoles. This was because, at that time, the tallest thing in Tianjin was the pair of flagpoles in front of the Temple of the Queen of Heaven. It was said that the flagpoles were originally the masts of an ocean-going ship, and each of them was supposed to be one hundred feet high. As to when they were put up there, well, stories differed. But if you stood underneath them and looked straight up, you could stare until you felt dizzy, and you still would not be able to see right to the tippy-top.

However, there was a man who lived by Imperial Guard Bridge who really deserved to be called a flagpole. How tall was he? At least four heads taller than any ordinary person! Any bird flying low would find itself ramming straight into him. When he walked through any of the city gates, he had to aim right for the centre, since they were all arch-shaped, and the highest point was in the middle – if he walked to either side, he would bang his

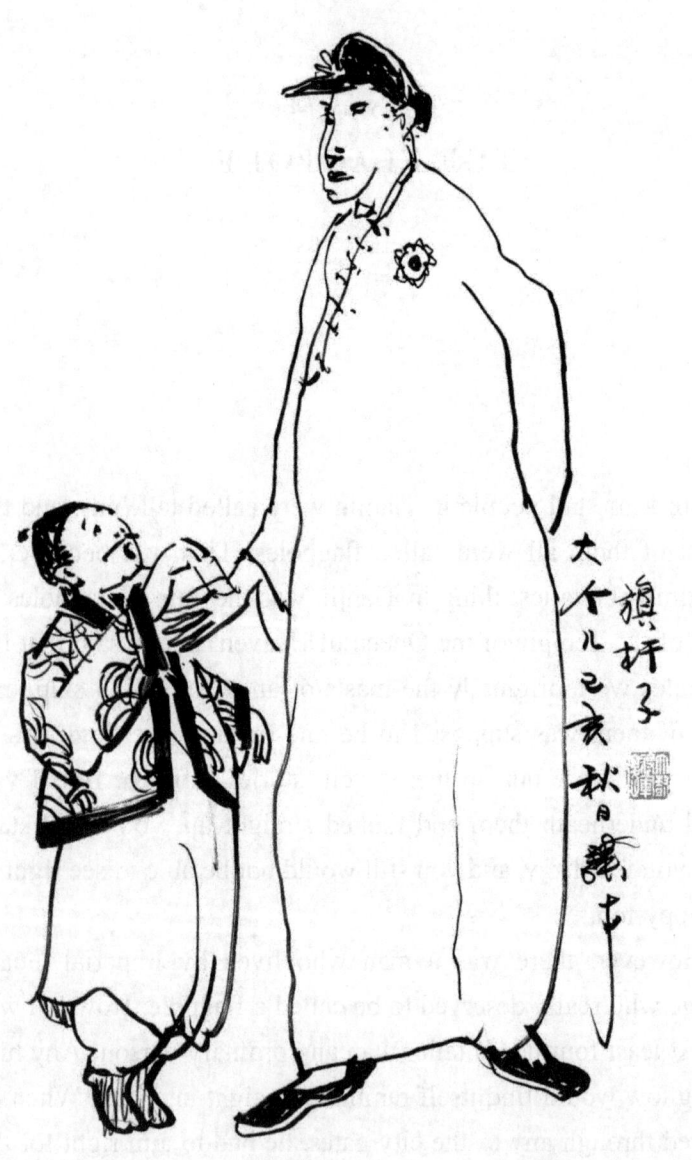

head. There was a half-brick missing on the left-hand side of the arch at the East Gate, and apparently he had knocked it out with his head. That was what people said at any rate; it is up to you whether you believe it.

He had been called a flagpole ever since he was a child. At twelve, he was already a head taller than everyone else; at fourteen, he was two heads taller; at eighteen, it was three heads; and by the time he was twenty, he was four heads taller. Since he was so tall, he had an enormous appetite; he ate like a wolf! An ordinary person might eat three buns with their meal at most, but he would eat eight and chase that down with four bowls of porridge.

You need a job if you are going to eat, and he only ever did three kinds of work: handing bricks or tiles up at a building site; washing the sign board on shops; and lighting lamps when it got dark. He could do these things without the ladder that would be necessary for anyone else. However, these kinds of jobs didn't turn up every day, and so he often went hungry. Of course, for him, going hungry was not entirely the fault of having no work to do, but because he was terribly shy. Whenever he walked down the road, the kids would treat him like some kind of freak, laughing at him, taunting him and throwing stones at him. He did not like it when people saw him – they would look at him with surprise and ridicule. He never wanted to get into trouble, but people seemed to go out of their way to annoy and upset him. This was not something that they could be blamed for, because he did look very frightening. One night, he went out with a can of oil in one hand and a little brand in the other with which to light the lamps, and he happened to come face-to-face with two people walking in the dark. When they saw him – this huge looming shadow as high as the eaves – they were so terrified that they started screaming and calling for help. They dropped the items they were carrying right there in the street, abandoning them where they fell, and ran for their lives, as if they had just seen a ghost.

He usually hid away in the house, rarely going out; mostly, he did not even go out into the courtyard. The other people who lived there, like sheep in a pen, could not see out over the tops of the walls, but when he was out there, he looked like a horse in a loose box, with half his body visible over the wall where everybody could see him – and it was a comical sight. Whenever people burst out laughing at him, he would rush back indoors and would often end up banging his head on the lintel of the door.

This big man stayed at home all day, every day. However, there was nowhere in the house where he could stand upright, and nowhere to put his long arms and legs. He could not move, and his stomach was empty, and the cupboards were bare. Bare cupboards are at the very least silent, but an empty stomach grumbles. When he got really starving, he would have to pull himself together and go out and get a job. But when it came to work like shifting loads down at the docks, how could he possibly do it? Other men might be able to lift sacks up onto their shoulders, but if he tried, it would be like hoisting a sack up to the roof. Besides which, without anything to eat, where was he going to get the strength?

He was afraid of people and never talked to anyone else – he seemed to have been born without the capacity for speech. If he saw one of the neighbours who lived on either side of him, he might nod his head. Nobody ever came to visit him – it seemed as though he filled the whole house. Who else could possibly fit inside? Because of this, nobody knew how the freak managed. There was no one to care about him; at most, they might speculate about whether he would ever get married. Who would want someone like that? If he had a wife, he would have to kneel down to kiss her.

One day after the Qingming Festival, he went out onto the streets to look for work, rushing here and there like a headless chicken. Suddenly, two middle-aged men in decent clothes came up to him with a smile and asked him: "We'll give you a job. Three meals a day and five coppers on top. Will you take it?"

Flagpole was stunned. He did not believe that such luck could fall to his lot and decided that the chances were that they were making fun of him. He asked: "What work?"

The pair of them said that they were from Xitou Park and they wanted him to stand at the gate to collect tickets. Visitors would buy their tickets at the ticket booth and then go to the entrance and hand it over to him – when he received the ticket, he could let them in. It was really simple and straightforward, and that was all they were asking him to do. It was a good job, and they would feed him three meals a day. What luck! The worst thing for him was having to go hungry so often, so if there was food involved, he was happy. He immediately agreed.

As soon as he agreed to take the job, the two men started to laugh, and then the one with a moustache said: "We heard about you a while back, and we've been looking for you for weeks! Today we were lucky and managed to bump into you, so we'd like you to start work tomorrow morning."

Flagpole could not figure out what they wanted him for.

The next day, he arrived at Xitou Park. His job was every bit as simple as the two men had said. He just stood at the gate to collect tickets and did not have to do anything else, and they fed him three meals a day. He could eat a dozen steamed buns in a sitting and nobody cared. In this way, he ate and ate until his stomach was bulging and hard as a rock. Before going to sleep, he would have to drink half a jug of cold water to kick-start his digestion. It was only then that he could begin to relax and lie down. However, the more he thought about it, the more baffled he was: anyone could do this job, so why did they want a lard-arse like him? The visitors all seemed to be dwarves – sometimes they had to stand on tiptoe to be able to put the ticket in his hand.

But gradually, everything became clear.

Once he began standing at the gate of the park, the number of visitors increased day by day, with one person telling ten, and ten telling a hundred. Within a couple of weeks, visitor numbers had actually doubled or tripled. The middle-aged man with a moustache who had hired him that day, whose name was Hao, was the director of the park. He now said that his clothes were too worn and patched. He did not look too good standing there for all the world like a gigantic beggar. Therefore, he asked a tailor to sew him a neat blue coat, which was longer than the curtains in the reception room attached to the director's office. He also asked Flagpole to cut his hair into a neat trim and gave him a special cap with a leather peak, which was big enough to cover a wine jar. It was new and interesting to dress up like this. While Director Hao was at it, he decided to gild the lily a bit and created a ribbon buttonhole for him. In this way, when he stood by the gate to the park, it was a very fine sight, and people came running from all corners of the city to see him. It was even more fun to actually buy a ticket and hand it up – when you put the ticket into the palm of his enormous fan-sized hand, he would emit a grunt like a buffalo, and that meant you were allowed to go in. Those who rushed to Xitou Park were not just going to stand around outside and watch him; they would all buy tickets and hand them over to him. It was a way to interact with a real freak – a very special moment. The park earned a lot of money from this.

Flagpole was an absolute treasure. You have to admire Director Hao's good idea and his quick-wittedness. In order to make Flagpole stand tall, looking even more magical and glorious than ever before, they had to feed him up. Director Hao ordered the cook to put plenty of meat and fish in his meals – Flagpole had never eaten so well in his life before. It seemed that each meal was better than the last, and his food put the heart into him. Pretty soon, his waistline seemed to have doubled. If he looked like a flagpole before, now he looked like a huge tree. The bigger he got, the stronger he seemed.

However, that made other people in the park resentful. They would secretly curse him as a useless freak who came running over here to eat everyone out of house and home and lord it over others. If a man is envied, trouble will follow.

There were many rich people in Tianjin. Some of them saw this extraordinary giant and were interested and amazed at the sight, and they would give him a tip. Flagpole would take it, but he knew that this money did not really belong to him. No matter whether it was a little or a large amount, he would give it to Director Hao. But when other people talked about this, they twisted the story, claiming that he kept back a huge amount of money for himself. Sooner or later, this gossip reached the ears of Director Hao. The first time, he did not believe it; the second time, he still did not believe it... but gradually, he started to wonder.

Director Hao said: "You lot always think the worst of everyone. So if he's been skimming, have you seen it?"

Well, they waited until after Flagpole had gone off work at the park one day to drag the director off to the main gate, where they put a ladder up next to one of the pillars and told him to go up and see for himself. There was a copper finial on top of the pillar, and a heap of cash had been stuffed under it, along with copper coins and some silver ingots – even some foreign money. Flagpole was so tall, and the finial was right there by his side. He was the only person who could have hidden the money there.

Director Hao was furious, and the very next day, when he was still in a rage, he cursed and screamed at Flagpole. He shouted about how he was such an ungrateful bastard, how heartless he was and how wicked. Flagpole just stood there and did not say a word. He didn't try to speak up for himself. He looked stiff and wooden, and the blood drained out of his face. In the end, he took off his nice coat and hat, and threw them into Director Hao's office. Then he turned around and walked away.

Afterwards, he was never seen again at Xitou Park. Two stories grew up around him, which spread far and wide. One story was that he'd stolen things and Director Hao had caught him red-handed and sent him straight to prison. The other story was that he wasn't a giant at all: the long coat concealed the stilts he was walking on. Nobody believed the second story – why would anyone do such a thing? What for? But the first story was also pretty quickly quashed by Director Hao himself.

Director Hao was not at all a stupid man. When the whole

thing died down, he started to mull it over: was it really Flagpole who had hidden all that money? If it was, why didn't he take it home? What was he doing putting it on top of the wall? He started to wonder whether the whole thing had not been a trap – someone was jealous that he got to eat meat and fish, and dressed up in nice clothing, and so came up with this way to get rid of him? However, after Flagpole left, where could he find food for three meals a day?

This was a disaster for Director Hao. With Flagpole gone, the park was deserted. Nobody bought tickets any more. A few days earlier, when Flagpole had been standing at the gate, it had been a fine sight... a temple festival every day. He couldn't do without Flagpole! He rushed around the old city, searching for him everywhere, hoping that he would bump into him in the same area that he had first seen him. He searched for weeks and weeks but simply could not find him, although he did locate his tumbledown house by the Imperial Guard Bridge. The door was locked, and in spite of banging on it for ages, nobody answered. Director Hao ordered someone to break open the door, but when he did so, he exclaimed in horror. Flagpole was lying face-up on the bed, but his body was stone-cold. He was dead, and nobody knew when he had passed away. Director Hao noticed that his corpse lay out flat but the stomach was concave – he must have died of starvation. He felt sorry for the man and regretted the way he had so brutally fired the innocent giant that day. Firing him had turned out to be no different from killing him.

Director Hao made enquiries of Flagpole's neighbours on either side, and nobody knew anything much about him. They'd only heard a few bits and pieces. Apparently, his family came from the Yimeng Mountains in southwestern Shandong

Province, and they had come to Tianjin along the Grand Canal. His father worked as a coolie, but both parents had died young. He didn't have any family or friends – he was all on his own. Who was going to bury him? Director Hao felt so bad about how he had treated poor Flagpole that he paid for a pinewood coffin for him. This would just be boards nailed together, no lacquer. He was eight feet tall, so the coffin would have to be eight feet six inches. The maker complained that he'd never had to put together such a big coffin before.

However, when the coffin was put together, Flagpole did not fit. They had measured him properly, so how come they could not get him into it? Was it possible that he had grown after death and so was now too big? The coffin maker said that he had never seen such a thing, or heard tell of the like. The dead ought to shrink if anything. How could this man grow taller? Maybe there was something special about this giant after all!

If the world does not make room for the tall in life, they will just grow bigger after death.

Director Hao put up a bit more money, and they lengthened the coffin by a foot. Then he could fit inside. Flagpole did not have any family or friends, so nobody attended his funeral. Director Hao did not want to go, but he hired some people to quickly bury him in the wasteland outside the South Gate.

After that, there were no more giants here, nor anyone with special, unusual abilities.

ON ILLUSTRATING MY NOVELS
BY FENG JICAI

Producing the illustrations for your own novels is a kind of hobby, and drawings for this purpose are different from other paintings.

When an author writes about a particular character, the voice and appearance must first be quite clear in his own mind – it is only afterwards that they can be described in writing. But if an author can bring his characters to life on the page, why does he need to draw them as well? Surely it is for an artist to provide the illustrations for a novel! Why should there be authors who like to illustrate their own work, like Hugo, Thackeray, Mayakovsky and so on? On the one hand, it is because these writers are good at drawing and painting; for those who know how to draw, they cannot stop themselves from trying to illustrate the images they see in their heads. If you look at a manuscript by Pushkin or Lermontov, are there not all kinds of little people drawn all over them? On the other hand, there are some authors who really care about the appearance of their books, the artistic qualities, such as the great Chinese novelist Lu Xun. Even though he did not know how to draw himself, he still designed the covers of many of the books that he wrote or edited. Even if you only consider the binding, Lu Xun's designs are most tasteful and elegant, with an aesthetically pleasing quality to them.

I draw the illustrations to my own novels for my own pleasure. Sometimes, even after I have finished writing, the characters are still vivid in my imagination. I originally trained as a painter, and so I end up feeling that I need to draw them to get them out of my system. When the time comes to send the manuscript off to the publisher, I send the illustrations along with the text. When the editor sees the illustrations I have provided, it may be that he finds them interesting and they get published along with the novel. In the 1980s, the fictional writings such as 'Three-Inch Golden Lotus' and 'The Visitor on a Snowy Night' I published in the literary magazine *Harvest,* as well as my 'Discussions on Wang Meng' and 'London in the Fog' published in *Wenhui Monthly,* were all printed with my own illustrations. To have the text and the pictures working together like this gives readers an extra pleasure while enjoying oneself at the same time. However, this was something that happened impromptu, almost like doodling. In recent years, I have been extremely busy and have had little time to write fiction. Mostly I have been writing essays on serious, thought-provoking topics, and so my practice in drawing my own illustrations came to an end.

My illustrations come easily to me. I also draw them when inspiration strikes: with whatever pen comes to hand when I reach across my desk, whether this is a fountain pen, a pencil, a ballpoint pen, or a felt-tip. To just sketch in my characters with a few simple lines gives my pictures a humorous quality; this must be why I also enjoy drawing my own manga. My manga have become part of my life with my family, since I often use comic incidents that happen in day-to-day existence as material, and my characters are usually my wife and children, my friends, neighbours, and myself. I draw these things for fun, and when I include myself, it is to poke fun at myself. Thanks to this regular practice, I have learned how to create a character with just a couple of lines, but since these drawings pertain to my private life with my family, I have never shown them to anyone else.

There was one occasion, however, when I did use this manga-style of drawing to illustrate one of my own books. This was back in the 1980s when I returned from a tour of the USA and wrote a collection of seventy or so essays comparing different aspects of life in China and the west, which were then published in a newspaper. These essays had a light-hearted comic touch which suited my style of drawing. So with one illustration for each essay, I quickly produced seventy pictures, which were later published together in a book: *Overseas Tales*.

This volume of tales had its illustrations produced in the same way. It was all very spur-of-the-moment. Having written this collection, I found the characters living on in my mind; furthermore, there is a humour about these tales which fits my manga-trained illustrative technique. I started by drawing the characters from a number of these tales in a notebook, but quite unexpectedly, the more I drew, the more I enjoyed it – in the end there was no getting out of it, and over the course of the next few weeks, I filled an entire sketch-pad, with some characters portrayed in a number of different poses and a variety of moods. I picked one character for each of my stories, and that is how this illustrated volume came into being.

Other people have already drawn illustrations for this volume; the pictures done by Namura Kimiko of Japan are very fine. However, what other people draw are their images of these extraordinary people; what I draw are mine. These characters were created by me; I know their tempers and what they ought to look like. Furthermore, I have lived in Tianjin my whole life, and I know its people, with their toughness and competitive streak, their generosity, their determination to be respected, and their refusal to back down. When I illustrate them, it is these qualities that I draw.

When all is said and done, here we have my collection of short stories that I have illustrated myself. Now I want to start all over again, writing and illustrating another book.

20 August 2015

TRANSLATOR'S AFTERWORD
BY OLIVIA MILBURN

Over the course of the last fifty years, Feng Jicai has made his mark in many fields: as a painter, poet, novelist, illustrator, architectural historian, and as an activist for the preservation of traditional Chinese culture. Through his many works of fiction, he has come to be regarded as the quintessential novelist of Tianjin, his home town. In *Faces in the Crowd: 36 Extraordinary Tales of Tianjin*, he takes an unsentimental look at the inhabitants of this city in the late 19th and early 20th centuries – a time when this great port city was in fact composed of two entirely different communities: the inhabitants of the old walled Chinese city, and the nine foreign concessions located to the south-east. During this period, Tianjin people found themselves living at the sharp end of global capitalism and colonial greed, and the city was a battleground between the forces of conservatism and those who enthusiastically embraced this new world. These tales provide a sometimes charmingly picaresque, sometimes chilling and bleak look at the way in which the residents of Tianjin adapted themselves in the struggle to survive.

The world described in this book no longer exists. This is not just a matter of the amount of time that has passed, but also due to the physical destruction of the old walled city in the process of modernisation and the relocation of the original inhabitants to concrete tower blocks far away from the places where they used to live and work. Where old skills and old businesses survive, they are only a shadow of their former selves. However, as long as Feng Jicai's writings are read and loved, the Tianjin that he has spent his life trying to save will not have been entirely lost.

ABOUT THE AUTHOR

Born in Tianjin in 1942, Feng Jicai is a contemporary author, artist and cultural scholar who rose to prominence as a pioneer of China's Scar Literature movement that emerged after the Cultural Revolution. He has published almost a hundred literary works in China and more than forty internationally. He is proficient in both Chinese and western artistic techniques, and his artwork has been exhibited in China, Japan, the US, Singapore and Austria. He has had a major influence on contemporary Chinese society with his work on the Project to Save Chinese Folk Cultural Heritages and his roles as honorary member of the Literature and Arts Association, honorary president of the China Folk Literature and Art Association and adviser to the State Council, among others. He is also dean, professor and PhD supervisor at the Feng Jicai Institute of Literature and Art, Tianjin University.

ABOUT THE TRANSLATOR

Olivia Milburn is professor of Chinese language and literature at Seoul National University. She completed her first degree in Chinese at St Hilda's College, University of Oxford, a master's in Oriental studies at Downing College, University of Cambridge, and a doctorate in classical Chinese at the School of Oriental and African Studies, University of London. She has authored several books including *Cherishing Antiquity: The Cultural Construction of an Ancient Chinese Kingdom*, *The Spring and Autumn Annals of Master Yan* and *Urbanization in Early and Medieval China: Gazetteers for the City of Suzhou*. In collaboration with Christopher Payne, she has translated two spy novels by Mai Jia, including the bestselling *Decoded*, from Chinese to English. In 2018, Milburn's translation work was recognised by the Chinese government with a Special Book Award of China, which honours contributions to bridging cultures and fostering understanding.

About SINOIST BOOKS

We hope you enjoyed this collection of stories featuring the extraordinary inhabitants of the Chinese port city of Tianjin.

SINOIST BOOKS brings the best of Chinese fiction to English-speaking readers. We aim to create a greater understanding of Chinese culture and society, and provide an outlet for the ideas and creativity of the country's most talented authors.

To let us know what you thought of this book, or to learn more about the diverse range of exciting Chinese fiction in translation we publish, find us online. If you're as passionate about Chinese literature as we are, then we'd love to hear your thoughts!

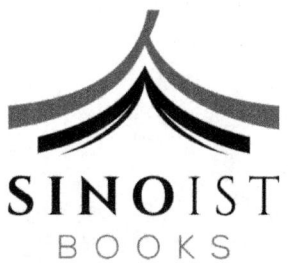

www.sinoistbooks.com
@sinoistbooks